MAKING A DIFFERENCE IN EDUCATION

What is working in education in the UK – and what isn't? This book offers a highly readable guide to what the latest research says about improving young people's outcomes in pre-school, primary and secondary education. Never has this issue been more topical as the UK attempts to compete in the global economy against countries with increasingly educated and skilled workforces. The book discusses whether education policy has really been guided by the evidence and explores why the failings of Britain's educational system have been so resistant to change, as well as the success stories that have emerged.

Making a Difference in Education looks at schooling from early years to age 16 and entry into further education, with a special focus on literacy, numeracy and IT. Reviewing a large body of research, and paying particular attention to findings that are strong enough to guide policy, the authors examine teacher performance, school quality and accountability, and the problematically large social gap that still exists in state school education today. Each chapter concludes with a summary of key findings and key policy requirements.

As a comprehensive research review, *Making a Difference in Education* should be essential reading for faculty and students in education and social policy, and of great interest to teachers and indeed to anyone who wants to know about the effectiveness of UK education policy and practice, and where they should be going.

Robert Cassen is Visiting Professor at the Centre for Analysis of Social Exclusion, London School of Economics, UK, and received an OBE for services to education in 2008.

Sandra McNally is Professor of Economics at the University of Surrey, UK, and Director of the Education and Skills Programme at the Centre for Economic Performance, London School of Economics, UK.

Anna Vignoles is Professor of Education at the University of Cambridge, Research Associate at the Institute for Fiscal Studies, and Visiting Professor at the Institute of Education, London, all in the UK.

'This is a first-rate and highly readable assessment of "what works" in pre-school, primary and secondary education, telling us where there is robust evidence, where it is only suggestive, and where more is needed. Politicians need better information if they are to succeed in making evidence-based policy. All too often it is not available to them in a form that is easy for them to use. Now they can find it here. *Making a Difference in Education* should be required reading for anyone in the education policy community and teaching professions, and will also be valuable to parents and school governors.'

– *Baroness Blackstone*

'This book is a refreshing alternative to the vacuous political rhetoric of "what works" and "evidence-based policy". It identifies where there is – and where there isn't – robust evidence to inform education policy, and provides an accessible and realistic assessment of what we know about quality and effectiveness in educational interventions.'

– *Professor Geoff Whitty, Director Emeritus, Institute of Education, University of London*

MAKING A DIFFERENCE IN EDUCATION

What the evidence says

Robert Cassen, Sandra McNally and Anna Vignoles

Routledge
Taylor & Francis Group

LONDON AND NEW YORK

First published 2015
by Routledge
2 Park Square, Milton Park, Abingdon, Oxon OX14 4RN

and by Routledge
711 Third Avenue, New York, NY 10017

Routledge is an imprint of the Taylor & Francis Group, an informa business

British Library Cataloguing in Publication Data
A catalogue record for this book is available from the British Library

Library of Congress Cataloging in Publication Data
Cassen, Robert.
  Making a difference in education: what the evidence says/Robert Cassen,
  Sandra McNally and Anna Vignoles.
    pages cm
  Includes bibliographical references and index.
  1. Education – Great Britain. 2. Education and state – Great Britain.
  3. Educational change – Great Britain. I. McNally, Sandra, 1972–
  II. Vignoles, Anna. III. Title.
  LA633.C37 2015
  370.941 – dc23
  2014042219

ISBN: 978-0-415-52921-1 (hbk)
ISBN: 978-0-415-52922-8 (pbk)
ISBN: 978-1-315-71235-2 (ebk)

Typeset in Bembo and Stone Sans
by Florence Production Ltd, Stoodleigh, Devon, UK

CONTENTS

ACKNOWLEDGEMENTS

We wish to thank the following for help and advice:

Andrea Berkeley (Teaching Leaders), Sara Bubb (Institute of Education (IoE)), Sue Burroughs-Lange (IoE), Richard Connor (British Educational Suppliers Association (BESA)), Claire Crawford (Institute for Fiscal Studies (IFS)), Lorraine Dearden (IFS), Michael Day (Roehampton University), Chris Dede (Harvard University), Feyisa Demie (Lambeth), E.A. Draffan (Southampton University), Jon Drori (Thoughtsmith), Simon Gallacher (Teach First), Jason Hill (Beanstalk), Aga Kelly (NAACE), Martin Knapp (LSE), Diana Laurillard (London Knowledge Lab), Richard Levene (BESA), Joseph Mintz (IoE), Marilyn Mottram (Ofsted), Richard Noss (London Knowledge Lab), Vanessa Pittard (DfE), James Richardson (Education Endowment Foundation), Delia Smith (Ark Academy), James Toop (Teaching Leaders), Robin Trew (University College London), Dylan Wiliam (IoE), Christopher Wood (Ofsted), Alf Wood (Bishop's Hatfield School).

While we have written our chapters separately, as indicated in the Table of Contents, we take collective responsibility for the book as a whole.

The authors alone are of course entirely responsible for any errors or shortcomings of the book.

1

INTRODUCTION

Robert Cassen, Sandra McNally
and Anna Vignoles

There is a lot of talk about 'evidence-based policy' in education. But what exactly does the evidence say?

This book reviews the key research in the fields we cover, namely education from early years to age 16 and entry into Further Education. We concentrate on England and the state sector, but refer to the rest of the UK where we can, and also draw on the experience of other countries when it is relevant. The research field of education is of course extremely broad and we have had to be necessarily selective in our choices of topic. We have therefore not addressed several important subjects, such as arts education, sport in schools, coaching, moral and social issues in various educational practices and we do not discuss Higher Education at all.

We have tried to reach conclusions about what is and is not effective in education in our topics. By 'effective' we mean what can reasonably be expected to achieve a given result: in particular what can improve outcomes for learners, and what can narrow the 'social gap', the association of disadvantage with diminished outcomes. It is a book about what 'works', in this sense.

The language of 'what works' has itself become contested in some quarters, for assuming a crude type of causality, or being asserted in relation to particular kinds of policies, or suggesting a set of simple-minded 'rules' for the education profession. We hope that we will be understood as adopting a nuanced approach to causality. It is well known that in quantum physics one can speak only of probabilistic relationships, not causation. Equally in some fields, causality can be and has been established with certainty. We know that the variola virus caused smallpox, and that vaccination prevented it; without that knowledge, smallpox would not have been eradicated. Much more than that, we could not live in a world without cause and effect, without knowing that given actions lead to given effects, at least most of the time. Yet social science lies somewhere short of this kind of certainty.

In social science and certainly in education, we can say at most that a measured relationship is highly unlikely to be the result of chance – sometimes we can even say how unlikely. But we can never be 100 per cent certain that all confounding factors have been fully accounted for. The randomised controlled trial or 'RCT' is often held up as the ultimate gold standard as a way of establishing causal relationships. In practice, if one were to adopt the results from a RCT into a policy measure, one would still have to be confident that the entire context would be the same as in the trial in every relevant respect. The physical world is relatively constant over time, so that we may rely on cause and effect at long intervals. But the social context changes, sometimes quite fast: we cannot be sure, for example, that a measure that 'worked' in education 20 years ago will have the same effects for the internet generation today or that something that 'worked' in Doncaster would work in Delhi. And societal factors may differ a great deal. Quite a few educational RCTs have been carried out in India, but because of the importance of context we do not refer to them in this book, as the conditions are so far from our own.

A 2012 paper from the Cabinet Office made a strong plea for more RCTs in public policy, including education.[1] They are standard practice in medicine for any new therapeutic methods and the arguments for their use in policy are clear. Simply evaluating whether an intervention or policy is associated with a change in a particular outcome is insufficient: one might wrongly conclude that it had (or had not) worked because of a change in the environment. RCTs give us confidence that there has been cause and effect. RCTs will also rule out 'selection bias', the possibility that individuals or institutions adopting an intervention may have some characteristic that makes the intervention more likely to succeed. An RCT can also give guidance about cost-effectiveness: depending on the magnitude of its effect and the cost, it will help to show whether an intervention is worth rolling out to scale. RCTs need not be expensive, yet we do not have all that many of them.

RCTs have their limitations. We need to know not only what works, but what works for whom and under what conditions. RCTs cannot always help us answer all these questions. We need many other kinds of research too, not least to find out what to trial in RCTs and crucially why particular policies work or don't work. But sensitively used, they are among the best kinds of evidence we can have when it comes to policy.

Indeed concern with effective policy-making motivates this book; there is much talk of 'evidence-based policy', so here we have tried to make clear where the evidence we discuss is based on RCTs or other, methodologically rigorous, statistical analysis that provides 'robust' findings. Equally, we have signalled where the evidence we present only amounts to observation or statistical correlation. How and to what extent evidence has been used in past policy is discussed and the book gives examples of research findings that have influenced policy and quite probably should not have done. Indeed sometimes research results are quoted in support of a policy long after they have been shown to be misleading.

We are however realistic. There is much 'policy-based evidence' rather than 'evidence-based policy'. Despite this, we hope that our book will provide some insight into the more robust evidence that is available on a range of important education issues. We start by highlighting some key issues that we think are critical for the education system in England.

The legacy of the past and the key issues

The large social gap – the tendency of pupils from disadvantaged backgrounds to do disproportionately badly in school outcomes at 11 and 16 – is a key problem in state school education today, and the subject of much media comment and policy discussion. Put briefly, the UK is an unequal society, and the educational system does not do enough to make up for a poor start in life. It also does not serve the post-16 age group well enough, either in stretching the better performers, or in providing clear and flexible routes in practical education. (This book does not in the main cover research on private, independent schools; they have a major role in the country's inequalities, but they account for only 7 per cent of pupils, and are largely unexamined here.)

A further big issue is how to improve the handling of vocational education and the Further Education (FE) sector. The FE sector absorbs significant resources, but is somehow the Cinderella of educational policy and indeed of research. While post-16 education is not a main subject of this book, we address vocational education in Chapter 11.

Gaps

A frequent observation about our education system is the large 'tail' of inadequately educated young people emerging into the world of work. The Confederation of British Industries (CBI) regularly complains that we are not turning out the people industry needs – according to them there is not just a lack of engineering or technological skills, but also of even basic literacy and numeracy and 'soft' skills that companies need. The CBI's 2013 education and skill survey pointed out that 36 per cent of pupils did not get an A*–C grade in GCSE English in 2012, and 42 per cent did not get one in maths. The survey said that even college and university graduates lack basic skills and that high proportions of firms report difficulties in recruiting the people they need. We are not, they lament, the 'global leader in the race for knowledge, skill and innovation' that we could and should be.[2] While one might dispute the details as expressed by the CBI, certainly there is a sentiment among policy-makers, business and the public that some parts of the education system are not fit for purpose.

The social gap relates to this concern. A common way to show the gap is to look at the achievement of pupils on free school meals (FSM). FSM is imperfect as a measure of disadvantage; but it is widely used because so often the data include it rather than other measures. FSM pupils are in fact half as likely as non-FSM pupils to score 5A*–C results in their GCSEs. More positively the socio-economic gap in the proportion achieving 5A*–Cs including English and maths was reduced a little in the 5 years to 2012.[3] However, this may somewhat mask the true situation – if you use postcode poverty rather than FSM, there is a continuous association between deprivation and school outcomes – the gap will not be closed just by improving results for FSM pupils.[4]

The problem begins before school: data from the Millennium Cohort show cognitive gaps between disadvantaged and better-off children as early as age 3 and gaps in vocabulary at age 5. In a much quoted study, Leon Feinstein showed that bright children from disadvantaged backgrounds fared worse at primary age than less bright children from better-off homes.[5] Socio-economic gaps in achievement then widen by age 11, as can be seen from English and maths results in primary schools, and then widen a little further by age 16. Again there are some positive elements to this story. While the socio-economic gap as measured by GCSE results relative to postcode-poverty has declined since the early 2000s, it may well widen again as a result of the recession that began in 2008. It is undoubtedly true that there is still a strong link between family income and educational results.[6] Related to the socio-economic gap in pupil achievement, there is a variety of learning difficulties going under the heading of special educational needs (SEN), which are only slowly being met – but these needs too are more common among pupils from disadvantaged backgrounds. The issues of SEN are addressed in Chapter 9.

As for teaching, we may quote Ofsted in 2012:

> Pupils in most need of the best teaching, such as lower attaining pupils and those with special educational needs, may not get it. They are often taught by the weakest teachers in the school. In secondary schools, they are more likely to be taught by non-specialists, whose subject knowledge is weak; in primary schools, by teaching assistants deployed too extensively with children who find learning difficult.[7]

Improving teaching – and not just for the disadvantaged – is a key need in UK education, addressed in Chapter 6. It has the most mileage for improving educational outcomes of almost any intervention in schools, yet policy has targeted school reform more usually than teaching.

It is also often said that our schools do not sufficiently stretch the better-performing pupils. An Ofsted report in 2013 noted that nearly two-thirds of those who achieve well in English in primary school (obtaining a level 5) do not get an A* or A at GCSE; for maths the proportion was more than a half, and a quarter did not even get a B.[8] Our more able maths pupils also lose ground relative to others internationally between the ages of 10 and 16.[9] Furthermore, our higher performers do not do as well as those of competitor countries.[10]

There are further problems for the disadvantaged. Schools vary greatly in quality, but the disadvantaged have less chance of getting into better schools – the UK has among the highest degrees of social segregation in schools in the developed world.[11] A 2013 report examined the top 500 comprehensive schools as ranked by the 5A*–C GCSE league table. It found they had less than half the national proportion of FSM pupils: 7.6 per cent compared with 16.5 per cent. Only 26 of the 500 schools took a higher proportion of FSM pupils than was present in their local authority. Much of this was due to the fact that many of these schools were able to select their pupils, or that better-off parents were able to buy properties in the schools' catchment areas. Some apparent selection is of course also due to parents' choices of schools. While comprehensive schools quite frequently achieve excellent results in 'challenging' circumstances, that is a matter for congratulation, rather than the norm.[12] Chapter 5 discusses school effectiveness and the role of school organisation.

It is not just the case that disadvantage accounts for so much underperformance, but it does so more in the UK or in England than in many other countries. Indeed international studies show we lie relatively high on the scale of the effect of social background on educational outcomes, even if by some measures we have been doing better in recent years.[13] But while the UK was sixth among OECD countries in the proportion having completed tertiary education,[14] it was in the bottom third in terms of its proportion of people aged 25–34 with completed upper Secondary school qualifications.[15] This reveals the great disparity in educational achievement between the upper and lower ends of the system.

Disadvantage has stronger effects among particular groups. This is particularly true of boys relative to girls. If you look at disadvantaged girls and boys, who come from the same homes and mostly go to the same schools, the girls do much better – there appears to be a distinct 'boy' problem. Among the disadvantaged, White British and Afro-Caribbean pupils perform less well than most other ethnic groups; the White British are of course the majority population, making up over 70 per cent of all pupils.[16]

There is also a geographical aspect to educational outcomes for the disadvantaged. While major urban centres, London most outstandingly, have made significant improvements in results for FSM students in recent years, a number of areas are lagging in this respect, particularly those with large rural communities and in several coastal towns.[17]

The social gap cannot be closed just by improving schools. They can make a big difference, but even if all secondary schools were 'outstanding', and the disadvantaged made the same improved progress that they already do in 'good' schools, a substantial gap would still remain.[18] This is because secondary schools inherit a large socio-economic gap in achievement from primary schools. Primary schools in turn admit poor children who are already substantially behind their better-off peers: a large part of the gap has to be addressed even before school, in the early years. Many of the relevant questions are reviewed in Chapters 3 and 4, on early years and parenting.

Improving the educational outcomes for disadvantaged children is not just a matter of equity – it is important for the children themselves and for the economy and society at large. We cannot have a productive, internationally competitive economy with such a large tail of badly educated people. One report has called it 'a waste of human resources on a grand scale'.[19] A host of studies have shown that besides contributing to economic growth, improving education for all would have positive consequences for health, employment and other desirable outcomes.[20] The 2013 report of the Social Mobility Commission called on the government to ensure that

> raising standards and closing attainment gaps are the twin objectives for all teachers and all schools . . . through the standards it sets, the inspection regimes it sanctions, the league tables it publishes and the reward mechanisms it deploys.[21]

Challenges ahead

The UK education system, and indeed many other education systems across the globe, faces some major challenges ahead. As a nation we should be investing more in education and ensuring that our workforce has greater levels of skill. Yet achieving this has proved difficult as the above discussion implies. Many of the economic problems that we face, in particular income inequality and the prevalence of low skilled and ill paid jobs, make it harder still to ensure a high skill level for our poorest students. In this book we present evidence on what may be effective in improving the system, though we also highlight the severe limitations to our knowledge about 'what works' in many instances. Here we emphasise some issues for the future.

As discussed above, in the UK, parental school choice and greater school autonomy within a quasi-market system have been proposed as the means to ensure that the school system works better. In Chapter 5 we show how in fact the evidence on the impact of these reforms is mixed. Certainly there are some potential concerns for the future. With greater levels of school autonomy, there has come a degree of fragmentation and a proliferation of different school types.[22] We can also expect some diversity to develop in the curriculum as some schools have more freedom than others in this respect. All in all, there will be far less centralised control of the system. This is indeed the purpose of the reforms, with the idea being that schools will be encouraged to take their own optimal path, and parents will be able to make choices from a more diverse range of schools.

Even if this approach does produce gains in average student achievement, the system may not benefit everyone. There is a particular concern about some of the functions previously performed by local authorities, such as provision for children with special educational needs, for pupil exclusions and for pupils with severe behaviour problems. Managing this may be far harder in a decentralised system, where local authorities have a more limited role, and where the interests of individual schools and their pupils come into conflict with the interests of a specific child. For instance, local authorities used to take an overview on whether a child should be excluded or not, knowing they would have to provide for that child somehow. An individual school, working alone, has less incentive to keep a disruptive child. Careful monitoring of children who may be particularly undesirable for schools to take on will be needed.

Another issue is that the quasi-market in education relies on information. Parents need good information to make sensible choices, otherwise they can only choose on the basis of factors other than academic quality, such as the types of student attending a school. Hence a good accountability system is essential. Yet measuring school quality is highly problematic. In Chapter 5 we discuss how the system had set up perverse incentives by using crude measures of pupil achievement, such as the proportion of children achieving 5 A★–C grades. These types of targets have driven teacher and school behaviour with unfortunate side effects, not least an over-emphasis on children near the margin of the target. This affects both high achievers and very low achievers. Reforms are now in place to encourage schools to use a broader range of measures.

Progress is still needed on how best to measure school quality. Indeed the Government is currently consulting on how to measure value-added in primary schools, a challenge made more difficult by the problems of assessing academic achievement in very young children. Overall we need to ensure we are measuring what matters, that we are not setting up perverse incentives, and that we are not placing an undue burden on teachers and schools. Measurement of pupil and school performance is important for a well-functioning and effective education system, but too much measurement, or the wrong kind, can be damaging. This issue will run and run.

Another key challenge is to ensure we have high quality and motivated teachers, as discussed in Chapter 6. There are a number of factors that make teaching a demanding career, not least long hours during term time, problems with behaviour management in some schools, and issues about career progression. It is crucial that we attract able people into teaching and that teaching is considered a high quality occupation. This has long been a challenge and will continue to be so.

With regard to managing teacher performance, the Coalition Government that came into office in 2010 introduced a stronger link between teacher performance and pay, but in practice operating this system will be difficult. Schools are not all well set up to manage complex human resource functions, and just as in the case of league tables, teacher quality has to be appropriately measured and perverse incentives avoided. We are a long way from being able to use as a measure the value added by the teacher to the pupils they teach. There is a clear danger associated with using snap-shot classroom observations of quality that may not be particularly strong predictors of pupils' achievement with that teacher. We also need to accept that if pay does become genuinely more flexible then this will, and indeed should, lead to competition for good teachers, particularly in shortage subjects. If a genuine market emerges in terms of teachers' pay, however, this will have consequences for the wage bill and for schools with limited resources trying to manage the process, particularly given the history of opposition to pay differentials within the teacher work force.

Perhaps the biggest challenge of all that we face in the UK is the danger of politicisation and an excessively frequent introduction of new initiatives. Education has been the subject of constant and perhaps one might say relentless change during the last 50 years, and particularly during the last two decades. Large and complex systems are slow to change and policy churn can be very damaging, particularly to the morale of those working within them. No sooner has one initiative been implemented than the system moves on, often with little attempt to consider whether the change has actually produced benefits. Many aspects of the UK education system have clearly improved in recent years, but the need for better evaluation of what we do in the system, ideally before policies are changed and implemented on a wide scale, is essential. Sensible piloting of potential policies is a more responsible way to implement policies; it would give more hope of finding out 'what works' in advance and also of convincing key stakeholders of why change is necessary.

Evidence and policy

We would argue that the need for evidence of 'what works' is crucial if we are to rise to the challenges outlined above. On the whole, while reliable evidence is lacking in some areas, we know a lot about what could work to improve school outcomes and close the social gap very significantly. Our book reviews a large body of research, paying particular attention to where the findings are strong enough to guide policy, or indicating where evidence is only suggestive. We have made efforts, in addition to the chapters mentioned above, to look specifically at literacy (Chapter 7), numeracy (Chapter 8) and information technology in the classroom (Chapter 10): they are all critical areas that deserve particular attention.

We have not been able to include a chapter on Arts education. There is, however, some evidence that it has a positive effect on other school outcomes, such as pre-school and primary pupils' early literacy skills, secondary school students' academic attainment, and young people's cognitive abilities (based on various measures of intelligence).[23] Given the intrinsic importance of Arts education as well, it is a matter of regret that we were unable to cover the topic.

There are of course other efforts to present the best research evidence and reflect on its quality, with a range of websites, university centres and charitable organisations devoted to the task, as well as the institutions of government. The Education Endowment Foundation 'Toolkit' and the US Government 'What Works Clearing House' are just two of the most frequently visited.[24] We refer to several throughout the book.

It should perhaps be noted that the Department of Education's expenditure on research is relatively modest. It is difficult to get an exact figure for this expenditure as it is paid out of several budgets, which include child care and other policy areas, but it amounts to upwards of £10 million. The Department also funds the

Educational Endowment Foundation to the tune of more than £10 million on an annualised basis, and projects such as Test and Learn with the National College of Teaching and Leadership. But the sums do not appear to approach the 0.88 per cent of total health expenditure that is spent on research by the NHS – to get close to that proportion the Department would have to be spending £50 million a year. The Cabinet Office paper cited earlier suggests an aspiration for educational research that is not reflected in actual expenditure.

We are aware, however, that evidence is far from the only force guiding policy – in fact it is sometimes completely absent. A careful study has examined how and why evidence plays the often limited part that it does in policy formation.[25] The study is particularly revealing about the rapidly changing scenery of policy-making on vocational and further education, listing the plethora of initiatives, agencies and reports that have come and – mostly – gone in recent years, as well as turnover in civil service and government responsibility. In one period of 7 years, 11 different ministers were in charge of basic skills.[26] Heads of schools and colleges more generally often say they would welcome a period of no new initiatives, and describe themselves as struggling to cope with the variety of legislation and official advice.

A book can only do so much. But for practitioners, researchers and policy makers alike, if they really do want to know what the evidence is on our topics, we hope they will find some answers here.

Notes

1 Haynes *et al.* (2012).
2 CBI (2013).
3 DfE data. See further Ofsted (2012).
4 Clifton and Cook (2012).
5 Feinstein (2003). See also Jerrim and Vignoles (2011) for a methodological critique.
6 Clifton and Cook (2012).
7 Ofsted (2012), p. 24.
8 Ofsted (2013a).
9 Jerrim and Choi (2013).
10 Clifton and Cook (2012).
11 OECD (2012a, b).
12 Sutton Trust (2013).
13 This is true specifically in mathematics as well – Jerrim and Choi (2013).
14 OECD (2013) p. 28; data for 2011.
15 McNally (2012).
16 Cassen and Kingdon (2007). See further Strand (2014).
17 Ofsted (2013b).
18 Clifton and Cook (2012).
19 LSE Growth Commission (2013) p. 17.
20 Ibid. and OECD (2013).
21 Social Mobility and Child Poverty Commission (2013), p. 23.
22 Mortimore (2013) calls it a 'mess'.
23 CASE (2010); Catterall (2009); Cultural Learning Alliance (2011); PWC (2010).
24 http://educationendowmentfoundation.org.uk/toolkit and www.whatworks.ed.gov respectively. A fairly complete list is given in Perry *et al.* (2010), p. 7.
25 Perry *et al.* (2010).
26 Ibid., p. 32. See also Stanton (2009).

Bibliography

CASE (2010) *Understanding the Drivers: Impact and Value of Engagement in Culture and Sport*, Culture and Sport Evidence Programme, London: Department of Culture, Media and Sport.

CBI (2013) *Changing the Pace*, CBI/Pearson education and skills survey 2013, London: Confederation of British Industries.

Cassen, R. and Kingdon, G. (2007) *Tackling Low Educational Achievement*, Report to the Joseph Rowntree Foundation, York: Joseph Rowntree Foundation.

Catterall, J. (2009) *Doing Well by Doing Good: A 12-Year National Study of Education in the Visual and Performing Arts*, Los Angeles, CA/London: I-group Books.

Clifton, J. and Cook, W. (2012) *A Long Division: Closing the Attainment Gap in England's Secondary Schools*, London: Institute for Public Policy Research.

Cultural Learning Alliance (2011) *Key Research Findings: The Case for Cultural Learning*, London: Cultural Learning Alliance.

Feinstein, L. (2003) 'Inequality in the early cognitive development of British children in the 1970 cohort', *Economica* 70(277): 73–98.

Haynes, L., Service, O., Goldacre, B. and Torgerson, D. (2012) *Test, Learn, Adapt: Developing Public Policy with Randomised Controlled Trials*, London: Cabinet Office.

Jerrim, J. and Vignoles, A. (2011) 'The use (and misuse) of statistics in understanding social mobility: Regression to the mean and the cognitive development of high ability children from disadvantaged homes', Department of Quantitative Social Science *Working Paper* no. 11–01, London: Institute of Education.

Jerrim, J. and Choi, A. (2013) 'The mathematics skills of school children: How does England compare to the high performing East Asian jurisdictions?' Department of Quantitative Social Science *Working Paper* no. 13–03, London: Institute of Education.

LSE Growth Commission (2013) *Investing for Prosperity: Skills, Infrastructure And Innovation*, London: London School of Economics.

McNally, S. (2012) *Report to the LSE Growth Commission: Education and Skills*, London: London School of Economics.

Mortimore, P. (2013) *Education Under Siege: Why there is a Better Alternative*, Bristol: Policy Press.

OECD (Organisation for Economic Co-operation and Development) (2012a) *Education at a Glance*, Paris: OECD.

OECD (2012b) *Equity and Quality in Education*, Paris: OECD.

OECD (2013) *Education at a Glance*, Paris: OECD.

Ofsted (Office for Standards in Education, Children's Services and Skills) (2012) *Annual Report: Schools*, London: Ofsted.

Ofsted (2013a) *The Most Able Students: Are they Doing as Well as they Should in Our Non-Selective Secondary Schools?* London: Ofsted.

Ofsted (2013b) *Unseen Children: Access and Achievement 20 Years On*, London: Ofsted.

Perry, A., Amadeo, C., Fletcher, M. and Walker, E. (2010) *Reason or Instinct: How Education Policy is Made and How We Might Make it Better*, Reading: CfBT Education Trust.

PWC (Pricewaterhouse Coopers) (2010) *Creativity, Culture and Education: The Costs and Benefits of Creative Partnerships*, London: Pricewaterhouse Coopers.

Social Mobility and Child Poverty Commission (2013) *State of the Nation 2013: Social Mobility and Child Poverty in Great Britain*, London: The Stationery Office.

Stanton, G. (2009) *Learning Matters: Making the 14–19 Reforms Work for Learners*, Reading: CfBT Education Trust.

Strand, S. (2014) 'School effects and ethnic, gender and socio-economic gaps in educational achievement at age 11', *Oxford Review of Education* 40(2): 223–245.

Sutton Trust (2013) *Selective Comprehensives: The Social Composition of Top Comprehensive Schools*, London: The Sutton Trust.

2

HOW DID WE GET HERE?

A selective history

Robert Cassen

> I hold it for indisputable, that the first duty of a State is to see that every child born therein shall be well housed, clothed, fed, and educated, till it attain years of discretion.
>
> John Ruskin, 1867

The foundation of state education in Britain was laid by the Education Act of 1870. There was a network of private, charitable and government supported schools before that, but the 1870 Act for the first time established a major role for government spending on schooling and did several important things. Counties were divided into school districts. Elected school boards were set up, empowered to raise rates to build schools and support them and to compel attendance. Poor families were exempted from fees and restrictions on funding secular schools were removed. It was still a long way from what had to be done. Compulsory attendance at school was not generally enforced until 1876 and was not made completely free until 1891. The low status and pay of teachers and the quality of schooling would long remain problems, but the Act was a watershed.[1]

We were in fact among the last countries in Europe to have compulsory education, a government department of education, or free education for everyone. If you look as far back as you can, you find a complicated story linked to social class, the Church and politics. While we did little in terms of educating our population, other countries were doing rather better. Some German municipalities had compulsory education in the sixteenth century; Massachusetts introduced it in the seventeenth; England was also well behind Scotland, Austria and Sweden. In Scotland, rural landlords were obliged to provide a school in each parish from the end of the seventeenth century and there were burgh schools in Scottish towns supported by municipal money. For a long time education in Scotland would remain substantially better than in England, and more accessible to the average child.

To be universal, education had to be compulsory – but to be compulsory it had to be non-denominational and free. This meant reconciling points of view among religious and dissenting groups, among sections of public opinion, and among politicians – all of which took a considerable struggle.

On the eve of the industrial revolution about 4 per cent of the English population was in school, rather lower than in Scotland, but higher than in Wales. The early years of industrialisation did not require an educated workforce either. In 1841 very few men and women had jobs that needed literacy. The demand for child labour kept growing at least up to the 1850s. But then there was a big rise in literacy, with women catching up with men in the second half of the nineteenth century. Scotland, one should add, reached 87 per cent literacy by 1855; its big expansion was earlier than England's. But by the end of the nineteenth century, literacy for both men and women in England was well over 90 per cent.

Secondary education, however, had a strong hierarchy. Workers' education stopped at elementary schooling for a very long time. In fact it was quite late before the distinction between primary and secondary schools was made, since such a high proportion of the population stopped their education very early. Grammar schools were endowed to teach everyone, rich and poor, though access for the poor was in reality limited and they mostly left after achieving basic skills – or without them. You can argue about whether 'push' or 'pull' accounted for the changes in the nineteenth century. The push came from educational reformers and some parliamentarians; the pull from the slowly increasing demand for skills in the economy.

By 1851 the distance between what was going on and what was needed was enormous. The Census Report of that year provides a snapshot of where things had reached. Only about half of children aged 6–12 were in school, and more boys than girls. Including nursery education and children up to 15 years of age, the average number of years of schooling for those who received any was only five per child; and as the Report notes, much of that education was of low quality. It judged about 14,000 of nearly 30,000 reporting private schools to be 'inferior', mainly 'Dame schools', 'only reading and writing taught, the latter not always'.[2]

Many social changes led the way to action. Child labour was diminishing, both as a result of earlier factory legislation and changes in the economy. The extension of the vote and industrial unrest – big building-trades strikes in the 1860s for example – reinforced the old arguments for social peace through education. In the parliamentary debate on the 1870 Act, members said that if people were going to vote and form unions, they had better be educated. There was also another argument that had been heard as early as the 1840s, but gained renewed strength with events like the Paris Exhibition of 1867: we were falling behind our competitors in America, France and Prussia, and education was part of the answer. Religion was still a key factor in the debate, prolonging it for months, but finally the 'conscience clause', exempting dissenters from specific religious instruction, gave the way out.

From the nineteenth to the twenty-first century

Providing a decent education for all, and a practical one, was still a long way off by 1900. That is hardly a surprise. What is more remarkable, is how real educational progress was dogged for so long by the same arguments and the same forces. There were always two main tasks for education; that it should fit people for life in the fullest sense, as citizens and as moral and cultural beings; and that it should equip them to earn a living and to contribute to national productivity. The sad thing was that the two were seen not as complementary, but as opposed to each other. The big problems of education – getting everyone into a good school, and ensuring the kind of education appropriate for each person's and society's needs, are with us still.

The appalling conditions of our industrial towns and cities in the nineteenth century have been well documented. People left the countryside in droves, some driven by the destruction of sheep farming and its associated jobs, some by other kinds of poverty. The pattern of our industrialisation laid the conditions for the profound inequality of the country, with the middle classes enjoying health and education vastly superior to that of working men and women. One detail of many will suffice: boys aged 13½ in an industrial school in 1883 were on average nearly 6 inches shorter than the sons of professional parents.[3]

On the eve of the First World War there were still grievous deficiencies in anything beyond elementary education. A report cited by Corelli Barnett found that of the 2.7 million 'juveniles' between the ages of 14 and 18, 81.5 per cent 'were enrolled in neither day schools nor in evening schools'. Just before the Second World War, things were not vastly better: only 20 per cent of 14-year-olds had any form of further full-time education. It was such a dereliction, and invidious comparisons with countries like Germany abounded. There were 40 day-continuation schools in England and Wales, with 20,000 pupils, compared with almost 3,200 *Berufsschulen* (vocational schools) in Germany, with over 1.8 million pupils, mostly compulsorily up to the age of 18. Over a wide range of German industries there was 100 per cent vocational training, compared with 10 per cent in the UK.[4]

Those who did get into proper secondary education in England were few, and most did not get very far. Only 19,000 finished their education in 1937, 1 in 132 of 14- to 18-year-olds. Only 8,000 of them came out with the Higher School Certificate and only half of them got to university. A mere 13,000 out of a total of 663,000 school-leavers had any kind of vocational schooling, mostly in junior technical schools.

Yet report after report since the 1860s had called for more education, academic and vocational; endless opinions were voiced about how detrimental the deficits were to the young people concerned and to national productivity, and about how much better these things were managed elsewhere. What was this very English disease?

Looking back over the centuries one can see several features of it. One was disputes arising because of concerns from religious groups – although religious groups have played a major role in English education. For example, some religious bodies resisted mass education in earlier times, and for four decades prior to the 1870 Act the Church of England in particular disputed the control of schools and curricula, while non-religious groups opposed the religious influence on schools.[5] Another was a strand of libertarianism or individualism, which did not want to see the state involved in education. Yet another was the role of the 'practical man' in business and industry, who did not see much point in book learning for his workers. Yet another was the unconcern, contempt or even fear with which much of the establishment regarded the 'lower orders'. For these reasons education was undervalued and governments were extremely tight-fisted in what they would spend on it. Of course there were any number of men and women who had totally different views. But politically they rarely prevailed.

Everything was going to be different after the Second World War. Or was it? We had a new Labour government intent on improving the lot of the people. But some things did not change, or did not change enough. A version of the old arguments continued to bedevil educational reform: that everyone should have the 'best' – and the best was an education incorporating moral values and high culture. The long domination of classical education had been somewhat eroded by the introduction of a growing number of science subjects over time; but it was still largely there in the 1930s, and with it the false dichotomy between cultural and practical subjects. The Spens Report on secondary education in 1938 noted that little had been done since 1900 to 'foster the development of secondary schools of quasi-vocational type designed to meet the needs of boys and girls who desired to enter industry and commerce at the age of 16'. And even more damningly, 'although 85 per cent of pupils did not remain at school beyond 16', the curriculum was 'still largely planned in the interests of pupils who intended to go to a University'.

So the vast majority of children left school with traces of Latin, English, religious knowledge and history, and some vestigial science. This was our 'liberal education'. Only in fairly recent times has our education system begun to be transformed away from one in which each stage is designed for those who will go on to the next, regardless of whether they will or not.

The Butler Act

The next landmark in education was the Butler Act of 1944. Preparations for it went on from 1941 under the wartime coalition government. When the Act was finally passed, it established free, compulsory schooling for children aged 5–15, under Local Education Authorities for the state sector. The Ministry clearly intended that there should be three types of state schools – Grammar, Secondary Modern, and Technical – and there would be at least part-time compulsory education up till the age of 18. But as David Bell, then Her Majesty's Chief Inspector, commented in a speech in 2004 commemorating 60 years of the Act, 'We are not even close to achieving this goal because we have not bridged the academic/vocational divide; we have only chipped away at it.'[6] The technical schools never got built; in fact we even lost many of those that we had. Religious education, however, was well served. The Act laid down that all schools must start the day with a corporate act of worship, although parents had the right of withdrawal. All schools had also to provide religious instruction even if non-denominational.

There is perhaps one strange aspect of the Act and its follow-up. Before it Butler had written that the first need 'was for industrial and technical training and the linking up of schools with employment'. In the run-up to the Act, however, for all the favourable reports on this issue, and the criticism of the modesty of financial proposals for vocational education, and a few meetings with representatives of industry and unions, little was done to fulfil that need.

While priorities were being argued over, the Norwood Committee to study curriculum issues reported in 1943. Its chairman was a classical scholar. The Report asserted the primacy of 'ultimate values'. It had three pages on the requirements of 'commerce' and seven pages on religion, and argued that traditional academic education is the best for everyone. When post-war educational reconstruction began, the third part of the Butler Act was largely ignored. Secondary Modern schools, with spending on each pupil about a third of that in Grammar schools, never seemed like something to 'link schools with employment'; and for 20 years the few technical schools that there were catered to 2 per cent or less of the school population. The so-called 'best' was truly the enemy of the good.

Moving on

The next steps in state education are more familiar. The 1960s and 1970s were a time of great concern about educational equality; there was the 1967 'Plowden Report' on primary education, which drew attention in particular to the poor performance of primary schools in disadvantaged areas,[7] and in its wake a two-volume study entitled *Educational Priority*, which emphasised the dependence of educational outcomes on conditions in homes and communities – it argued that equality of opportunity without equality of conditions 'is a sham'.[8] Both the *Educational Priority* study and Plowden argued for positive discrimination. The perceived inequities of the Grammar/Secondary Modern divide – not least the possibility that pupils were wrongly sorted by the 11+ exam, and the big differences in teaching quality between the two types of schools – were addressed by the move to Comprehensives in the 1960s and 1970s. It was of course controversial and the debate about Grammar schools and Secondary Moderns still continues today.[9]

O-Levels became GCSEs in 1984 and the practice of marking to a curve (that is, ensuring an unvarying distribution of grades) ended. The National Curriculum arrived in 1988, along with parental choice and the language of competition in our school system. Other big steps were the range of initiatives introduced by New Labour to drive up standards: Sure Start, Excellence in Cities, Education Action Zones, Pupil Referral Units, Literacy Hours. More autonomous schools were introduced in the late 1980s and over time have become a more important part of our system. 'Academies' were introduced in 2000, and a considerable impetus was given to Faith schools; there were also a number of changes in the methods of school financing, and very major increases in the budget for education. By the start of the twenty-first century our education system had begun to look much as we know it today.

One big failing, which is still with us, is the lack of progress with vocational, technical and business education. Yes, there was the Technical and Vocational Education Initiative in 1982, and the Youth Opportunities Scheme, also in the early 1980s. But they had limited positive impact. A belated – and also limited – start had been made in further technical education somewhat earlier. We acquired our first Colleges of Advanced Technology in 1963 (70 years after Germany), and our first Business School in 1965 (66 years after Harvard). The process of adapting the education system to the needs of the economy as well as that of the individual and society had barely begun even by the 1960s.

We wonder whether any other country has had so unsettled an approach to practical education as England? Since the 1980s there have been continued efforts to change policy. The last Labour government had the Tomlinson Report of 2004 on 14–19 education, which proposed a radical change to secondary education, with specified paths to higher and further education, flexibility for students between those paths, and new methods of assessment. But its far-reaching proposals were set aside, not least because they meant doing away with A-levels, a political hot potato with an election looming soon after Tomlinson reported. The Labour government also proposed a new system of Diplomas for vocational education, and 'Pathfinder' schools were given the task of trying it out.

While the Pathfinders achieved good results in the main, the Coalition Government that came into office in 2010 scrapped the scheme, not least on grounds of its expense and complexity. The same government also dropped the Educational Maintenance Allowance, replacing it with a more limited bursary scheme. Policies and additional funding were put in place to strengthen the role of apprenticeships, and a major review of vocational education was commissioned.[10] The pace of policy change has certainly been relentless, even if many issues remain unresolved.

Notes

1 For education history, see generally Cressy (1980); Curtis (1967); Durkheim (1956); Lawson and Silver (1973); Maclure (1990); Mitch (1992); Orme (2006); Purvis (1991); Vincent (2000).
2 Wales was worse off than England: parliamentary reports showed that over 85 per cent of children 5–15 were not in day schools in 1819–21; for England the figure was over 70 per cent; both made progress, but by 1862 more than half such children were still not in school in Wales, while in England the figure was closer to 40 per cent.
3 Barnett (1996). Even in 2012 men in Social Class I (skilled professional) still had 7 years more life expectancy than men in Social Class v (manual unskilled), according to ONS data.
4 Ibid.
5 On the 1870 Act, see further Maclure (1990).
6 'Change and continuity: reflections on the Butler act', speech to commemorate the sixtieth anniversary of the 1944 Education Act, reprinted in *The Guardian* 21 April 2014.

7 Plowden Report (1967).
8 Halsey (1972), vol. 1 p. 11.
9 Atkinson *et al.* (2006); Manning and Pischke (2006).
10 Wolf (2011).

Bibliography

Atkinson A., Gregg, P. and McConnell, B. (2006) *The Result of 11+ Selection: An Investigation into Opportunities and Outcomes for Pupils in Selective LEAs*, CMPO Working Paper no. 06/150. Bristol: Centre for Market and Public Organisation, University of Bristol.

Barnett, C. (1996) *The Audit of War: The Illusion and Reality of Britain as a Great Nation*, London: Pan Macmillan.

Cressy, D. (1980) *Literacy and the Social Order: Reading and Writing in Tudor and Stuart England*, Cambridge: Cambridge University Press.

Curtis, S.J. (1967) *History of Education in Great Britain*, London: University Tutorial Press.

Durkheim, E. (1956) *Education and Sociology*, trans. S. Fox, Glencoe, IL: Free Press.

Halsey, A.H. (ed.) (1972) *Educational Priority: Educational Priority Areas – Problems and Policies*, vols 1 and 2, sponsored by the Department of Education and Science and the Social Science Research Council, London: Her Majesty's Stationery Office.

Lawson, J. and Silver, H. (1973) *A Social History of Education in England*, London: Methuen.

Maclure, S. (1990) *A History of Education in London 1870–1990* (2nd edn), London: The Penguin Press.

Manning, A. and Pischke, J. (2006) *Comprehensive versus Selective Schooling in England and Wales: What Do We Know?* London: Centre for the Economics of Education, London School of Economics.

Mitch, D.F. (1992) *The Rise of Popular Literacy in Victorian England: The Influence of Private Choice and Public Policy*, Philadelphia, PA: University of Pennsylvania Press.

Orme, N. (2006) *Medieval Schools: From Roman Britain to Renaissance England*, New Haven, CT: Yale University Press.

Plowden Report (1967) *Children and their Primary Schools*, A Report of the Central Advisory Council for Education (England) London: Her Majesty's Stationery Office.

Purvis, J. (1991) *A History of Women's Education in England*, Milton Keynes: Open University Press.

Vincent, D. (2000) *The Rise of Mass Literacy: Reading and Writing in Modern Europe*, Malden, MA: Polity Press.

Wolf, A. (2011) *Review of Vocational Education*, London: Department for Education.

3

THE EARLY YEARS

Anna Vignoles

Introduction

A theme throughout this book is the recognition that developing children's skills, broadly defined, is critically important since these skills have a huge impact on children's economic and social success in life. We know that having good skills is essential to: securing success in the education system; getting a good job and to becoming a higher earner; as well as potentially improving one's health, happiness and general well-being. It is also evident that due to a range of influences, by the time individuals enter adulthood they vary substantially in their capabilities and have quite different prospects of achieving success in education and other aspects of life. We know, for instance, that children from poor families tend to be already up to a year behind their more advantaged peers educationally, even by the age of 3.[1] This stark difference in the earliest years of life then results in much worse outcomes for poor children later on. The key to changing this is improving our understanding of what causes some children to fall behind so early on in their lives and finding ways of providing early education that counters this. As is evident throughout this book, in the field of education in many instances we still lack robust evidence of 'what works'. However, this is one area where the evidence *is* convincing and relatively conclusive, largely due to a number of extremely robust early childhood experiments conducted in the US over a number of decades.

In this chapter we start by considering the evidence on why the early years are so important to children's development and how we can improve the early environments of children. Of course what really matters is whether we can design early years education to improve children's outcomes at scale, particularly the outcomes for children from the most disadvantaged backgrounds. We therefore review the effectiveness of a number of different large-scale programmes that have been trialled in various locations and we consider the limited evidence available on their relative costs and benefits. This evidence is encouraging about the potential for state interventions to improve children's early outcomes. We end by discussing briefly the ways in which early years policy in the UK has developed, in response to this evidence base. It is worth noting that the focus of this particular chapter is the early years and the ways in which educational provision can help children during this period. The issues discussed also relate to the importance of parenting, a topic that is predominantly covered in the next chapter.

So why are early years so important?

We know that a major factor that drives differences in individuals' cognitive and non-cognitive skills is the family environment in which a child is raised (or indeed the lack of family environment experienced by those in social care), an issue discussed in detail in Chapter 4 on parenting.[2] The research community, if not the policy world, has long recognised that families have a far greater influence on children's development than the school system and that this influence impacts on children long before they go to school. Indeed as long ago as 1966, the influential Coleman report highlighted the fact that most of the differences we observe in terms of children's skills and education achievements are in fact attributable to family background rather than their schooling per se. That said, parents are not the only influence on children, and the experiences of the child in the education system and in their community also matter. We also know that differences in children's skills emerge very early in their lives and the implication of this is that the education children receive in the early years is key to getting children on the right track.

To some extent the early years are important simply because this is the period during which we first observe differences emerging between children, in terms of their development, and particularly between more and less socio-economically advantaged children. However, this period is also potentially critical for biological reasons and because some attempts to improve children's skills appear to be more effective when targeted during this period.

Why might early intervention be more effective? There is evidence from neurology and child health that this is because the brain is more malleable at earlier ages, meaning that it can be influenced to a greater extent. Further, early years programmes have more time to impact on children. Get a child's basic reading, writing and mathematics right in primary school and there is a greater chance that this success will be built on as they go through the education system. The early years are also potentially important because of the interaction between a child's genetic endowment and their environment and the impact this has during critical periods of brain development in the first few years of life.

The literature on the impact of genes on children's cognitive and non-cognitive skills is growing rapidly. Empirical evidence suggests that there is a relatively strong relationship between a parent's IQ and their child's IQ. This holds even for children who are adopted at birth and hence not exposed to their biological parents. This might imply a strong role for genes, yet a number of research studies using genetic data have not found strong links between specific genes and cognitive outcomes.

This does not of course prove that genes are unimportant: rather it is likely that a larger number of genes are implicated but that no single gene explains much of the variation in a child's IQ or indeed other aspects of their cognitive skill. The 'new science' of epigenomics also tells us that we should no longer think along the lines of the traditional dichotomy of nature versus nurture. Rather we are increasingly learning that in fact the earliest environments that children are exposed to actually change the biology of children's development by altering their gene expression. This evidence confirms the importance of the earliest years, when the child is in the womb and in infancy, and the potential impact of this period on children's cognitive and non-cognitive development.

What this means is that we need to be cautious about attributing the large differences in cognitive skills we observe across children solely to genetic endowment. There is scope for parents, the state and indeed other agencies to intervene to mediate the effect of a child's genetic endowment and their environment. This is evident from the fact that there are large differences across countries in the extent of the inequality in children's developmental outcomes, suggesting that the institutional setting that a child is born into can indeed influence their skill development and consequently that genetic endowment cannot be the only explanation for poor outcomes.[3]

We also know that there are strong inter-generational forces at work that go beyond the genetic. Even allowing for differences in parental IQ, it is the case that parents who acquire more education themselves have children with higher levels of cognitive skill. In other words, the process of being educated (for the parent) appears to have a causal positive impact on their children's development, over and above any impact from the parent having a higher IQ in the first place.[4] Equally, whether or not the family lives in poverty directly influences children's educational achievement. This suggests that there may indeed be scope for state policies and programmes to improve children's outcomes by focusing on parental skills and indeed the quality of their parenting (as discussed in the next chapter), as well as the material resources available to poor families. Certainly one needs to think about the impact that educating parents has on their children's development when considering how much state subsidy to provide for adult education. Even if improvements in parents' education and skills do not directly benefit the adults themselves or the economy, we need to be aware that there are likely to be inter-generational benefits for their children that should be taken into account when calculating the benefit from state investments in their education and skills.

As has been said, there has been some misinterpretation of the neurological evidence to suggest that because early years programmes have been more effective this implies that we should focus only on the early years. Clearly this is not the case, children need support throughout their educational careers and again some neurological studies actually suggest the brain can be influenced much later than in infancy, well into early adulthood and beyond. Specifically personality traits, so called non-cognitive skills, appear more malleable in later life than IQ per se. Further, it appears that if early years programmes to improve children's skills are not then

---

HEAD START

What is it?

- Head Start is a US Federal programme that has evolved considerably over time.
- It provides a high quality pre-school education for 3- and 4-year-olds from poor families.
- The programme helps parents in a number of ways, including providing additional advice and support on health and nutrition issues and parenting approaches.

What does the programme aim to do?

The programme seeks to improve children's school readiness.

Evidence of effectiveness

High quality trials show positive short run impact from Head Start but the effect peters out over time for some.

---

built upon as they age, some of the benefits of early intervention may be lost. This has been shown most clearly by US researchers Janet Currie and Sally Thomas (2000) who found that the US pre-school programme Head Start, aimed at helping disadvantaged children, had a minimal longer-run impact on ethnic minority children since they went on to poor quality schools after the initial investments made in them. Since the early investments were not sustained, this group of children did not reap long-term benefits. So while in this chapter we focus on the impact of early years education, we need to be aware of the need for ongoing investment in our children if long-term gains are to be secured.

As well as being cautious about over-emphasising the importance of the early years and ignoring the need for sustained investment throughout childhood, there is also a danger that we focus overly much on children's cognitive skills. Certainly the focus of many early years programmes is on building children's cognitive skills to prepare them for entry into the education system. Yet research suggests that we should be thinking more broadly about the kinds of skills that need to be developed in our children. There do seem to be complementarities between different types of skills at the same age. For example, children who are able to behave appropriately in class are more likely to benefit from classroom instruction and hence behavioural skills and cognitive skills would be mutually reinforcing in this instance. We also know that in the longer run individuals who have good non-cognitive skills, such

SURE START

What is it?

- A UK government programme introduced in the late 1990s and targeted at disadvantaged families and their children.
- It is a pre-school intervention that focuses on high quality childcare, as well as integrated support on parenting, education and health issues.
- Originally a neighbourhood based programme, Sure Start is now delivered through Sure Start Centres.

What does the programme aim to do?

The programme seeks to improve children's early cognitive and non-cognitive development.

Evidence of effectiveness

Evaluations have not always found positive impacts from Sure Start. It is a less intensive (and hence less costly) programme than many of the US programmes. This may explain why results have not been as positive for this programme as compared with some US initiatives. However, more recently there is evidence of some positive health and parenting impacts, as well as some positive academic impacts.

as more positive attitudes to education, higher aspirations, better attention skills, good social adjustment, self control and self belief, will have better prospects in the education system and indeed in the labour market.[5] Cognitive and indeed non-cognitive skills also influence other life outcomes. Both cognitive and non-cognitive skills reduce the chances of a person getting in trouble with the police and having poor physical and mental health later in life.[6] This suggests that when designing policies for the early years period we need to consider ways in which we can simultaneously improve children's cognitive and non-cognitive skills; but the evidence on the impact of existing interventions on children's non-cognitive skills is more limited than for cognitive skills.

What can we do in the early years to improve children's outcomes?

So if we know that the early years are a critical time in terms of the development of a child's cognitive and non-cognitive skills, how can we design the early education system to improve outcomes for children? A range of influences impact on a child's development in the early years and the importance of the family cannot be overstated. The home-learning environment, the financial resources available to the family, the cultural resources available to the family and the level of the parents' education have all been found to be important in determining the cognitive and non-cognitive skills (for example, behaviour, including hyperactivity) of the child.

The home-learning environment includes factors such as whether the child is read to regularly, parental time with the child, whether the parents have high educational expectations, the extent of the learning opportunities presented to the child and the quality and warmth of parent–child interactions. All these factors have been found to have an important impact on a child's success in school and consequently later in life, over and above any impact from coming from a more economically advantaged family with better-educated parents.[7] It is important to clarify what this means. It suggests that in fact the home-learning environment and a child's socio-economic background are not one and the same thing. Certainly the chance of having a supportive home-learning environment is higher for a child from a wealthier background, but it is equally true that many children from poor backgrounds also have a good home-learning environment.[8] This is of course crucial in policy terms as it suggests that by helping parents change what they do at home we can influence children's outcomes, even if we cannot necessarily have a major impact on the socio-economic resources at their families' disposal.

There are two main sets of programmes that aim to help children in poor families and there is considerable overlap between them. First, there are programmes that are designed to specifically intervene with parents to improve their parenting. These programmes are reviewed in the next chapter. Second, there are programmes that are predominantly focused on providing early years education to help poor children achieve. These latter programmes often include a parenting element so to some extent the distinction between them is somewhat arbitrary.

There is remarkably consistent and robust evidence that the quality of pre-school education experienced by the child is crucially important and that pre-school programmes really can improve a poor child's outcomes[9] right through into adolescence.[10] For instance, the quality of pre-school experienced by the child has been found to have a large impact on both children's non-cognitive development (e.g. sociability, independence, concentration) and, to an even greater extent, their cognitive achievement.[11]

A particularly influential study in England, namely the Effective Provision of Pre-School Education (EPPE) project, tracked infants and young children in the earliest years of their lives and concluded that those who had higher quality pre-school provision had better cognitive skills and indeed better behavioural outcomes.[12] This positive effect of pre-school education continued to be evident as the children progressed through primary school. The impact of high quality pre-school also appears to be greater for certain types of children, such as ethnic minority children, migrant children and more economically disadvantaged children.[13] Why might this be? Well to determine the impact of attending pre-school we also need to understand the alternative. If a child is not in pre-school, they will be receiving different types of care, from parents, grandparents, childminders and the like. Children in different circumstances will therefore experience different types of alternative care. We must also be mindful that in many countries the majority of mothers with young children now work and so families will definitely need non-parental childcare of some kind or another (parental leave issues are considered in Chapter 4). Hence the impact of pre-school will depend not just on the quality of the pre-school but on the quality of any alternative care. If children from minority ethnic groups or those from poorer households receive poorer alternative care when they do not attend pre-school, this might be one explanation of why pre-school appears to benefit these groups most.

Of course some early years programmes are likely to be more effective than others. Below we consider the specific types of programmes that have been found to work.

Are there effective pre-school programmes?

One of the first experiments to determine whether a high quality pre-school education could make a difference was the Perry Pre-school random experiment conducted in the 1960s.[14] This programme was specifically focused on African American infants (3 years old) who had been identified as being cognitively disadvantaged on the basis that they scored below 85 on a standard IQ score. These children were then randomly allocated to either the pre-school programme or no pre-school at all. The programme lasted 2 years and involved about 2½ hours of pre-school a day and additional weekly home visits. Since this programme took place a long time ago it is particularly useful to look at the long-term effects of high quality pre-school and indeed researchers have analysed the outcomes for these children at age 40.

The programme did not bring about permanent gains in children's IQ per se but it did produce gains in their cognitive achievement and in their non-cognitive skills (e.g. self control). For instance, adults who undertook the pre-school programme were around 20 per cent more likely to graduate from high school and around 19 per cent less likely to have had multiple arrests. Overall, the Perry Pre-school Experiment has been found to have long term benefits by reducing participants' likelihood of committing crimes, increasing their education achievement and reducing the probability that they are in receipt of welfare payments.[15] The programme was also found to yield a good return (10–16 per cent) on the investment made, in the sense that the monetary value of the benefits produced, for both the individuals themselves and the wider community, exceeded the costs of the programme. However, one must be careful when drawing lessons from this programme: it was a relatively intense and costly programme, involving very few individuals targeted specifically for their low levels of achievement, and it is not clear that the results would hold for a less intense intervention delivered at scale.

A later 1970's programme, called the Abecedarian Project, was also conducted as a random experiment in North Carolina. This project was particularly important because it was very prescriptive in the content of the pre-school education provided and because it provided an intense high quality programme that started at a very early age (around 4½ months). Further, the programme lasted longer than most others, covering a 5-year period. The programme itself involved daily care for the child of around 6–8 hours a day and had very low child–adult ratios (1:3 for infants, 1:6 at age 5). Again, this programme was targeted largely at African American children who were at risk because their mothers had low education, low family income and other risk factors. In terms of the effects of the programme, the participants were followed up to the age of 21 and the programme was found to have a large impact on children's reading (1.8 grade level increase), mathematics (1.3 grade level increase) and some quite small improvements on child IQ. In the longer run, participants were far more likely to graduate high school, attend college, get a skilled job, not become a teen parent and not commit crime.[16]

Some of the effects from the Abecedarian Project are startlingly large. For example, around one third of those who received this programme attended university, where as just over one in ten of those in the control group did. This illustrates that pre-school can make a very large impact on children's outcomes but in this instance the very early intervention and the intensive nature of the programme were key and despite the high cost of this programme it still showed a positive return when the costs were compared with the benefits.[17]

A more recent US programme is Head Start, which is similar to the UK's Sure Start in that it is a general pre-school programme targeted at disadvantaged mothers and their children. The programme involved a combination of home visits to disadvantaged families and childcare with support and advice provided in specific child centres. The programme was aimed at children from birth to age 3. One particular outcome from the Head Start programme was to improve the quality of parenting i.e. the nature of the parent's interactions with the child.[18] Although Head Start was found to be effective its effects varied across different types of student. For example, as noted earlier, it had minimal longer-run impact on ethnic minority children. One interpretation of the somewhat more limited effects from Head Start as compared with the Abecedarian Project is that a pre-school intervention needs to be sufficiently intense and targeted to have a large impact.

In the UK, Sure Start has been modelled on the US Head Start programme in that it is an early years programme that is not particularly intense. The original intention for the Sure Start programme was to target additional resources on deprived infants by building children's centres in deprived areas, providing integrated children services and support for parents under one roof. These centres offer advice and help with parenting, as well as practical assistance of an educational or medical kind. Although the children's centres are generally located in more deprived areas, many of the beneficiaries of the facilities on offer are not necessarily the most deprived children since any child who is living in the neighbourhood can normally use the services. In terms of impact, some earlier assessments of Sure Start found very mixed results and it was by no means clear that the programme was effective.

More recent studies have suggested that Sure Start has improved children's cognitive skills and indeed their educational achievement. This is cautiously encouraging, given that the Sure Start programme is somewhat less intensive, in terms of resources, than some of the earlier US early years programmes. More recently the Coalition Government has made changes to the Sure Start programme, not least driven by budget cuts as a result of the 'austerity measures'. Specifically, there has been a shift in emphasis towards greater accountability and monitoring of the work of children's centres, better evaluation of impact and even payment by results to encourage providers to improve outcomes. It is too early to judge the results of these changes but it is likely that the programmes will become more focused on the most disadvantaged children.

In contrast to schemes focused on disadvantaged children, more general schemes, such as subsidy for childcare or guarantees of universal child care have not always produced positive outcomes. For example, in Quebec a scheme of highly subsidised childcare was introduced in the late 1990s, eventually resulting in childcare being available for all children under 5 at the highly subsidised cost of $5 per day. Baker *et al.* (2008) found that it actually had a negative impact on children's non-cognitive outcomes (specifically, the child's level of aggression, motor skills, social skills and incidence of illness). The scheme was popular, many parents took advantage of it and it did increase the numbers of mothers working but the researchers also found it resulted in an increase in problematic parenting and poorer parental well-being. This evidence relies on short run outcomes that are simply reports by the parent of the well-being of the child and themselves. Hence some caution is needed when interpreting these results. One possible explanation for the result is that the scheme encouraged mothers to work more and this may have had a negative impact on their outcomes or caused additional stress in the mothers or both.[19] This is a tentative explanation however.

However, the study does illustrate two key points. First, pre-school provision needs to be of high quality to be effective, so cheap childcare does not necessarily work. In this instance, the subsidised childcare included childminders and provision that may have been of variable quality. Second, the impact of childcare in the early years depends on the alternative childcare that children would have experienced. Hence low cost childcare may be inferior to maternal care, particularly if the mother is more educated and has good parenting skills. If policies are introduced that encourage more educated mothers and those with good parenting skills to work, this may potentially be detrimental to their children's development in the earliest years, whereas such policies may be positive for children from more disadvantaged backgrounds. Certainly universal childcare provision has proven to have a positive impact on child outcomes in Norway and Germany, for example, but in the case of Norway the positive impact was only sizeable for children from families with income below the median or migrants,[20] and in the case of Germany it was only beneficial for migrant children.[21]

Generally therefore, the evidence is that high quality pre-school provision can be very beneficial, at least for disadvantaged children. Programmes that are more intensive and last over an extended period of time are likely to be more effective, and when initial investments are then reinforced by follow up investment, outcomes are likely to be better.[22] Of course this begs the question as to what we mean by high quality. By and large more structured pre-school education programmes have been found to be more effective,[23] as have programmes that employ more qualified staff. However, this remains a highly contentious issue. While employing more qualified staff to work in pre-school settings appears to be beneficial, in the sense of producing a higher quality learning environment, it is less clear that there is a strong relationship between lower child to staff ratios and child outcomes except in the very first years of life. This is an area where there is very little in the way of experimental evidence and hence being sure of 'what works' is difficult. Our reading of the evidence is that while lower child to staff ratios are not a guarantee of high quality provision, employing sufficient numbers of more educated and qualified staff is likely to be beneficial. There is also agreement that for pre-school interventions to be effective they must be of high quality, over an extended period of time (more than a year).

One point we have made repeatedly in this chapter, however, is that while policies to improve children's cognitive skills that are targeted on the early years may be potentially more effective, this does not mean that all policies aimed at the early years produce improvements in children's outcomes. Some programmes aimed at the early years may be ineffective and we still need to know which programmes are most effective and why. We must determine what precisely we can do in the early years to bring about gains in children's skills, particularly for children from disadvantaged family backgrounds. Further, while early intervention is a necessary first stage, subsequent investment in older children and youth is needed if the gains made in the earliest years are to be sustained into adulthood. In other words, while later attempts to improve children's skill levels (particularly their cognitive skills) may be less effective if the children do not have a good basis on which to build, early investment in children alone may be insufficient to produce long-term improvements in the skills of children.

One could indeed argue that early high quality pre-school is successful because it helps the children in ways that their families cannot, in a sense it substitutes for poor parenting. An alternative approach however, is to attempt to influence the quality of parenting that a child receives directly, with parenting programmes that teach parents how to parent effectively. Such parenting programmes vary enormously in their scope and impact, ranging from parent education through to home visiting and mentoring, as reviewed in the next chapter.

Are recent reforms to the UK early years system encouraging?

In the UK at least, politicians have recognised the strength of the evidence on the effectiveness of early years programmes. Hence during the last decade or so, there has been a great deal more policy emphasis on this important period of child development and some serious financial investment, particularly under the previous Labour Government. For example, the amount spent on early years (including childcare and Sure Start) increased approximately four fold in England from 1997 to 2009.[24] It is important we understand what this increase in resources was spent on and whether or not it appears to have had a positive impact.

One of the major policy initiatives under the last Labour Government in the UK was the universal provision of nursery school places. Specifically, all 3- and 4-year-olds were entitled to at least part-time provision in a nursery or other kind of pre-school setting. This meant that such places were available even to disadvantaged children, whose mothers did not work and who would not otherwise have chosen or been able to afford any pre-school education. Indeed by 2010 there was evidence that this entitlement had ensured that a higher proportion of disadvantaged young children accessed formal pre-school and hence the gap in enrolment between more and less advantaged children narrowed.[25] The results of this policy will of course take time to be evident in children's longer run educational achievement and economic success, though the evidence discussed above on the importance of pre-school would suggest potential academic and social benefits for children from this policy. Indeed a recent review of trends over time has suggested that not only did the number of children living in poverty fall under the period of high investment under the previous Labour Government, but the gap between more and less advantaged children was reduced. This was particularly the case in gaps in terms of low birth weight, infant mortality and cognitive and non-cognitive skills.[26]

It is also significant that the subsequent Coalition Government continued to make this investment in pre-school and in fact extended free pre-school provision to 2-year-olds from disadvantaged backgrounds. One challenge however, is to ensure that this provision is of high quality, as discussed by Gambaro et al. (2013). Early results from this programme indicate cognitive and social development benefits but only for children who secured a place in a higher quality pre-school, and quality can be quite variable.[27] For example, some nursery schools will have qualified staff and quite formal provision, whereas some pre-school play group and other settings will be more informal with a lower proportion of qualified staff. While child to adult ratios are regulated by law, there is no doubt that there is much variability in the quality of provision.

Conclusions and policy implications

It is clear that the earliest years of a child's life, from the mother's womb through to primary school, are critical in terms of children's development. Families in particular play an important part in determining children's educational and life success and the impact of families starts very young. This does not, however, leave the state helpless to intervene to improve the educational performance of young children from homes where the children are at risk of low educational achievement – far from it in fact. There is good evidence that a number of programmes aimed at developing very young children's cognitive and non-cognitive skills have been highly successful. Further, cost benefit analyses have shown that some of the intensive, high cost and high quality interventions are worthwhile investments and produce valuable gains for children relative to the cost of provision.

Successful and high quality early years interventions have a number of features. High quality programmes offer a good learning environment for children but easily quantified measures, such as child to adult ratios, are not by any means the only or most important determinant of the quality of provision. Hence when trying to monitor quality we need to look more broadly than at such simple metrics, focusing on the quality of staff and the quality of their interactions with children. Successful interventions are also often targeted at more disadvantaged children. Whether or not a programme has a positive impact on children's cognitive skills depends on what alternative care or provision the child would have received. Hence subsidised state interventions in the early years can be very effective for disadvantaged children who would otherwise have experienced worse care.

We do, however, need to be cautious. There is some rather mixed evidence that some pre-school interventions may lead to worse non-cognitive outcomes and in particular poorer behaviour. It is unclear whether this is a long term effect but future research does need to focus on understanding any potential negative impact from very early (low quality) childcare interventions and ways of mitigating this.

Of course not all attempts to improve children's cognitive skills in the early years have been successful. Where programmes are not intensive enough and where they are not followed up by further investment, the effects of a good pre-school programme often peter out. Policy makers therefore need to recognise that if we are to secure the future of children currently at risk of poor educational achievement we will need to do a number of things. We need to intervene at the earliest possible point and ideally pre-birth. We must accept that we need to compensate for poor parenting and we need to invest intensively and over a long period of time. We must also acknowledge that investments need to be sustained throughout a child's schooling.

Key findings

- The impact of family background and parents on children's development is critically important.
- Children need high quality early years care but simple measures, such as the child to adult ratio, are not necessarily good indicators of quality.
- Intensive, high cost and high quality interventions in very early childhood can be effective in overcoming the negative effects of coming from a socially disadvantaged family.

Key policies

- To overcome social disadvantage we need to intervene with high quality and intensive early education programmes.

- These programmes must be followed up with further investments in children throughout their schooling if they are to be effective in the long run.
- Early years education often attempts to compensate for poor quality parenting and it is likely that an early years education programme should be accompanied by a parenting intervention (see next chapter).
- Programmes will need to be intensive and hence may be high cost, and therefore will need to be targeted on the more disadvantaged pupils, particularly if such investments are to be sustained throughout a child's schooling.

Notes

1 Feinstein, (2003).
2 See Heckman *et al.* (2006) for an economic perspective.
3 See UNICEF (2008) for a discussion of cross country differences in child outcomes.
4 See for example, Behrman and Rosenzweig (2002); Black *et al.* (2005); Black *et al.* (2005); Carneiro *et al.* (2007); Blanden *et al.* (2007); Brown *et al.* (2009); Cunha and Heckman (2008); Ermisch *et al.* (2012); Todd and Wolpin (2007).
5 Carneiro *et al.* (2006); Feinstein and Duckworth (2006); Murnane *et al.* (1995).
6 Carneiro *et al.* (2007).
7 Propper and Rigg (2007); Sylva *et al.* (2007).
8 Sylva *et al.* (2004).
9 Anderson *et al.* (2003); Gilliam and Zigler (2000).
10 Manning *et al.* (2010).
11 Camilli *et al.* (2010).
12 Sammons *et al.* (2002).
13 Barnett (1992, 1995); Currie (2001); Carneiro and Heckman (2003); Blau and Currie (2006); Cunha *et al.* (2006).
14 Heckman *et al.* (2008a).
15 Heckman *et al.* (2010).
16 Campbell *et al.* (2001, 2002).
17 Leonard and Barnett. (2002).
18 Love *et al.* (2005).
19 See Brooks-Gunn *et al.* (2010) for a discussion of the neutral impact of mothers' working and the benefit of part-time, as opposed to full-time work.
20 Havnes and Mogstad (2010).
21 Dustmann *et al.* (2012).
22 Feinstein *et al.* (1999); Goodman and Sianesi (2005); Schütz *et al.* (2008).
23 Lewis and Vosburgh (1988).
24 Stewart (2013).
25 Speight and Smith (2010).
26 Stewart (2013).
27 Smith *et al.* (2009).

Bibliography

Anderson, L.M., Shinn, C., Fullilove, M.T., Scrimshaw, S.C., Fielding, J.E., Normand, J. and Carande-Kulis, V.G. (2003) 'The effectiveness of early childhood development programs: A systematic review', *American Journal of Preventative Medicine* 24: 32–46.

Baker, M., Gruber, J. and Milligan, K. (2008) 'Universal child care, maternal labor supply and family well-being', *Journal of Political Economy* 116(4): 709–745.

Barnett, W.S (1992) 'Benefits of compulsory pre-school education', *Journal of Human Resources* 27(2): 279–312.

Barnett, W.S (1995) 'Long-term effects of early childhood programs on cognitive and school outcomes', *The Future of Children* 5(3): 25–50.

Barnett, W.S (1998) 'Long-term cognitive and academic effects of early childhood education on children in poverty', *Preventative Medicine* 27(2): 204–207.

Berger, L. M., Hill, J. and Waldfogel, J. (2005) 'Maternity leave, early maternal employment and child health and development in the US', *The Economic Journal* 115: F29–F47.

Behrman, J. and Rosenzweig, M. (2002) 'Does increasing women's schooling raise the schooling of the next generation?', *American Economic Review* 92(1): 323–324.

Black, S., Deveruex, P. and Salvanes, K. (2005) 'From the cradle of the labour market? The effect of birth weight on adult outcomes?', *The Quarterly Journal of Economics* 122(1): 409–439.

Blakemore, S. (2010) 'The developing social brain: Implications for education', *Neuron* 65(6): 744–747.

Blakemore, S. and Choudhury, S. (2006) 'Development of the adolescent brain: Implications for executive function and social cognition', *Journal of Child Psychology and Psychiatry* 47(3–4): 296–312.

Blanden, J., Gregg, P. and Macmillan, L. (2007) 'Accounting for intergenerational income persistence: Non-cognitive skills, ability and education', *Education Journal* 117: C43–C60.

Blau, D and Currie, J. (2006) 'Pre-school, day care and afternoon care: Who's minding the kids?', *Handbook of the Economics of Education*, 2: 1163–1278.

Borghans, L., Duckworth, A. L., Heckman, J. J. and ter Weel, B. (2008) 'The economics and psychology of personality traits', *Journal of Human Resources* 43(4): 972–1059.

Bradley, R. (2002) 'Environment and parenting'. In M. Bornstein *Handbook of Parenting*, 2nd ed., Hillsdale. NJ: Lawrence Erbaum Associates, pp. 281–314.

Bradley, R. and Corwyn, R. (1999) 'Parenting'. In L. Balter and C.S. Tamis-LeMonda, *Child Psychology: A Handbook of Contemporary Issues*, Philadelphia, PA: Taylor and Francis, pp. 339–362.

Brooks-Gunn, J., Wen-Jui, H. and Waldfogel, J. (2002) 'Maternal employment and child cognitive outcomes in the first three years of life: The NICHD study of early child care', *Child Development* 73(4): 1052–1072.

Brooks-Gunn, J., Wen-Jui, H. and Waldfogel, J. (2010) 'Maternal employment and child development in the first 7 years', *Monographs of the Society for Research in Child Development* 75(2): 1–147.

Brown, S., McIntosh, S. and Taylor, K. (2011) 'Following in your parents' footsteps? Empirical analysis of matched parent-offspring test scores', *Oxford Bulletin of Economics and Statistics* 73(1): 40–58.

Burgess, S., Gregg, P., Propper, C., Washbrook, E. and the ALSPAC Study Team (2002) 'Maternity rights and mothers' return to work', CMPO *Working Paper* no. 02/055, University of Bristol.

Camilli, G., Vargas, S., Ryan, S. and Barnett, W.S. (2010) 'Meta-analysis of the effects of early education interventions on cognitive and social development', *Teachers College Record* 112(3): 579–620.

Campbell, F.A., Pungello, E., Miller-Johnson, S., Burchinal, M. and Ramey, C.T. (2001) 'The development of cognitive and academic abilities: Growth curves from an early childhood educational experiment', *Developmental Psychology* 37(2): 231–242.

Campbell, F.A., Ramey, C.T., Pungello, E., Sparling, J. and Miller-Johnson, S. (2002) 'Early childhood education: Young adult outcomes from the abecedarian project', *Applied Developmental Science* 6(1): 42–57.

Carneiro, P. and Heckman, J.J. (2003) 'Human capital policy'. In J.J. Heckman, A.B. Krueger and B.M. Friedman (eds) *Inequality in America: What Role for Human Capital Policies?*, Cambridge, MA: MIT Press, pp. 77–239.

Carneiro, P., Heckman, J.J. and Vytlacil, E.J. (2006) 'Estimating marginal and average returns to education', unpublished manuscript, University of Chicago, MA: Department of Economics.

Carneiro, P., Crawford, C. and Goodman, A. (2007) 'The impact of early cognitive and non-cognitive skills on later outcomes', CEE Discussion Paper no. 92. Available at: http://cee.lse.ac.uk/ceeper cent20dps/ceedp92.pdf (accessed 6 January 2014).

Carneiro, P.K. Loken, K. and Salvanes, K. (2010) 'A flying start? Long term consequences of maternal time investments in children during their first year of life', IZA Discussion Paper no. 5362.

Chatterji, P. and Markowitz, S. (2004) 'Does the length of maternity leave affect maternal health?', NBER Working Paper no. 10206, Cambridge, MA: National Bureau for Economic Research.

Chowdry, H., Crawford, C. and Goodman, A. (2010) 'The role of attitudes and behaviours in explaining socio-economic differences in attainment at age 16', *Longitudinal and Life Course Studies* 2(1): 59–76.

Coleman, J.S. (1966) *Equality of Educational Opportunity*, Washington, DC: U.S. Department of Health, Education and Welfare, Office of Education.

Crawford, C., Goodman, A. and Joyce, R. (2010) 'Explaining the socio-economic gradient in child outcomes: The inter-generational transmission of cognitive skills', *Longitudinal and Life Course Studies* 2(1): 77–93.

Cunha, F. and Heckman, J.J. (2007) 'The technology of skill formation', *American Economic Review* 97(2): 31–47.

Cunha, F. and Heckman, J.J. (2008) 'Formulating, identifying and estimating the technology of cognitive and noncognitive skill formation', *Journal of Human Resources* 43(4): 738–782.

Cunha, F. and Heckman, J.J. (2009) 'The economics and psychology of inequality and human development', *Journal of the European Economic Association* 7(2–3): 320–364.

Cunha, F., Heckman, J.J. and Schennach, S. (2010) 'Estimating the technology of cognitive and non-cognitive skill formation', *Econometrica* 78: 883–931.

Cunha, F., Heckman, J.J, Lochner, L. and Masterov, D.V (2006) 'Interpreting the evidence on life cycle skill formation'. In Hanushek, E.A and F. Welch (eds) *Handbook of the Economics of Education*, Amsterdam: North-Holland, pp. 697–812.

Currie, J. (2001) 'Early childhood education programs', *Journal of Economic Perspectives* 15(2): 213–238.

Currie, J. and Thomas, D. (2000) 'School quality and the longer-term effects of Head Start', *Journal of Human Resources* 35(4): 755–774.

Currie, J. and Thomas, D. (2001) 'Early test scores, school quality and SES: Longrun effects on wage and employment outcomes', *Research in Labor Economics* 20: 103–132.

Currie, J. and Moretti, E. (2003) 'Mother's education and the intergenerational transmission of human capital: Evidence from college openings', *Quarterly Journal of Economics* 118(4): 1495–1532.

De Coulon, A., E. Meschi and A. Vignoles (2008) 'Parents' basic skills and children's cognitive outcomes', Centre for the Economics of Education Discussion Paper 104. Available at: http://eprints.lse.ac.uk/23653/1/ceedp104.pdf (accessed 6 January 2014).

Desforges, C. and Abouchaar, A. (2003) *The Impact of Parental Involvement, Parental Support and Family Education on Pupil Achievement and Adjustment: A Literature Review*, Research Report no. RR433, Sheffield: DfES.

Dustmann, C. and Schonberg, U. (2008) 'The effect of expansions in maternity leave coverage on children's long-term outcomes', IZA Discussion Paper no. 3605.

Dustmann, C., Raute, A. and Schonberg, U. (2012) 'Does universal child care matter? Evidence from a large expansion in pre-school education', mimeo. Available at: www.ucl.ac.uk/~uctpb21/Cpapers/KiGa_october22_final.pdf (accessed 6 January 2014).

Ermisch, J., Jantti, M. and Smeeding, T. (2012) *The Intergenerational Transmissions of Advantage*, New York: Russell Sage Foundation.

Esping-Andersen, G. (2004) 'Unequal opportunities and the mechanisms of social inheritance'. In M. Corak (ed.) *Generational Income Mobility in North America and Europe*, Cambridge: Cambridge University Press, pp. 284–314.

Evangelou, M. and Sylva, K. (2003) *The Effects of the Peers Early Education Partnership (PEEP) on Children's Developmental Progress*, Brief No: RB489, London: Department for Education and Skills.

Feinstein, L. (2003) 'Inequality in the early cognitive development of British children in the 1970 cohort', *Economica* 70(277): 73–97.

Feinstein, L. (2004) 'Mobility in pupils' cognitive attainment during school life', *Oxford Review of Economic Policy* 20(2): 213–229.

Feinstien, L. and Duckworth, K. (2006) *Development in the Early Years: Its Importance of School Performance and Adult Outcomes*, London: Centre for Research on the Wider Benefits of Learning, Institute of Education, University of London.

Feinstein, L., Robertson, D. and Symons, J. (1999) 'Pre-school education and attainment in the national child development study and British cohort study', *Education Economics* 7(3): 209–234.

Gambaro, L., Stewart, K. and Waldfogel, J. (2013) 'A question of quality: Do children from disadvantaged backgrounds receive lower quality early years education and care in England?',

CASE *Discussion Paper* no. 171. Available at: http://sticerd.lse.ac.uk/dps/case/cp/CASEpaper 171.pdf (accessed 6 January 2014).

Garces, E., Thomas, D. and Currie, J. (2002) 'Longer-term effects of Head Start', *American Economic Review* 92(4): 999–1012.

Gilliam, W. and Zigler, E.F. (2000) 'A critical meta-analysis of all evaluations of state-funded pre-school from 1977 to 1998: Implications for policy, service delivery and program evaluation', *Early Childhood Research Quarterly* 15(4): 441–473.

Goodman, A. and Sianesi, B. (2005) 'Early education and children's outcomes: How long do the impacts last?', *Fiscal Studies* 26(4): 513–548.

Gregg, P., Washbrook, E., Propper, C. and Burgess, S. (2005) 'The effects of a mother's return to work decision on child development in the UK', *The Economic Journal* 115(501): F48–F80.

Havnes, T. and Mogstad, M. (2010) 'Is universal childcare leveling the playing field? Evidence from non-linear difference-in-differences', IZA Discussion Paper no. 4978.

Heckman, J., Stixrud, J. and Urzua, S. (2006) *The Effects of Cognitive and Noncognitive Abilities on Labor Market Outcomes and Social Behavior*, no. w12006, London: National Bureau of Economic Research.

Heckman, J., Malofeeva, L., Pinto, R. and Savelyev, P. (2008a) 'The effect of the Perry Pre-school Program on the cognitive and non-cognitive skills of its participants', unpublished manuscript, University of Chicago, MA, Department of Economics.

Heckman, J., Moon, S.H., Pinto, R., Savelyev, P. and Yavitz, A. (2008b) 'A reanalysis of the HighScope Perry Pre-school Program', unpublished manuscript, University of Chicago, MA, Department of Economics.

Heckman J., Moon S.H, Pinto R., Savelyev P., Yavitz, A. (2010) 'The rate of return to the HighScope Perry Pre-school Program', *Journal of Public Economics* 94(1–2): 114–128.

Jerrim, J., Vignoles, A., Lingham, R. and Friend, A. (2013) 'The socio-economic gradient in children's reading skills and the role of genetics', June, Institute of Education mimeo.

Leonard, N. and Steven Barnett, A. (2002) *Benefit-Cost Analysis of the Abecedarian Early Childhood Intervention*, New Brunswick, NJ: National Institute for Early Education Research.

Lewis, R.J. and Vosburgh, W.T. (1988) 'Effectiveness of kindergarten intervention programs: A meta-analysis', *School Psychology International* 9(4): 265–275.

Liu, Q. and Skans, O. (2009) 'The duration of paid parental leave and children's scholastic performance', IZA Discussion Paper no. 424.

Love, J., Kisker, E., Ross, C., Constantine, J., Boller, K., Chazan-Cohen, R., Brady-Smith, C., Fuligni, A., Raikes, H., Brooks-Gunn, J., TarulRo, L., Schochet, P., Paulsell, D. and Vogel, C. (2005) 'The effectiveness of Early Head Start for 3-year-old children and their parents: Lessons for policy and programs', *Developmental Psychology* 41: 885–901.

Machin, S. and McNally, S. (2004) 'The literacy hour', IZA Discussion Paper no. 1005.

Maguire, E.A., Gadian, D.G., Johnsrude, I.S., Good, C.D., Ashburner, J., Frackowiak, R.S. and Frith, C.D. (2000) 'Navigation-related structural change in the hippocampi of taxi drivers', *Proceedings of the National Academy of Science, USA* 97(8): 4398–4403.

Manning, M., Hommel and Smith (2010) 'A meta-analysis of the effects of early years developmental prevention programs in at-risk populations on non-health outcomes in adolescence', *Children and Youth Services Review* 32: 506–519.

Murnane, R., Willett, J. and Levy, F. (1995) *The Growing Importance of Cognitive Skills in Wage Determination*, no. w6076, London: National Bureau of Economic Research.

Olds, D.L. (2006) 'The nurse-family partnership: An evidence-based preventative intervention', *Infant Mental Health Journal* 27: 5–25.

Propper, C. and Rigg, J. (2007) *Socio-Economic Status and Child Behaviour: Evidence from a Contemporary UK Cohort*, London: CASE, LSE.

Reynolds, A. J. and Temple, J.A. (2009) 'Economic returns of investments in pre-school'. In *A Vision For Universal Prekindergarten*, eds E. Zigler, W. Gilliam and S. Jones. Cambridge: Cambridge University Press, pp. 37–68.

Ruhm, C. (2000) 'Parental leave and child health', *Journal of Health Economics* 19(6): 931–960.

Rutter, M. (2006) *Genes and Behaviour: Nature-Nurture Interplay Explained*, Oxford, UK: Blackwell.

Sammons, P., Sylva, K., Melhuish, E., Siraj-Blatchford, I., Taggart, B. and Elliot, K. (2002) *Measuring the Impact of Pre-School on Children's Cognitive Progress Over the Pre-School Period*, EPPE Technical Paper 8a, London: Institute of Education.

Sammons, P., Sylva, K., Melhuish, E., Siraj-Blatchford, I., Taggart, B. and Grabbe, Y. (2007) *Effective Pre-School and Primary Education 3–11 Project (EPPE 3–11): Influences on Children's Attainment and Progress in Key Stage 2: Cognitive Outcomes in Year 5*, London: Institute of Education, University of London.

Schütz, G., Ursprung, H.W. and Wößmann, L. (2008) 'Education policy and equality of opportunity', *Kyklos* 61: 279–308.

Shonkoff, J.P. and Phillips, D.A. (eds) (2000) *From Neurons to Neighborhoods: The Science of Early Childhood Development*, Washington, DC: National Academy Press.

Smith, R., Purdon, S., Schneider, V., La Valle, I., Wollny, I., Owen, R., Bryson, C., Mathers, S., Sylva, K. and Lloyd, E. (2009) 'Early education pilot for two year old children evaluation', Department for Children, Schools and Families Research Report DCSF-RR134.

Smolensky, E. and Gootman, J. (eds) (2003) *Working Families and Growing Kids: Caring for Children and Adolescents*, Washington, DC: National Academy Press.

Speight, S. and Smith, R. (2010) *Towards Universal Early Years Provision: Analysis of Take-Up by Disadvantaged Families from Recent Annual Childcare Surveys*, London: Department for Education.

Stewart, K. (2013) 'Labour's record on the under fives: policy, spending and outcomes 1997–2010', CASE *Discussion Paper* SPCCWP04, London: London School of Economics.

Sylva, K., Siraj-Blatchford, I. and Taggart, B. (2003) *Assessing Quality in the Early Years: Early Childhood Environment Rating Scale Extension (ECERS-E): Four Curricular Subscales*, Stoke on Trent, UK and Stirling, NJ: Trentham Books.

Sylva, K., Melhuish, E., Siraj-Blatchford, I. and Taggart, B. (2007) *Promoting Equality in the Early Years*, Report to the Equalities Review, London: Cabinet Office.

Sylva, K., Melhuish, E., Sammons, P. Siraj-Blatchford, I. and Taggart, B. (2004) 'The effective provision of pre-school education (EPPE): Project findings from the pre-school period', EPPE Brief 2503, London: Institute of Education.

Tierney, J. and Grossman, J. (1995) *Making a Difference: An Impact Study of Big Brothers/Big Sisters*, Philadelphia, PA: Public/Private Ventures.

Todd, P.E. and Wolpin, K.I. (2007) 'The Production of cognitive achievement in children: Home, school and racial test score gaps', *Journal of Human Capital* 1(1): 91–136.

UNICEF (2008) *The Child Care Transition: A League Table of Early Childhood Education and Care in Economically Advanced Countries*, Florence: UNICEF.

Valenzuela, M. (2009) 'Can cognitive exercise prevent the onset of Dementia? Systematic review of randomised clinical trials with longitudinal follow-up', *American Journal of Geriatric Psychiatry* 17(3): 179–187.

Waldfogel, J. (2002) 'Child care, women's employment and child outcomes', *Journal of Population Economics* 15(3): 527–548.

Waldfogel, J. (2004) 'Social mobility, life chances and the early years', *CASEpaper* 88, STICERD, London: London School of Economics.

Webster-Stratton, C. (1998) 'Preventing conduct problems in Head Start children: strengthening parenting competences', *Journal of Consulting and Clinical Psychology* 66: 715–730.

Wößmann, L. and Schütz, G. (2006) *Efficiency and Equity in European Education and Training Systems*, Analytical Report for the European Commission, Munich, Germany: Institute for Economic Research, University of Munich.

4

PARENTS AND PARENTING

Anna Vignoles

Introduction

In the previous chapter we discussed the importance of the early years and acknowledged that a major factor driving differences in children's skills and educational achievement is the family in which the child is raised or indeed the lack of a family environment experienced by those in social care. While the family is not the *only* factor influencing a child's outcomes, the role of parents and parenting cannot be overstated.

In this chapter we start by considering why we are interested in parents and parenting and highlight why we think this is an important policy issue. We then go on to ask how important parents and parenting are for children's outcomes before considering how specific aspects of parenting appear to influence children's outcomes. We start by evaluating the importance of parental resources, before moving on to their knowledge, attitudes and finally their parenting practices. This evidence base tells us what parents themselves might do to foster better child development. We then discuss the long-term effectiveness of particular programmes that have been adopted in various countries to improve parenting, especially programmes targeting parents whose children are at risk of poor outcomes. Considering these programmes and their effectiveness will provide some sense of what might work in terms of interventions to help parents to parent more effectively.

Why are we interested in parents and parenting?

Children in good home-learning environments, with additional financial and cultural resources available to them, do better in terms of their cognitive and non-cognitive skill. But what constitutes a good home-learning environment? Different studies define this in different ways, but we use the term to describe an environment that maximises children's learning and in this chapter we present the evidence that describes just such an environment. The knowledge, education and skills that parents have, and potentially their genetic endowment, affect how well their children do in school, though the latter is the subject of much controversy. The way parents look after and parent their children also influences their children's outcomes. For example, we know that children will do better if their parents read regularly to and with them, spend more time with them, have high expectations of them and present them with a range of educational and learning opportunities. Further, children who experience certain parenting styles also appear to do better both in education and later in life: parental warmth towards their children, particularly in the early years, is important. This implies that 'good' parenting, i.e. parenting that may help children achieve academically and developmentally, is not only about financial resources but also about parenting practices.[1]

Certainly parenting has become a major policy issue, with politicians of all hues commenting on the effectiveness or otherwise of parents.[2] Topics of particular note in the media and among politicians include: the apparent poor parenting of children who have major behavioural problems (especially conduct disorders); the increasing prevalence of non-traditional (single parent/cohabiting) households and the implications of this for children; and more generally the impact of family breakdown on children. Solutions put forward to solve these apparent social ills include a greater emphasis on traditional family structures (i.e. marriage), the censuring of parents who are found to be negligent or inadequate in some way and, more positively, programmes to support and educate young people on how to be good parents. However, the evidence behind many of these proposed solutions is weak and it remains an important and controversial question as to whether and how the state should intervene to help parents to parent more effectively. There is now recognition, by the UK Government at least, that there is no longer such a thing as a 'typical' family[3] but knowing this does not necessarily make it easier to provide appropriate help to families. What is clear is that public policy can *potentially* influence parents' behaviour and hence impact on children, and so considering the issue of parenting should be central to any strategy to improve children's academic outcomes and their wellbeing.

So how important are parents and parenting?

Despite parents being very concerned about the schools that their children attend, researchers have long recognised that the family environment that the child experiences is relatively more important for their development. In 1966 an influential report written by sociologist James Coleman demonstrated the crucial importance of a child's family background in determining their future outcomes, including its education achievement. Since then, most empirical studies have suggested that children's family circumstances have a greater impact on educational success than the school they attend or even which teacher they have.[4] This is not to say that schools and teachers do not matter. In circumstances where parents are really struggling to parent well, it may well be that schools and individual teachers, potentially at least, play an even more important role. However, when we look at differences across children in terms of their academic and their non-cognitive outcomes, it is apparent that a child's family environment is a better indicator of their likely success or otherwise, than their school.

There are of course a number of ways in which parents influence their children's cognitive and non-cognitive outcomes. The most obvious way is that they provide a genetic endowment to their children. There is much controversy about the exact relationship between specific genes and children's education achievement, their IQ, or indeed a range of other cognitive and non-cognitive outcomes. We do not propose to discuss the biological evidence in detail here, but there are a number of important points to make on the topic of heritability. First and foremost, while non-biological studies using twins and siblings have implied a strong genetic link for many outcomes, what is proving harder to determine is which specific genes cause the intergenerational transmission of the outcomes. We are therefore not yet in a position to say with confidence the extent of heritability of particular outcomes of interest, say reading or mathematical skills. Second, it is increasingly apparent that the nature versus nurture dichotomy is too simplistic. Indeed, as we discussed in the previous chapter, recent research from epigenomics has discovered that the earliest environments that children are exposed to actually change the biology of child development and it is the interplay of genes and environment that influences child outcomes.[5] Hence this new area of genetic research suggests that families are important not least because they provide the child's physical and emotional environment from conception onwards.

Thus even genetic research would suggest that the role of parents and families goes well beyond the genes they pass on to their children. Parents influence their children's outcomes via the resources they have available for raising their child, the skills, knowledge and attitudes that they have and of course their parenting practices. We now consider each of these in turn.

What difference do parental resources make?

Despite decades of policies designed to improve access to education by children from poorer backgrounds, by some measures social inequality in education achievement actually worsened in the UK during the 1980s and early 1990s, although it does appears to have improved somewhat since then.[6] Hence despite much effort to try to improve the education achievement of poor children, the economic and social circumstances into which a child is born continues to predict their education achievement. This does not mean of course that all poor children necessarily have bad outcomes. Many poorer parents have children who achieve well at school. Nonetheless, poorer parents have less economic resources at their disposal and there is evidence that low family income and poverty causes children to achieve less well in school.[7] Further, poverty in *early* childhood, when many families and particularly single parent families are more economically vulnerable, is particularly detrimental to children's educational achievement later on.[8] Even though single parenthood per se has not been found to have a negative impact on children's cognitive development, there is no doubt that the economic distress associated with being a single-parent household often can.

The mechanisms by which poverty and low income might affect a child are perhaps obvious. Families with greater economic resources can potentially buy nutritionally superior food, live in well-heated houses, purchase more educational toys and books and, critically, can buy better quality childcare and schooling. That said, much of the apparent relationship between family income and child achievement is actually down to factors other than income. For example, poorer families tend to have younger parents and the children of young mothers in particular do worse in school.[9] Families with low income are also more likely to have parents who have mental health problems and this too is associated with poorer educational achievement of children.[10] Additionally, if parents have to work more, they are likely to spend less time with their children and there is some evidence that full-time work by mothers in the very early years of a child's life can be detrimental to their child's social development (though this is by no means conclusive evidence).[11] In terms of fathers, while there is little evidence that the quantity of time fathers spend with their children matters, there is some evidence that the *quality* of the time that fathers spend with their children does influence their school success and fathers in low-income households may be less able to spend quality time with their children.[12]

There are of course a number of other factors associated with low income. The poorest families tend to experience greater marital and partnership instability and live in more deprived neighbourhoods with more deprived schools.[13] Some of these factors have been causally linked to poor child achievement. It also appears to be the case, perhaps unsurprisingly, that the children who are most likely to be negatively affected in terms of their cognitive development will be those who experience a number of these risks simultaneously.[14]

In summary, the economic resources available to the child and the family do appear to play a role in influencing the child's educational outcomes, but largely because having low income is also associated with a number of other difficulties within the family. Therefore we cannot conclude that improving children's outcomes is simply a question of providing higher incomes for the poorest families. Any policy solution to low achievement by poor children needs to focus not just on increasing the income of the poorest families but also tackling these other related problems. We know that parents' involvement in their children's lives is crucially important, that children will do better in a stable home where their intellectual interests are stimulated and parents discuss things with their children.[15] They will do better in homes where education is valued and parents have high aspirations and high involvement in their child's schooling. Poorer children are far less likely to experience such environments and the big policy challenge is to help these vulnerable families build more supportive environments despite the many economic and social difficulties they face.

How important is parental knowledge?

As well as the time and resources that parents give their children, the education, knowledge and skills that parents have also influence their children's outcomes. In particular parents with higher IQs and more education have children who do better in school.[16] This evidence suggests that parental education causally influences children's outcomes, so it is not simply that more educated parents tend to have higher incomes and live in better family environments, rather it is the education of the parent that impacts directly on the education achievement of the child. Of course an educated parent may have children with greater levels of academic achievement simply because the parent has a stronger genetic endowment to pass on to the child. However, even in studies that have been able to allow for differences in parental IQ, it is still clear that more educated parents have children who do better educationally. This is partially because more educated parents provide more stimulation to their children, they talk more often to their children and engage their children in conversation more, and hence they help develop their child's cognitive skills. For example, more educated parents have a wider vocabulary and are more likely to use this vocabulary when speaking to their children and hence their children also tend to have a wider vocabulary at an earlier age.[17] It is also the case that educated mothers are more likely to breastfeed their children, vaccinate their children and undertake other parenting practices that may be more beneficial. Certainly there is good causal evidence of the benefit of breastfeeding for children's cognitive development, and of the benefits of breastfeeding for longer.[18]

Indeed children who have more educated mothers generally do better on a wide range of outcomes.[19] This is critical from a policy perspective as it suggests that there will be very long-term inter-generational benefits from education. When we are making decisions about how to invest the more restricted state budgets that we currently have, we need to be mindful that the pay off from education can, quite literally, take another generation to be fully realised.

How do parental attitudes influence children's outcomes?

While parental education, knowledge and skills clearly influence a child's development and education achievement, parental aspirations and parental expectations have also been found to be important. Whether the parent expects the child to do well in school and whether the parent aspires for the child to have educational and economic success does appear to influence the child's actual achievement. Again this is not simply because parents who have high aspirations also have higher income and live in more advantaged circumstances. Even allowing for this, researchers have found that high parental aspirations and expectations are strongly related to children's achievement.[20] Some of this relationship may be because parents with higher educational aspirations actually get more involved in their children's education, support them more in their homework and place greater emphasis on school work in the home.[21] Again, one has to think carefully about the policy implications of these findings. It is not enough to encourage all parents to have higher educational aspirations for their children, rather we need to encourage parents to both have high aspirations *and* help their children achieve them via their engagement with their education. Recent data from the Millennium Cohort Study suggests that more than around 80 per cent of the richest fifth of mothers aspire or expect their child to go to university; for the poorest mothers that falls to just under 40 per cent, still a relatively high proportion.[22] By and large aspirations were even higher for all minority ethnic groups as compared with whites.[23] Given that overall less than 40 per cent of young people go on to university in the UK, these appear to be quite high levels of aspiration, even if a smaller proportion of poorer families have such high aspirations for their children. However, it is also *how* parents help their children realise those expectations that matters as we discuss below.

What parenting practices appear to be more effective?

The home-learning environment of the child and the parenting routines and styles adopted by the parents do appear to influence the child's outcomes.[24] Of course separating out the impact of parental education, skill and ability from parenting practices is very difficult indeed.[25] Nonetheless UK evidence indicates that the home-learning environment is at least as important as, or even more important than parents' socio-economic status per se.[26] This is of course reassuring for policy-makers. While policy might struggle to influence the socio-economic status of a parent or indeed parental education levels, introducing programmes designed to help parents improve their parenting practices seems a more tractable solution. It still requires us, however, to have a good idea about what makes for an effective parenting approach.

There are a number of theories that explain what makes for effective parenting, the main ones being social learning theory, attachment theory, parenting styles theory and the model of human ecology (as set out by The National Academy of Parenting Research[27]). Social learning theory suggests that positive child behaviour can be reinforced by rewarding the child for good behaviour and by ignoring or punishing inappropriate behaviour. Hence some of the parenting programmes discussed below focus on helping parents improve the behaviour of their children by building on the premise that positive behaviour should be rewarded and inappropriate behaviour ignored or sanctioned. Attachment theory is not necessarily in contrast to social learning theory but focuses on the need for children, and specifically young infants, to form a strong emotional bond with their mother or primary caregiver. Some parenting programmes focus on getting the parent(s) to respond more to their child's attempts to get their attention, building their sensitivity and helping them form a responsive and strong bond with their child.

The theory of parenting styles links the behaviour of the child with specific parenting practices. Parenting programmes based on this theory encourage parents to combine parenting warmth with clear boundaries (authoritative parenting) and high levels of attention to boost their children's confidence and improve their behaviour. Finally, the model of human ecology recognises that the child develops in a way that is influenced by the interactions between the child, their family, school, community and wider society. There are therefore factors within these environments that can increase a child's risk of poor outcomes or indeed factors that can protect the child. Parenting programmes based on this model try to strengthen protective factors to mitigate the differing levels of risk faced by each child, though the specifics of how they might do this varies across programmes.

Of course these theories can help guide our thinking on what makes for a good parenting programme, but we really need to know what works in practice, based on robust empirical evidence. Such programmes need to be informed by the evidence on the impact of parenting practices, and they need to encourage positive practices such as reading to the child or adopting clear boundaries and authoritative parenting approaches. Work on the influential *Effective Provision of Pre-school Education* study[28] has suggested that there are a number of key behaviours that are important positive aspects of parenting in the early years. These include reading to the child, playing with alphabets and numbers, going to the library, painting, drawing, singing, rhyming, taking children on visits and arranging for children to play with their friends at home. So parenting programmes are likely to try to encourage parents to engage in such activities but also draw on the theories described above about *how* to parent. Programmes will also need to recognise that while parental involvement in their child's education is indeed crucially important, this involvement tends to reduce as the child ages. So programmes need to be age appropriate, with perhaps quite different approaches in adolescence. One of the challenges when designing programmes for adolescence is also that children themselves affect how parents parent, so for example a child who is higher achieving in school will tend to encourage parents to be more involved in their education. Equally a child who is in difficulty may have the opposite effect.[29] While there is evidence from later in adolescence that parents can influence their child's achievement positively through supporting their learning in the home, for example through homework or outside reading, etc., this is undoubtedly a greater challenge.[30] We will now consider the effectiveness of some specific programmes largely but not exclusively aimed at the parents of younger children.

What is the long-term impact of specific parenting programmes?

Clearly families have a huge impact on children.[31] The question is how can we help families do better for their children? In the previous chapter we included a review of various interventions that are specifically targeted on the earliest years of a child's life. There is no doubt about the critical importance of early intervention, especially for the most disadvantaged children. However, the evidence on the impact of early years programmes is mixed, programmes are quite diverse and many are not fully evaluated. For some early years programmes there is simply

CHILDREN MOST AT RISK

Some children experience extremely disadvantaged childhoods, acutely bad parenting and significant neglect and stress or even abuse. These children are at severe risk of a range of poor outcomes, including poor health, poor cognitive development, poor non-cognitive skills and premature death.

We know that stress and insecure relationships in the first years of life can have a particularly detrimental impact on a child's non-cognitive skills in the longer term. This is a major mechanism through which poor parenting can have such a negative impact on children and particularly their likelihood of developing conduct disorders.

Children who have experienced such weak parenting can lack a range of important non-cognitive skills that have been found to be important for longer term educational and economic success, including:

- 'Grit'
- Conscientiousness
- Persistence
- Self-control
- Optimism
- Motivation
- Willpower.

In the US there is some evidence that children from very wealthy families can also experience problems developing good non-cognitive skills, again largely because of emotional distance from their parents and excessive parental criticism. See for example various studies by Suniya Luthar and colleagues.

Some parenting programmes have been found to be effective in preventing neglect and abuse, as well as improving children's non-cognitive skills. These effective programmes often revolve around intensive parent-child psychotherapy, support based on attachment theory that seeks to build secure relationships in the family, and education and training targeted specifically to help parents or carers meet the needs of children who have experienced acute stress in their lives.

Two examples of effective programmes are:

The Incredible Years Programme, which has been shown to reduce the risk of conduct disorders in children and to be cost effective (McGilloway *et al.* 2009; O'Neill *et al.* 2011)

Nurse-Family Partnership, which has been shown to reduce child maltreatment and associated outcomes (Olds *et al.* 1986; Krugman *et al.* 2007 and see review by MacMillan *et al.* 2009) no good evidence of a long run positive effect. Indeed some do not even produce positive short-term effects.[32] However, the previous chapter did highlight the fact that some family-focused early years interventions and parenting programmes *can* help improve outcomes for children. Here we discuss the evidence on what works in terms of parenting programmes more generally, including programmes targeted at children in both primary and secondary school.

It should be pointed out that many, if not most, of the parenting programmes introduced both here in the UK and in the US are actually focused on either preventing abuse or neglect, or improving the behaviour and mental health of children and young people, rather than their academic attainment per se. We do not consider the specific issue of child abuse and neglect here[33] but some more general early years and parenting programmes, such as the Nurse Family Partnership, have been found to be effective in reducing the likelihood of abuse or neglect. Although the primary aim of such programmes is often to influence behaviour and outcomes such as youth crime and antisocial behaviour,[34] many of these inter-ventions also potentially impact on educational achievement. Examples of such programmes include Strengthening Families Strengthening Communities, which aims to build better relationships between parents and children, or Parent-Child Interaction Therapy for Primary Age Children and Functional Family Therapy for older children, both of which address conduct disorders in children.

One example of a parenting programme that is primarily focused on child behaviour but that has been found to influence children's education achievement is First Step to Success.[35] The programme is designed to help children who might develop aggression and antisocial behaviour. It involves an individual behaviour coach working with the student, their friends and their teacher. A major component of the programme is also a parent-training element and the parent aspect of the programme is relatively intense (45 minutes of coaching per week for 6 weeks). The parent coaching sessions are designed to improve parent–child communication, as well as other aspects such as confidence development. The programme had a positive impact on children's behavioural outcomes but had no impact on their reading or literacy. However, the programme did show some positive impact on academic performance overall, which is promising.

The Child-Parent Centre Education Programme is a typical example of a parent programme that has focused more directly on the educational achievement of children, and also has the advantage of meeting (with some limitations) the 'What Works Clearinghouse'[36] standard of evidence for its effectiveness.[37] This programme is designed to provide both education and family support in pre-school (age 3) and primary school (up to age 9). The support is aimed at improving children's language and mathematical skills and involves both teachers and parents. The intervention includes work with families and specifically provides parenting education, home visits and health services. The long-run impact of the study is impressive with those in the programme going on to complete more schooling, being more likely to graduate from high school and more likely to go to university than the comparison group. This study reminds us perhaps that a successful parenting programme is likely to be intensive and may have greater impact if it is focused on younger children.

Some programmes have been targeted on fathers. We have already noted that the quality of the time that fathers spend with their children is important in fostering good child development. Further, the key determinant of the relationship between the father and his children turns out to be the quality of the relationship between the father and the mother (and this holds whether married or divorced). Hence programmes that *involve* fathers and mothers, rather than programmes only aimed at mothers or indeed aimed solely at fathers, appear more likely to be effective. In 1999 Lloyd undertook a comprehensive review of the evidence on fathers and their impact on children's outcomes and found that programmes that promote an 'authoritative style of parenting' are particularly likely to be effective for fathers, as are programmes that focus on issues of co-parenting. One such programme is the Incredible Years,[38] discussed in the previous chapter. Other programmes, specifically Triple P,[39] the Supporting Fathers Involvement Project,[40] and the Marriage and Parenting in Stepfamilies Intervention,[41] have been evaluated and found to be effective in terms of improving both fathers' and children's behaviour and interactions.[42] All these programmes stress the importance of authoritative parenting in particular.

Given the evidence cited earlier that the age of the mother influences the child's likelihood of success, with younger mothers having lower achieving children, some parenting programmes are specifically targeted at teen mothers. One such programme is Chances for Children Teen Parent-Infant Project. This programme is provided to young mothers attending high schools in New York City. Activities for this programme include individual and group interventions that aim to improve teen mothers' education and coping skills, as well as prevent destructive relationships from interfering with the healthy development of the mother and child. Teen fathers are encouraged to participate in the service and individual counselling is provided by social work staff when appropriate.

The programmes described above are generally flagship programmes, large scale, costly, intensive and targeted towards very vulnerable families. As has been said, many are aimed at improving child behaviours and preventing conduct disorders in children both of which have significant negative impacts on a child's academic and social outcomes. The consensus certainly appears to be that many programmes impact positively on children's behaviours.[43] However, there is limited research that has tried to calculate both the costs and the benefits of such programmes: what work there indicates that such programmes are likely to be good investments. Bonin *et al.* (2011) have estimated the potential cost savings from adopting a typical effective parenting programme for a typical 5-year-old with a clinical conduct disorder. They found the cost savings to be large in relation to the costs of the average programme. The cost savings largely arise from reductions in costs of health, education, social care and intervention from the criminal justice system. They estimated that a typical programme would save the public purse more than £16,000 per family, which is considerably more than the average cost of the programmes, which at that time ranged from £1,000–2,000 (2008/2009 prices). O'Neill *et al.* (2011) have undertaken a cost benefit analysis based on the results of a randomised controlled trial testing the impact of *The Incredible Years* programme described earlier. They estimated a rate of return on the investment in the programme to be around 13 per cent. Clearly such calculations are based on a number of strong assumptions about the financial benefits arising from these programmes and inevitably such estimates tend to be broad brush. However, these numbers are encouraging and suggest that such programmes, though relatively expensive, are likely to provide good value for money in the longer term even when assessed in purely monetary terms. When one considers the broader benefits that may not be so readily monetised, serious consideration should be given to further investments in such programmes.

There is another set of programmes that are generally somewhat lower cost and focused on a wider group of parents. These programmes address the specific issue of improving parental involvement and engagement of parents with their children's education. They often involve getting parents to come into their children's schools to learn about what they are doing, getting parents to support homework activities and generally strengthening the link between the parent and the school. These programmes are underpinned by evidence that has found strong links between parental involvement and children's outcomes. For instance, Jeynes (2005) reviewed 77 studies that had looked at the relationship between parental involvement in children's education and children's achievement during compulsory schooling. This meta-analysis concluded that parental involvement is very clearly highly related to children's achievement. More involved parents have children who do better in school. The study tried to examine which particular aspects of parental involvement are most effective and concluded that while reading with children, talking to them and having high expectations are all important, parental expectations and aspirations are particularly important. The result held across different ethnic groups. A follow-up piece by Jeynes in 2007 focused on older children in urban secondary schools. Again, the findings suggested that parental involvement is important even at this age and this holds across ethnic groups. So there appears to be no doubt that parental involvement can help children achieve and that such programmes should particularly strive to raise parental expectations.

The evidence on the effectiveness of parental involvement programmes suggests they have moderate effects. It appears to be hard to design a programme that can bring about large increases in parental involvement and in turn large improvements in children's achievement. An important and very high quality systematic review by Nye and others in 2006 looked at the most rigorous evidence of the impact of parent involvement programmes in *primary* education. This review ended up focusing on 19 randomised controlled trials of programmes, which sought to engage parents in their children's education. The results were encouraging. These programmes did, on average, improve parental involvement and this in turn had an impact on children's academic achievement. There was no clear relationship between the length of the programme and its impact but one key result was that parents becoming involved in academic enrichment activities outside of school had a beneficial impact. This is consistent with another meta-analysis (of just seven studies) by Senechal and Young[44] who found that training parents how to teach their children literacy did indeed have a positive significant impact on their literacy skills. Other reviews of family literacy programmes have also found that they can produce a positive impact, though in many cases this impact is quite modest in size.[45]

So are there other ways that we can teach parents how to be better parents? Might formal parenting lessons be a good option to pursue? It is certainly a solution that has often been suggested by policy-makers and other stakeholders in the UK. A survey by Layzer and others in 2001 concluded in fact that most parent education programmes had at best modest impacts and were not likely to make a major difference to children's academic achievement. Many programmes had no impact at all and designing parent education that is effective is clearly challenging. That said, those programmes that were more focused on vulnerable families and children and more intense were more likely to be effective. This is a similar message to the one that comes out of the early years evidence reviewed in the previous chapter: programmes that are likely to be successful will tend to be intensive and aimed at the most needy families.

What are the lessons for policy?

In terms of child development, and particularly children's cognitive achievement, the influence of parents appears to be greater than the influence of schools or even teachers, despite the evidence on the importance of the latter. This raises the question about what policy can do to improve children's achievement, since improving schools or recruiting and retaining the highest quality teachers would appear to be the obvious way that policy makers might aim to affect children's outcomes and intervening in families appears to be more difficult. For children in the most vulnerable families, or indeed children in care, it is possible we might design schools that would have a much greater impact on children, to offset the lack of good parenting experienced by some children. Indeed in the US, KIPP schools[46] that provide 24/7 support to children and wrap around care from 7 a.m. to 7 p.m., are an attempt to design schools that perform the functions normally undertaken by parents. However, for the majority of children who are not in vulnerable families, the message to take away is that parents matter a great deal and there is some evidence to suggest that the influence of effective parenting may outweigh any negative impacts from attending a lower quality school.

We can also conclude that what matters about parents is not only the resources they provide for the child, in the way of income and a good physical home environment, but more importantly their education, aspirations and methods of parenting. Parents with more education and higher aspirations, who parent in a warm but authoritative manner, will tend to have children who have higher educational achievement. The specifics of what type of parenting approach works are known, but to a limited extent. There is evidence that warm parenting but with clear boundaries is effective. That is not specific guidance for a parent trying to improve their parenting approach. What parents need to know is what to do. Some things are obvious, such as reading to the child. Some are both more controversial and difficult to implement, such as authoritative parenting.

Finally, even if we agree on what style of parenting we think parents should use, it is more difficult to know how to affect the way in which parents do their parenting. Some policies that can be introduced to support parents may have an obvious impact, such as ensuring sufficient parental leave entitlements to enable them to take time with their newborn and form an initially strong bond. However, going beyond this to introduce policies to help parents improve their parenting style is more difficult. In this chapter we presented examples of effective parenting programmes (or programmes that include a parent education component) that have been successful in raising education achievement and some that have proved to provide good value for money in the long term. We need to build on this knowledge further and most importantly we need to evaluate more of the parenting programmes that we implement. Programmes that foster parental involvement with their children's schools appear to be a particularly promising avenue to explore further. A number of such programmes have been found to be effective and they are generally not as costly as some of the more intensive parenting programmes.

The evidence on parenting also raises some particularly thorny issues from a policy perspective. First, we have shown that parents matter a great deal, partly in terms of the genetic endowments they give their children, but particularly in the resources they provide them with, the way they raise their children and their aspirations for their children. If we take a deficit model of parenting, we need to be telling parents who do not have these advantages how to improve their parenting to maximise the chances for their children. Many will be uncomfortable both with the state determining what makes for a good parent, and with the state telling parents how to parent. We have no such qualms about schools or teachers of course, in that the state both determines what makes for an effective school and an effective teacher, and has regulatory procedures to ensure that the school operates in a manner consistent with what the state has determined is the optimal approach. Whether we are comfortable applying similar reasoning to parents is of course a philosophical question, but one that it would behove us to debate more openly than we currently do.

The evidence here also has huge implications for schools and teachers and the way in which we hold both accountable for children's achievement. We have provided convincing evidence that parents matter perhaps even more than schools for a child's development. Yet parents and their parenting are issues that schools may need to take as given. Schools certainly don't necessarily have the authority or means to improve the parenting of their pupils, though some may strive to do so. Thus what we can reasonably expect schools to do is partially determined by the parenting environment their pupils are faced with.

In the UK at least, we have acknowledged this to some extent by measuring the success of schools in terms of value-added measures, taking the child's initial level of achievement into account when judging whether the school has been successful. However, in other respects we do have a tendency to blame the schools for under-achieving pupils when, at least to some extent, the evidence indicates that many of the factors that determine whether a pupil achieves in school are outside the control of the school itself. Clearly developing programmes that involve parents with their children's education and school are a starting point but even with such programmes we still need to acknowledge the crucial impact that parents have on their children and the fact that this may limit the ability of schools to improve the education achievement of some pupils. Again, this requires a more open debate about the role of schools and the expectations on parents.

Key findings

- Many studies suggest that the influence of parents is generally greater than the influence of schools.
- Parents matter, not just for the resources they provide the child but for their own educational achievement, for their attitudes towards education, for their aspirations and for their methods of parenting.
- Parents with more education and higher aspirations, who parent in a warm but authoritative manner, will tend to have children who have higher educational achievement.

Key policies

- There are effective programmes listed in this chapter that can help parents improve their parenting and many are likely to provide good value for money in terms of reducing children's antisocial behaviour and improving their academic outcomes in the longer term.
- Encouraging greater parental involvement with their children's school can be effective and is relatively cheap, and more could be done to trial such interventions at scale.
- While schools can certainly help under-achieving pupils, many of the factors that determine whether a pupil achieves in school are outside the control of the school itself and this requires a more open debate about the role of schools and the responsibilities of parents.

Notes

1 Propper and Rigg (2007); Sylva et al. (2007); Bornstein and Bradley (2002).
2 Cabinet Office and the Department for Children, Schools and Families (2008).
3 Ibid.
4 See for example, Haveman and Wolfe (1995).
5 See Carey (2012).
6 Blanden and Machin (2004); Galindo-Rueda et al. (2004); Raffe et al. (2006).

7 Ermisch (2008); Kiernan and Huerta (2008).
8 Magnuson and Duncan (2002).
9 Hawkes (2010).
10 Kiernan and Mensah (2011).
11 Belsky and Eggebeen (1991); Vandell and Ramanan (1992); Gregg *et al.* (2005).
12 Goldman (2005); Flouri (2005).
13 Haveman and Wolfe (1995); Iacovou and Berthoud (2000).
14 Rutter (1981, 2009).
15 Desforges and Abouchaar (2003).
16 See for example, Behrman and Rosenzweig, (2002); Black *et al.* (2005); Black *et al.* (2005); Carneiro *et al.* (2007); Blanden *et al.* (2007); Brown *et al.* (2011); Cunha and Heckman (2008); Cummings *et al.* (2011), Ermisch *et al.* (2012); Todd and Wolpin (2007).
17 Bornstein and Bradley (2002) summarises this evidence, see also Clegg and Ginsborg (2006).
18 Oddy *et al.* (2011) and references therein.
19 Carneiro *et al.* (2007).
20 Goodman *et al.* (2011); Flouri and Hawkes, (2008).
21 Flouri and Buchanan (2004); Gutman and Akerman (2008).
22 Goodman *et al.* (2011).
23 Ibid.
24 Kelly *et al.* (2011); Kiernan and Mensah (2011).
25 Cunha and Heckman (2008).
26 Melhuish *et al.* (2008); Dearden *et al.* (2011).
27 The National Academy for Parenting Research (NAPR) is funded by the Department for Education. This Academy is building an evidence base on effective parenting. The purpose of this is to inform parenting intervention programmes and specifically to provide robust evidence to practitioners so that their support for parents can be more effective, particularly when trying to help parents in challenging circumstances. We draw on this evidence in this chapter.
28 Melhuish *et al.* (2008).
29 Desforges and Abouchaar (2003).
30 Harris and Goodall (2008).
31 Cummings *et al.* (2011).
32 Waldfogel (2004).
33 See MacMillan *et al.* (2009) for a review of evidence on effective interventions
34 Farrington and Welsh (2003 and 2007); Moran *et al.* (2004); Piquero *et al.* (2009).
35 Walker *et al.* (2009).
36 The 'What Works Clearinghouse' requires randomised controlled trial 'gold standard' evidence on the effectiveness of education programmes as found at http://ies.ed.gov/ncee/wwc/.
37 Reynolds *et al.* (2011).
38 Webster-Stratton and Hammond (1997).
39 Sanders *et al.* (2000).
40 Cowan *et al.* (2009).
41 DeGarmo and Forgatch (2007).
42 Though these programmes have not been included in the 'What Works Clearinghouse' and are not based on random control trials.
43 Bywater *et al.* (2009)
44 Senechal and Young (2008).
45 Van Steensel *et al.* (2011).
46 See Chapter 3 for details of these KIPP (Knowledge is Power Program) schools.

Bibliography

Barnes, J., Ball, M., Meadows, P., McLeish, J. and Belsky, J. (2008) *Nurse-Family Partnership Programme: First Year Pilot Sites Implementation in England.* London: Department for Children Schools and Families.

Barlow, J. (2006) 'Home visiting for parents of pre-school children in the UK'. In C. McCauley, P. Pecora and W. Rose, *Enhancing the Well-Being of Children and Families Through Effective Interventions*, London: Jessica Kingsley, pp. 70–81.

Behrman, J. and Rosenzweig, M. (2002) 'Does increasing women's schooling raise the schooling of the next generation?' *American Economic Review* 92(1): 323–334.

Belley, P. and Lochner, L. (2007) 'The changing role of family income and ability in determining educational achievement', *Journal of Human Capital* 1: 37–89.

Belsky, J. and Eggebeen, D. (1991) 'Early and extensive maternal employment and young children's socio-emotional development: Children of the National Longitudinal Survey of Youth', *Journal of Marriage and the Family* 1083–1098.

Black, S., Devereux, P. and Salvanes, K. (2005) 'From the cradle of the labour market? The effect of birth weight on adult outcomes?', *The Quarterly Journal of Economics* 122(1): 409–439.

Blanden, J. and Gregg, P. (2004) 'Family income and educational attainment: A review of approaches and evidence for Britain', *Oxford Review of Economic Policy* 20: 245–263.

Blanden, J. and Machin, S. (2004) 'Educational inequality and the expansion of UK higher education', *Scottish Journal of Political Economy*, Special Issue on the Economics of Education, 51: 230–249.

Blanden, J., Gregg, P. and Macmillan, L. (2007) *Accounting for Intergenerational Income Persistence: Non-Cognitive Skills, Ability and Education*, CEEDP, 73. London: Centre for the Economics of Education, London School of Economics and Political Science.

Bonin, E., Stevens, M., Beecham, J., Byford, S. and Parsonage, M. (2011) 'Costs and longer-term savings of parenting programmes for the prevention of persistent conduct disorder: A modelling study', *BMC Public Health* 11: 803.

Bornstein, H. and Bradley, R.H. (2002) *Socio-Economic Status, Parenting and Child Development (Monographs in Parenting Series)*, Brunswick, NJ: Lawrence Erlbaum Associates.

Brown, S., Mcintosh, S. and Taylor, K. (2011) 'Following in your parents' footsteps? Empirical analysis of matched parent-offspring test scores', *Oxford Bulletin of Economics and Statistics* 73(1): 40–58.

Bywater T., Hutchings J., Daley D., Whitaker C., Tien Yeo S., Jones K., Eames C. and Edwards R. (2009) 'Long-term effectiveness of a parenting intervention for children at risk of developing conduct disorder', *British Journal of Psychiatry* 195: 318–324.

Cabinet Office and the Department for Children, Schools and Families (2008) *Families in Britain: An Evidence Paper*, London: The National Archives.

Carey, N. (2012) *The Epigenetics Revolution: How Modern Biology is Rewriting Our Understanding of Genetics, Disease, and Inheritance*, New York: Columbia University Press.

Carneiro, P., C. Crawford and A. Goodman (2007) *The Impact of Early Cognitive and Non-Cognitive Skills on Later Outcomes*, CEE Discussion Paper no. 92, London: Centre for Economic Performance, London School of Economics.

Clegg, J. and Ginsborg, J. (2006) *Language and Social Disadvantage*, Chichester: Wiley.

Coleman, J.S. (1966) *Equality of Educational Opportunity*, Washington, DC: U.S. Department of Health, Education, and Welfare, Office of Education.

Cowan, P., Cowan, P.C., Kline-Pruett, M., Pruett, K. and Wong, J.J. (2009) 'Promoting fathers' engagement with children: Preventative interventions for low-income families', *Journal of Marriage and Family* 71(3): 663–679.

Cummings, C., Dyson, A. and Todd, L. (2011) *Beyond the School Gates: Can Full Service and Extended Schools Overcome Disadvantage?* Oxford: Taylor & Francis.

Cunha, F. and Heckman, J.J (2008) 'Formulating, identifying and estimating the technology of cognitive and noncognitive skill formation', *Journal of Human Resources* 43(4): 738–782.

Dearden, L., Sibieta, L. and Sylva, K. (2011) *The Socio-Economic Gradient in Early Child Outcomes: Evidence from the Millennium Cohort Study*, no. 11.03, IFS Working Papers.

DeGarmo, D.S. and Forgatch, M.S. (2007) 'Efficacy of parent training for stepfathers: From playful spectator and polite stranger to effective stepfathering', *Parenting: Science and Practice* 7: 331–355.

Demack, S., Drew, D. and Grimsley, M. (2000) 'Minding the gap: Ethnic, gender and social class differences in attainment at 16, 1988–1995', *Race, Ethnicity and Education* 3: 112–141.

Desforges, C. and Abouchaar, A. (2003) *The Impact of Parental Involvement, Parental Support and Family Education on Pupil Achievements and Adjustments: A Literature Review*, London: Department for Education and Skills Research Report 443.

Dozier, M., Peloso, E., Lindhiem, O., Gordon, K., Manni, M., Sepulveda, S., Ackerman, J., Bernier, A. and Levine, S. (2006) 'Developing evidence-based interventions for foster children: An example of a randomised clinical trial with infants and toddlers', *Journal of Social Issues* 62(4): 765–783.

Ermisch, J. (2008) *Origins of Social Immobility and Inequality: Parenting and Early Childhood Development*, London: National Institute of Economic Research.

Ermisch, J. and Francesconi, M. (2000) 'Cohabitation in Great Britain: Not for long, but here to stay', *Journal of the Royal Statistical Society* 163(2): 153–171.

Ermisch, J., Jantti, M. and Smeeding, T. (2012) *The Intergenerational Transmissions of Advantage*, New York: Russell Sage Foundation.

Farrington, D.P. and Welsh, B.C. (2003) 'Family-based prevention of offending: A meta-analysis', *Australian and New Zealand Journal of Criminology* 36(2): 127–151.

Farrington, D.P. and Welsh, B.C. (2007) *Saving Children from a Life of Crime*, Boulder, CO: Westview Press.

Flouri, E. (2005) *Fathering and Child Outcomes*, Chichester: Wiley.

Flouri, E. (2006) 'Parental interest in children's education, children's self-esteem and locus of control, and later educational attainment: Twenty-six year follow-up of the 1970 British birth cohort', *British Journal of Educational Psychology* 76: 41–55.

Flouri, E. and Buchanan, A. (2004) 'Early fathers' and mother's involvement and child's later educational outcomes', *British Journal of Educational Psychology* 74: 141–153.

Flouri, E. and Hawkes, D. (2008) 'Ambitious mothers, successful daughters: The relationship between mothers' educational aspirations for their children early in life and earnings attainment and self-efficacy in adult life', *British Journal of Educational Psychology* 78: 411–433.

Galindo-Ruedo, F., Marcenaro-Gutierrez, O. and Vignoles, A. (2004) 'The widening socio-economic gap in UK higher education', *National Institute Economic Review* 190(1): 75–88.

Gardner, R. (2003) *Supporting Families: Child Protection in the Community*, Chichester: Wiley.

Goldman, R. (2005) *Fathers' Involvement in their Children's Education*, London: National Family and Parenting Institute.

Goodman, A. and Gregg, P. (2010) *Poorer Children's Educational Attainment: How Important are Attitudes And Behaviour?* York: Joseph Rowntree Foundation.

Goodman, A., Gregg, P. and Washbrook, L. (2011) 'Children's educational attainment and the aspirations, attitudes and behaviours of parents and children through childhood in the UK', *Longitudinal and Life Course Studies* 2(1): 1–18.

Gregg, P., Washbrook, E., Propper, C. and Burgess, D. (2005) 'The effects of a mother's return to work decision on child development in the UK', *The Economic Journal* 115(501): F48–F80.

Gunmar, M. and Fisher, P. (2006) 'Bringing basic research on early experience and stress neurobiology to bear on preventative interventions for neglected and maltreated children', *Developmental and Psychopathology* 18(3): 651–677.

Gutman, L. and Akerman, R. (2008) *Determinants of Aspirations*, London: Centre for Research on the Wider Benefits of Learning, Institute of Education, University of London.

Harris, A. and Goodall, J. (2008) 'Do parents know they matter? Engaging all parents in learning', *Educational Research* 50(3): 277–289.

Haveman, R. and Wolfe, B. (1995) 'The determinants of children's attainments: A review of methods and findings', *Journal of Economic Literature* 33: 1829–1878.

Hawkes, D. (2010) 'Just what difference does young motherhood make: Evidence from the MCS'. In Duncan, S., Edwards, R. and Alexander, C. (eds), *Teenage Parenting: What's the Problem?* London: The Tufnell Press, pp. 69–84.

Iacovou, M. and Berthoud, R. (2000) *Parents and Employment: An Analysis of Low-Income Families in the British Household Panel Survey*, London: Stationery office.

Jaffee, S.R., Moffitt, T.E., Caspi, A. and Taylor, A. (2003) 'Life with (or without) father: The benefits of living with two biological parents depend on the father's antisocial behaviour', *Child Development* 74: 109–126.

Jeynes, W.H. (2005) 'A Meta-analysis of the relation of parental involvement to urban elementary school student academic achievement', *Urban Education* 40(3): 237–269.

Jeynes, W.H. (2007) 'The relationship between parental involvement and urban secondary school student academic achievement: A meta-analysis', *Urban Education* 42(1): 82–110.

Kelly, Y., Sacker, A., Del Bono, E., Francesconi, M. and Marmot, M. (2011) 'What role for the HLE and parenting in reducing the socioeconomic gradient in child development?', *Archives of Disease in Childhood* 96: 832–837.

Kiernan, K. and Huerta, M. (2008) 'Economic deprivation, maternal depression, Parenting and Chidlren's cognitive and emotional development in early childhood', *British Journal of Sociology* 59(4): 783–806.

Kiernan, K. and Mensah, F. (2011) 'Poverty, family resources and children's early educational attainment: The mediating role of parenting', *British Educational Research Journal* 37(2): 317–336.

Krugman, D., Lane, W.G., Walsh, C.M. (2007) 'Update on child abuse prevention', *Current Opinion in Pediatrics* 19(2007): 711–718.

Layzer, J.I., Goodson, B.D., Bernstein, L. and Price, C. (2001) *National Evaluation of Family Support Programs. Final Report Volume A: A Meta-Analysis.* Washington DC: Administration for Children, Youth and Families (DHHS).

Lloyd, E. (1999) *What Works in Parenting Education? Summary.* London: Barnardos.

Luthar, S. and Sexton, C. (2004) 'The high price of affluence'. In R.V. Kail (ed.) *Advances in Child Development,* vol. 32, San Diego, CA: Academic Press, pp. 126–162.

Luthar, S. and Latendresse, S. (2005) 'Children of the affluent: Challenges to well-being', *Current Directions in Psychological Science* 14(1): 153–171.

McCauley, C., Knapp, M., Beecham, J., McCurry, N. and Sleed, M. (2004) *Young Families Under Stress: Outcomes and Costs of Home-Start Support,* York: Joseph Rowntree Foundation.

McGilloway, S., Bywater, T., Ni Mhaille, G., Furlong, M., O'Neill, D., Comiskey, C., Leckey, Y., Kelly, P. and Donnelly, M. (2009) *Proving the Power of Positive Parenting: A Randomised Controlled Trial to Investigate the Effectiveness of the Incredible Years BASIC Parent training program in an Irish Context: (Short-term Outcomes),* Dublin: Archways.

Machin, S. and Vignoles, A. (2004) 'Educational inequality: The widening socio-economic gap', *Fiscal Studies* 25: 107–28.

MacMillan, H., Wathen, N., Barlow, J., Fergusson, D.M., Leventhal, J.M. and Taussig, H. (2009) 'Interventions to prevent child maltreatment and associated impairment', *The Lancet* 373(9659): 250–266.

Magnuson, K.A. and Duncan, G.J. (2002) 'Parents in poverty', *Handbook of Parenting* 4: 95–121.

Meghir, C. and Palme, M. (2005) 'Educational reform, ability, and family background', *American Economic Review* 95: 414–424.

Melhuish, E.C., Phan, M.B., Sylva, K., Sammons, P., Siraj-Blatchford, I. and Taggart, B. (2008) 'Effects of the home-learning environment and preschool center experience upon literacy and numeracy development in early primary school', *Journal of Social Issues* 64: 95–114.

Moffitt, T. E., Caspi, A., Harrington, H. and Milne, B.J. (2002) 'Self-efficacy, goal orientation and fear of failure as predictors of school engagement in high school students.' *Development and Psychopathology* 14(1): 179–207.

Moran, P.B., Vuchinich, S. and Hall, N.K. (2004)'Associations between types of maltreatment and substances use during adolescence', *Child Abuse and Neglect* 28(5): 565–574.

Nye, C, Turner, J. and Schartz, C (2006) *Approaches to Parent Involvement for Improving the Academic Performance of Elementary School Children,* Norway: Campbell Collaboration, Campbell Library of Systematic Reviews.

Oddy, W., Li, J., Whitehouse, A., Zubrick, S. and Malacova, E. (2011) 'Breastfeeding Duration and Academic Achievement at 10 Years', *Pediatrics* 127(1): e137–145.

Olds, D.L. (2006) 'The Nurse-Family Partnership: an evidence-based preventative intervention, *Infant Mental Health Journal* 27: 5–25.

Olds, D.L., Henderson Jr, C.R., Chamberlin, R. and Tatelbaum, R. (1986) 'Preventing child abuse and neglect: A randomised trial of nurse home visitation', *Pediatrics* 78: 65–78.

O'Neill, D., McGilloway, S., Donnelly, M., Bywater, T. and Kelly, P. (2011) 'A cost-benefit analysis of early childhood intervention: Evidence from a randomised controlled trial of the incredible years parenting program', *European Journal of Health Economics* 14(1): 85–94.

Piquero, A.R., Farrington, D.P., Welsh, B.C., Tremblay, R. and Jennings, W.G. (2009) 'Effects of early family/parent training programs on antisocial behavior and delinquency', *Journal of Experimental Criminology* 5(2): 83–120.

Propper, C. and Rigg, J. (2007) *Socio-Economic Status and Child Behaviour: Evidence From a Contemporary UK Cohort,* London: CASE, London School of Economics.

Quinton, D. (2004) *Supporting Parents: Messages from Research,* London: Department of Health, Department for Education and Skills.

Raffe, D., Croxford, L., Iannelli, C., Shapira, M. and Howieson, C. (2006) *Social-Class Inequalities in Education in England and Scotland,* Special CES Briefing no. 40, Edinburgh: Centre for Educational Sociology.

Reynolds, A.J., Temple, J. A., Ou, S.R., Arteaga, I.A. and White, B.A.B. (2011) 'School-based early childhood education and age-28 well-being: Effects by timing, dosage, and subgroups', *Science Express* 333(6040): 360–364.

Ruhm, C. (2000) 'Parental leave and child health', *Journal of Health Economics* 19(6): 931–960.

Rutter, M. (1981) 'Stress, coping and development: Some issues and some questions', *Journal of Child Psychology and Psychiatry and Allied Disciplines* 22(4): 323–356.

Rutter, M. (2006) *Genes and Behaviour: Nature-Nurture Interplay Explained.* Oxford, UK: Blackwell.

Rutter, M. (2009) 'Understanding and testing risk mechanisms for mental disorders', *Journal of Child Psychology and Psychiatry* 50(1–2): 44–52.

Rutter, M., Moffitt, E. and Caspi, A. (2006) 'Gene–environment interplay and psychopathology: Multiple varieties but real effects', *Journal of Child Psychology and Psychiatry* 47: 226–261.

Sammons, P. (1995) 'Gender, ethnic and socio-economic differences in attainment and progress: A longitudinal analysis of student achievement over 9 years', *British Educational Research Journal* 21: 465–485.

Sammons, P., Sylva, K., Melhuish, E., Siraj-Blatchford, I., Taggart, B., and Elliot, K. (2002) *Measuring the Impact of Pre-School on Children's Cognitive Progress Over the Pre-School Period*, EPPE Technical Paper 8a, London: Institute of Education.

Sammons, P., Sylva, K., Melhuish, E., Siraj-Blatchford, I., Taggart, B. and Grabbe, Y. (2007) *Effective Pre-School and Primary Education 3–11 Project (Eppe 3–11): Influences on Children's Attainment and Progress in Key Stage 2: Cognitive Outcomes in Year 5*, London: Institute of Education, University of London.

Sanders, M.R. (1999) 'Triple P-positive parenting program: Towards an empirically validated multi-level parenting and support strategy for the prevention of behaviour and emotional problems in children', *Clinical Child and Family Psychology Review* 2(2): 71–90.

Sanders, M.R., Markie-Dadds, C., Bor, W. and Tully, L.A. (2000) The Triple P-positive parenting program: A comparison of enhanced, standard and self-directed behavioural family intervention for parents of children with early onset conduct problems, *Journal of Consulting and Clinical Psychology* 68: 624 – 640.

Senechal, M. and Young, L. (2008) 'The effect of family literacy interventions on children's acquisition of reading from kindergarten to grade 3: A Meta-Analytic Review', *Review of Educational Research* 78(4): 880–907.

Shonkoff, J. P. and Phillips, D.A. (eds) (2000) *From Neurons to Neighborhoods: The Science of Early Childhood Development*, Washington, DC: National Academy Press.

Sylva, K., Melhuish, E., Siraj-Blatchford, I. and Taggart, B. (2007) *Promoting Equality in the Early Years*, Report to the Equalities Review, London: Cabinet Office.

Todd, P.E. and Wolpin, K.I. (2003) 'On the specification and estimation of the production function for cognitive achievement', *Economic Journal* 113 (485): F3–F33.

Todd, P. E. and Wolpin, K.I. (2007) 'The production of cognitive achievement in children: Home, school and racial test score gaps', *Journal of Human Capital* 1(1): 91–136.

Utting, D., Monteiro, H. and Ghate, D. (2007) *Interventions for Children at Risk of Developing Antisocial Personality Disorder*, London: Cabinet Office.

Van Steensel, R., McElvany, N., Kurvers J. and Herppich S. (2011) 'How effective are family literacy programs?: Results of a meta-analysis', *Review of Educational Research* 81(1): 69–96.

Vandell, D.L. and Ramanan, J. (1992) 'Effects of early and recent maternal employment on children from low-income families', *Child Development* 63(4): 938–949.

Waldfogel, J. (2004) *Social Mobility, Life Chances, and the Early Years* CASEpaper 88, STICERD, London: London School of Economics.

Walker, H.M., Seeley, J.R., Small, J., Severson, H.H., Graham, B.A., Feil, E.G. and Forness, S.R. (2009) 'A randomised controlled trial of the first step to success early intervention: Demonstration of program efficacy outcomes in a diverse, urban school district', *Journal of Emotional and Behavioral Disorders* 17(4): 197–212.

Webster-Stratton, C. and Hammond, M. (1997) 'Treating children with early-onset conduct problems: A comparison of child and parent training interventions', *Journal of Consulting and Clinical Psychology* 65: 93–109.

5

SCHOOLS

Organisation, resources and effectiveness

Sandra McNally

Introduction

It is self-evident that the quality of schooling matters for children's educational attainment. But it is far less clear how much schools matter compared with other important factors. Several studies investigate how much of the difference in educational attainment we observe between children can be attributed to schools versus families and peers. They all suggest that families are much more important.[1] Furthermore, even before pupils start school, there is a large gap in cognitive ability between children from high and low socio-economic backgrounds. There are also gaps by ethnic background and even according to whether or not children are born in the summer.[2] This shows that 'education' is not something that begins only at school and that inequality is evident at an early stage. That said, some recent papers show that schools in particular contexts in the US have had an enormous impact on a student's educational attainment.[3] But the context of these studies cannot necessarily be generalised to other settings. These schools (for example, charter schools in Boston; the Harlem Children's Zone in New York) are attended by disadvantaged children and they receive a range of services and levels of resources not typically provided by schools (e.g. a much longer school day and year, after school tutoring).

Even in the more typical case, it is difficult to completely separate the influence of families and schools. Many people look for somewhere to live partly based on the quality of local schools. Apart from convenience, an additional incentive to locate near a 'good' school is that it greatly improves the chances that a child will gain entry to a popular school. This is because most schools in England use distance from the school as a criterion for selecting students when the school is oversubscribed. It is unsurprising that academic research finds that a 'school quality' premium is incorporated into property prices. In England, research evidence suggests that this is about 3 per cent of the average value of a home.[4] What this means in practice is that we observe the children of more affluent families attending schools with higher average levels of achievement and when they themselves go on to have higher levels of achievement it is difficult to determine the role that the school, as distinct from the family, plays in this.

Another difficulty in understanding the influence of educational institutions on attainment is that schools can be differentially effective for different types of student. For example, some schools may enable their weaker students to make more progress than average but may not do particularly well for their high ability students. Most research only estimates school effectiveness for the 'average' student. Recent work for England confirms that some schools are more effective at the bottom of the educational distribution whereas others are more effective at the top, implying that researchers and parents alike need to be considering the effectiveness of the school for children with differing levels of prior attainment.[5]

Despite these issues, we know that school characteristics are important for influencing a person's future educational attainment. In this chapter, we look at some of the mechanisms. We focus on (1) school resources; (2) the institutional environment; and (3) school type.

School resources: does more money make a difference?

One of the long disputed questions in academic literature is whether additional school resources have an effect on raising pupil attainment. 'Resources' are usually measured as school expenditure or class size. The question is not about spending per se (which of course is necessary) but whether additional spending is a good use of resources at typical levels found in developed countries. If one just correlates school spending with pupil outcomes, it is not unusual to find a negative association! This is because in many European school systems at least, spending is dispro-portionately allocated to schools in disadvantaged areas (which tend to have lower results). Similarly, in many schools, weaker students are placed in smaller classes. Even allowing for these issues, many studies find a very weak relationship between school resources and educational attainment. Often it is not clear whether this is because studies have not *fully* dealt with these issues or whether the relation-ship really is quite weak. Academics differ greatly in how to interpret the literature. For example, in various papers Eric Hanushek has argued that accumulated research suggests no clear, systematic relationship between resources and student outcomes.[6] However, others place more weight on studies with a particularly strong method-ological design and many of these show positive results.[7] Research in the last 10 years has tended to support positive effects of school resources on attainment, although there is a wide range of estimates about the magnitude of the effect.[8]

There have been several recent studies looking at this issue for English using a census of all pupils (the National Pupil Database) and expenditure data for all schools. They are careful to control for many other factors that differ between these schools (e.g. the proportion of students eligible to receive free school meals). There are two studies evaluating the relationship between expenditure and attainment in secondary schools specifically.[9] Both find a small positive effect of resources on pupil attainment. This is consistent with results from earlier work that evaluated the effects of a government programme (Excellence in Cities), which involved allocating additional resources to schools in disadvantaged, urban areas. The research involved comparing schools that participated in the programme with other similar schools, before and after the programme was introduced.[10] Again, small positive effects are found.

There have been two recent papers about the effects of school expenditure in primary schools. The first of these studies uses the National Pupil Database between 2002 and 2007 – a period of time in which there was a large increase in school expenditure in England.[11] They find evidence of a consistently positive effect of expenditure across subjects. The magnitude is a little bigger than that found for secondary schools but still modest. A more recent paper uses a very different strategy from the other studies using English data.[12] The study applies to schools in urban areas that are close to local authority boundaries. The percentage of poor children in these schools is much higher than the national average (28 per cent are eligible to receive free school meals, compared with 16 per cent nationally). The strategy uses the fact that closely neighbouring schools with similar pupil intakes can receive markedly different levels of core funding if they are in different education authorities. This is because of an anomaly in the funding formula used by central government to allocate funding to local authorities. This formula includes an 'area cost adjustment' to compensate for differences in labour costs between areas whereas in reality teachers are drawn from the same labour market and are paid according to national pay scales. Thus, schools on either side of a local authority boundary can receive very different levels of funding even though in all other respects they are similar to each other. The paper shows that this difference is associated with a sizeable differential in pupil achievement at the end of primary school. For example, for an extra £1,000 of spending, the effect is equivalent to moving 19 per cent of students currently achieving the expected level (or grade) in maths (level 4) to the top grade (level 5) and 31 per cent of students currently achieving level 3 to level 4 (the expected grade at this age, according to the National Curriculum).

The magnitude of these effects is consistent with the existing literature on this, which has largely been from the US. Certainly the magnitude of the effects is high enough to pass an approximate cost–benefit test. Also, the study finds that effects of expenditure are greater in schools with more disadvantaged students. This is a general feature of the school resources literature – increases in resourcing are usually, though not universally, found to be more effective in disadvantaged schools and/or for disadvantaged students at all phases of education.[13] This is an important finding. Even if across the system marginal changes in funding do not have a dramatic effect on pupil achievement, the evidence implies that targeting resources on disadvantaged students is likely to produce bigger gains in achievement. Crucially therefore, it is more efficient (as well as equitable) to target resources on these students. All of this bodes well for the 'pupil premium' policy, which provides additional resources

LONDON SCHOOLS

London is a success story in educational terms. Disadvantaged students have higher achievement in inner London than in the rest of the country.

- London students are 21 percentage points more likely to get 5 A*–C grades at GCSE (including English and mathematics) as compared with elsewhere in England, according to recent work by the Institute for Fiscal Studies (Greaves *et al.* 2014).
- In 2013, around half of London's poorer students who were eligible for FSM achieved 5 A*–C grades at GCSE (including English and mathematics) – just under a third do so in the rest of the south east of England.
- This improvement in London is not just due to students taking GCSE vocational equivalents and London students are more likely to continue on to Key Stage 5 than students elsewhere.

Some other urban areas have also shown rapid improvements in educational achievement at GCSE, including Birmingham and Manchester, though these have not necessarily translated into higher rates of staying on into Key Stage 5.

Part of the reason for the success of London schools is that they have a high proportion of students from minority ethnic backgrounds and on average many, though not all, ethnic groups make more educational progress than White pupils.

The success of London schools is not just about ethnic composition however. Greaves *et al.* (2014) have shown that much of the recent improvement in London at GCSE actually stems back to improvements in primary schools in London in the late 1990s and early 2000s.

The reason for this improvement in primary outcomes for disadvantaged pupils is not clear, though Greaves *et al.* 2014 suggest that timing is such that it occurred just as the National Literacy and Numeracy strategies were being introduced. Machin and McNally (2008) have suggested the literacy hour had a positive impact on achievement.

Of course London secondary schools have had to build on and maintain any advantage that disadvantaged children have as they enter secondary schools. Secondary schools therefore have played an important role in London's success and flagship programmes, such as London Challenge, Teach First and other big initiatives in London, may have helped them do that. Certainly there is research that suggests that London Challenge has been beneficial (Hutchings *et al.* 2012). It appears that some local authorities also played a part in London's school improvement: those whose work has been documented include Tower Hamlets (Woods *et al.* 2013) and Lambeth (Demie 2005, 2013).

for disadvantaged students who are eligible for Free School meals. It is too early to evaluate the impact of the pupil premium on student outcomes, and schools have used the money in a variety of different ways, but on the basis of this existing evidence we might expect it to produce an increase in pupil achievement. The caveat however, is that schools may not target the additional resource specifically on more deprived students within their school and this might limit its impact. Even more crucially, this policy operates in a context where many schools have seen a fall in their overall budget, which may offset any positive impact from the premium. In fact pupil premium funding constitutes a relatively small proportion of schools' total income. [14]

In a time of fiscal constraints, much of the current effort to improve school performance lies in trying to improve the institutional environment in which schools operate. However, even before austerity much education policy in the last few decades has been focused on the institutional arrangements of our school system in an attempt to provide the levers with which to bring about improvements in pupil achievement. This is the section to which we now turn.

The institutional environment: importance of choice, competition and accountability?

In England, there has been a concerted effort to increase parental choice, competition between schools and accountability of schools for the performance of students. If the 'market' works well, parents should be able to make an informed choice about what school to send their child to, and schools should have an incentive to improve performance because their funding is linked strongly to pupil numbers. The idea is that choice and competition would drive up educational standards.

The mechanisms to improve parental choice include the provision of better information about what actually goes on in schools. Publicly available information comes in two main forms: school performance (or 'league') tables and inspection reports from the statutory agency responsible for monitoring schools' performance (Ofsted). Both forms of information are available online. 'League tables' were introduced in 1992 for secondary schools and 1996 for primary schools in England. They consist of measures of performance in tests at age 11 (for primary school) and age 16 (for secondary school). Since 2002/2003, 'value added' measures have also been included, which look at the average gain in test scores (rather than their level). More recently (from 2006) the context has also been adjusted (i.e. to take account of a student's ethnicity, eligibility for free school meals, etc.).

On the positive side, these measures can be very helpful to parents. In England it has been shown that parents using these key indicators would make better decisions if they use the measures rather than ignore them completely.[15] In the US an experiment was conducted that tested the effect of giving information on school test scores to lower income families.[16] This shows that parents receiving the information were more likely to send their children to higher performing schools – and children who actually went to these schools did better than they would have done otherwise.

On the negative side, measures can be misleading. This can arise for statistical reasons – for example, value-added measures can be quite unstable from year to year and this statistical fluctuation is often not informative about actual changes in school quality.[17] Even when the measures are informative, they only provide information on school performance for the average student and this is only of limited use to a parent seeking the best match between the needs of their child and what the institution provides. In addition, education and schooling serves many purposes and these measures focus purely on test score achievement. This may not provide a broad assessment of a school's quality. Various ways have been suggested in which league tables could be improved in this respect, including the provision of statistical measures that assess the value added by a school for students of differing ability or from different socio-economic backgrounds.[18] Fortunately, other publicly available information is also provided by the reports of the Schools Inspectorate (Ofsted). Despite controversy about how Ofsted rates schools, and in particular what their observations of teaching tell us about quality, research does show that the performance ratings in these reports help predict measures of school quality in ways that are not contained in the league tables.[19]

Another potential negative consequence of measuring school quality is that it might encourage behaviour designed to look good on the actual measures while not really improving school quality (or actually neglecting aspects of school quality that are not measured). For example, teachers might concentrate attention on students who are close to the performance threshold and ignore students further away from it. They might teach only what is on the test and ignore broader aspects of education. They might encourage students to take 'easy courses' rather than courses that would stretch them. These sorts of behaviours have been documented both in the US and England.[20] However, evidence for England shows that when schools do badly on an inspection, they do genuinely improve over the following years.[21] This appears to be driven by greater effort, rather than perverse behaviour such as concentrating only on students near the performance threshold. The research evidence therefore indicates a potential trade-off. Test based measures do appear to improve school quality and thus serve an important role in the accountability system. That said, we must be mindful that we need to mitigate their negative impact and ensure they do not have major unforeseen effects on the behaviour of teachers and schools. Going forward, one of the major policy challenges in this area is the need to develop the accountability system further to monitor performance of the system, while also providing teachers and schools the professional autonomy they need to maintain a well functioning broadly based education system.

Even when the information from such measures provided is useful, parents might have limited ability to act on it. While parents can apply to any state school (since the 1980s), schools are permitted to discriminate if there is over-subscription, in accordance with an enforced Code of Practice. The most important over-subscription criterion is usually proximity to the school. As discussed in the introduction, there is evidence from England and other countries that parents act on available information when they are purchasing a home.[22] Of course, the link between choice and parental income means that many parents are unable to exercise meaningful choice because of their lower income (i.e. they cannot afford to live very close to a popular school). Furthermore, higher socio-economic groups have better information and understanding of school performance.[23] Thus, 'school choice' (although good in itself) is a blunt instrument for addressing attainment gaps by family background. In fact, a worry has been that 'school choice' might increase social segregation across schools. There has been research investigating trends in social segregation in the school system and confirmed that there has not been an increase in socio-economic based segregation across schools since major reforms introduced in the late 1980s.[24] This may be because school choice was already a reality before that time (i.e. parents have long been able to influence their child's school by choosing the location of their house), or it may be that segregation has not increased because there has been some benefit to low-income parents (who were most constrained prior to the market reforms). However, the situation may change again as more choice is introduced to the market (e.g. with the introduction of Free Schools).

Parental choice and incentives for schools to perform well should give rise to competition between schools. In the international literature, there have been many attempts to investigate whether increased competition gives rise to improved educational attainment. However, the international evidence is 'voluminous and mixed'[25] and there are few papers that evaluate the impact of school competition in England. However, research using school-level data on English secondary schools finds that those with the best examination performance have grown more quickly.[26] The authors argue that increased competition between schools led to improved exam performance. The first pupil-level analysis on this subject relates to primary schools in the South East of England.[27] The authors find no relationship between the extent of school choice in an area and pupil performance. The study also suggests that there is no causal relationship between measures of school competition and pupils' educational attainment. The only case where choice and competition might be beneficial is in the case of faith schools. This might be because many faith schools are voluntary aided and have greater autonomy than other state schools (e.g. there is less representation from the local authority on the board of governors; they control their own admissions, although they must adhere to the Code of Practice). This suggests that competition might play a more important role in school performance if schools were more autonomous. Faith primary schools are attended by about a fifth of all pupils.

One way to improve choice and competition is to allow schools a lot more freedom on such matters as pay and conditions of staff and what actually goes on in schools. We now go on to discuss this.

Does school type matter?

We first discuss publicly funded schools with a greater degree of autonomy than average. Then we discuss evidence about the merits of academically selective versus non-academically selective schools. Finally we discuss evidence about the efficacy of schools that operate entirely outside the public sector.

Granting schools greater autonomy

Several countries have enabled a certain proportion of state funded schools to operate with greater autonomy than the norm. The structure and rules differ between (and sometimes within) countries but they also have much in common – for example, 'Charter Schools' in the US, 'Free Schools' in Sweden and 'academies' in England. The rationale is that by giving schools more freedom, they might be better able to respond to local circumstances and become more innovative.

In England, 'academies' are run by their sponsors (where relevant) and/or a board of governors, though they vary substantially, both in terms of their student intake and in terms of their ethos, etc. They have responsibility for employing all staff, agreeing pay and conditions, freedom over most of the curriculum (except for core subjects) and all aspects of school organisation. The programme commenced in 2000 and was originally devised for a limited number of schools in disadvantaged areas (about 200 under New Labour). The programme has massively expanded under the Coalition Government and is no longer aimed specifically at schools in disadvantaged areas. From 2010, any school that has been rated as 'outstanding' by Ofsted is allowed to become an academy on a fast-track route. Other schools may also apply, with some additional conditions. There are also schools that appear to be pressurised or required to become academies. Over time, many of the original requirements to become an academy have been removed.[28] As of June 2014, there were 3,922 open academies.[29]

As the expansion of the academies programme is very recent, it is too soon to make a judgement on the overall impact of the programme. Although there are reports that show the overall performance of academies and other schools, research that evaluates the *academy policy* must compare 'like with like' and this is not straightforward. Also, it takes a number of years before we can realistically judge the effects of such a policy. However, there has been an evaluation of schools that became academies up to 2008/2009.[30] The authors compare average educational outcomes in schools that became academies and similar schools, before and after the conversion took place. There are three main findings. First, schools that became academies started to attract higher ability students. Second, there was an improvement in performance at GCSE exams – even after accounting for this change in student composition. Third, neighbouring schools started to perform better as well. This might either be because they were exposed to more competition (and thus forced to improve their performance) or it might reflect the sharing of academy school facilities (and expertise) with the wider community. However, another recent study has investigated the beneficiaries of this original policy.[31] It found that the benefits were entirely concentrated among students of medium-high prior attainment (as measured by attainment at the end of primary school). The policy did nothing to help the lowest achieving students. These students did the same as they would have done without the policy. Since students from disadvantaged families are more likely to be found in this low-ability group, one might infer that the policy was not particularly effective for improving the attainment of disadvantaged students. Thus, although we will not know about the effects of the expanded academies policy for a few years, current evidence gives no reason to think it will be particularly beneficial for low ability students (of which many are from economically disadvantaged backgrounds). Even though it is too early to evaluate the effectiveness of the expanded academies policy, it is noteworthy that half of those inspected in 2012–2013 have received a judgement from Ofsted as 'requires improvement' or 'inadequate'.[32] Of course, this does not prove anything about the academies policy (because we need to know the counter-factual, and research on the early academies suggests that it takes some time for such schools to become effective).[33] However, it suggests that we cannot expect the academies policy to be a 'quick fix' schools' improvement policy.

Another related initiative is the introduction of 'Free Schools'. In this case, parents, teachers or other non-profit organisations can set up a school that has a similar degree of autonomy as an academy. Since the first such schools opened in September 2011, we will not know for some time how effective this programme has been on those students directly affected by the programme and their surrounding communities. However, it is noteworthy that at least in principle, this policy opens the window for interested groups to start a school that might explicitly focus on particular neighbourhoods (e.g those with high poverty). On the other hand, there is no guarantee that many 'Free Schools' will be set up with this objective in mind and the funding to set up these new schools displaces that which would otherwise go to existing schools. It is notable that the most robust Swedish evidence on the effectiveness of 'Free Schools' finds evidence for only small positive effects.[34]

Finally, there are some risks attached to the new strategy of creating a lot more autonomy for schools:

1 Too many 'independent' state schools might undermine the ability of local authorities to plan for and provide centrally provided services (e.g. for students with special needs) to schools in their region.
2 When a school becomes an academy, regulation moves from the local authority to a more centralised authority. In 2014 the DfE announced the appointment of eight Regional Schools Commissioners to take on this task. They would be advised by four-person strong Head Teacher Boards elected by and from academies in each region. But without further details it was not clear that the system would adequately substitute for the kind of supervision and support for schools previously exercised by local authorities and local communities.
3 No market – public or private – is composed of only successful institutions. Furthermore, one cannot predict with certainty what management or institutions will be successful. In the private sector, firms open and close all the time. However, in the public sector, there is no natural mechanism to facilitate this essential aspect of markets. The worry with academies is that it

might prove hard to close down or remove the management of unsuccessful schools in a timely manner and of course shutting a school is likely to affect drastically the children who are currently enrolled.

An important question for policy is not only the effects of autonomous schools, but in what spheres and contexts all schools should be made more autonomous. For example, it has been argued that decisions that require significant local knowledge (such as hiring and budget allocations) should be made at the school level. On the other hand, decisions should be made at a higher level where standardisation is important (e.g. setting course offerings and requirements).[35] In the UK, most schools ('community schools') have more limited autonomy compared with academies or Free Schools, though their autonomy over staffing and other decisions has increased in recent years. It has been argued that localising hiring and making pay and conditions more flexible would put these schools on a similar footing to these other schools and help to overcome the problem of regional disparities in teacher pay.[36]

The extent to which a more autonomous school is successful depends, of course, on the qualities of those making the decisions. The typical conclusion drawn by quantitative leadership researchers is that school leaders have small and indirect effects on student outcomes that are essentially mediated by teachers.[37] However, there are some studies that find a moderately strong effect of school leadership on student outcomes.[38]

Academically selective versus non-selective schools

Countries differ in how and when 'ability tracking' takes place in education. This means at what stage students are selected into different educational institutions depending on their ability. Countries that track students into different schools at age 10/11 include Austria, Germany, Northern Ireland and Hungary. In other countries, including Britain (apart from in a few areas), Canada, Norway, Sweden and the US, education at this age is comprehensive (i.e. students of all abilities are taught in the same schools though not necessarily in the same classes). There have been important changes over time. European countries used to be more selective in how children were educated in the nineteenth and early twentieth century. The idea of comprehensive education gathered support in the post Second World War period.

There are two main questions in this literature: (1) Within an academically selective (or tracked) system, how does getting into the 'academic track' influence students' outcomes? (2) What happens to average outcomes if a country changes from an academically selective system to a comprehensive system? (as happened in Britain in the 1960s and 1970s). There are many studies in the UK that try to answer these questions. However, a strong critique by Alan Manning and Steve Pischke demonstrates how difficult it is to overcome the 'selection problem' and casts doubt over most of the literature that has tried to address this in a UK context.[39]

In the context of question (1) this selection problem arises because it is difficult to separate out the effect of getting into the 'academic track' from the effect of high student ability. With regard to question (2), it is difficult to separate out the effects of educational reform across areas when these areas change in other ways at the same time as the educational reform.

One of the more convincing studies for the UK on the effects of attending the 'academic track' (i.e. grammar schools) in a selective context makes use of student-level data in a particular Local Education Authority in Northern England (East Ridings) in the 1970s.[40] This was at a time before the education system was reformed in England. The author looks at what happened to students who just made the cut-off to enter grammar schools compared with students just below the cut-off. His estimates appear to rule out very large effects of attending grammar schools on test scores. However, there are potentially large effects on the number and academic content of courses followed. A more contemporary study about local authorities that still have grammar schools shows that pupils from more disadvantaged backgrounds are much less likely to be selected for grammar schools, even though it is beneficial for the few that enter relative to the alternative in those areas. However, the study also implies that this alternative (i.e. the schools where most disadvantaged students go) would have been better if they operated within a comprehensive system.[41]

When it comes to evaluating reforms from a selective system to a comprehensive system, more convincing evidence comes from other countries, particularly Scandinavia.[42] All these studies use data on cohorts born before and after the reforms and make use of the fact that they were introduced at different times across different regions. They all find beneficial effects from the move towards a comprehensive system on average educational attainment and that effects were stronger for lower socio-economic groups. This suggests that going back to a more selective system (in England) would not improve educational outcomes. A difficult aspect of the policy debate is that people tend to confuse the positive effects from attending an academically selective school for students who manage to get into one (such as a grammar school) from the overall effect on educational attainment from having a selective system compared with a comprehensive system, which needs to take account of the impact of a selective system on those who fail to get into a grammar school.

Of course, it is possible for some element of selectivity to take place within schools. For example, schools might use 'streaming' (i.e. in which higher and lower ability groups are taught separately for every subject) or some form of 'setting' (i.e. in which this only applies for some subjects). There is a big literature on the consequences of different forms of grouping arrangement. However, again it is difficult to compare pupil performance in schools that use grouping with an unknown counterfactual in schools that do not use grouping. In reality some grouping of students by achievement level occurs both within classrooms and within schools and it is the extent of this selectivity and the age at which schools start to segregate students that varies. Our reading of the evidence is that when one takes account of other differences across pupils and schools, school grouping policies can explain little of the variation in student achievement.[43] This is entirely consistent with our earlier observation that schools and indeed differences in school resourcing levels can only explain a relatively modest amount of the variation in achievement across different pupils.

Publicly funded and privately funded schools

In England, most schools are funded by the state with about 7 per cent of students going to private or independent schools. Independent schools have even greater autonomy in how they operate compared with academies. For example, they can select pupils on the basis of ability whereas this is prohibited for most state schools in England. Independent schools are funded entirely by student fees (although they have favourable tax treatment) and have much greater resources at their disposable compared with state schools. For example, average class size is about 25 pupils in state primary schools whereas it is only 13 pupils in private schools.[44] Teachers in private schools are more likely than those in state schools to possess post-graduate qualifications and to be specialists in shortage subjects.[45]

It is no surprise that raw achievement differs greatly between these school types because pupils going to independent schools often come from very privileged backgrounds, they are more likely to be academically selected and the resources available to independent schools are so much greater. The many ways in which state schools differ from independent schools make it difficult to ascertain why pupils attending these schools differ in their academic attainment. Also, researchers do not usually have good data on independent schools. However, there has been some research about whether there is a wage premium in the labour market for people who went to an independent school after taking account of family background characteristics. This study shows a very substantial wage premium.[46] Three and a half years after graduation from university, men and women who went to independent schools earn more than those who went to state schools by 8 per cent and 6 per cent respectively.

We cannot tell the extent to which this better performance is due to the additional resources available to independent schools or whether it has something to do with the way in which these schools are run (resulting from their greater autonomy). Furthermore, the fact that pupils come from relatively privileged backgrounds removes a whole set of problems that state schools in deprived neighbourhoods have to deal with. Thus it is hard to make policy inferences from the difference in outcomes achieved by students in state schools and independent schools.

Key findings

- Schools can make a difference to students' educational attainment. However, there is no 'magic bullet' to suddenly transform all schools into institutions that dramatically change the life chances for all of their students.

- Resources matter – especially for disadvantaged students. Given national budget constraints, it is important to find additional ways to improve the performance of our education system.
- While some aspects of school accountability (such as school inspections) appear to have improved school performance, despite the huge amount of policy attention focused on introducing choice and competition into the school system, it is not clear that this has actually led to an overall improvement in standards.
- Improving standards is not the only reason to increase parental choice. However, one should be aware that because residential choice, parental income and schools' over-subscription criteria are all linked, 'choice' is less available to low-income parents than to higher-income parents.
- It might well be the case that improving school autonomy will help both parental choice and school competition and thus drive up standards. But this approach is not without significant risks. As we decentralise our education system greater differences in school quality may well emerge across different areas. Further, the central planning necessary to provide for children with special educational needs or to deal with fluctuations in pupil numbers in different areas, will get more difficult. In this respect, English policy is moving into uncharted territory.

Key policies

- Continue to protect schools from cuts in public spending.
- Develop an accountability system that is an effective instrument for monitoring the performance of the education system (especially with respect to disadvantaged students) while allowing teachers and schools professional autonomy. The government announced in the autumn of 2013 a new set of criteria as performance measures for schools, to be introduced in 2016. It is too soon to comment on the likely effects of these criteria, but more sophisticated measures than the 5 A*–C target would be welcome.
- Many schools have control over their own admissions policies subject to staying within the Code of Practice (e.g. academies, Voluntary Aided schools, Foundation schools, Free Schools). School leaders and governors in these schools should be mindful of the inequitable effect their admissions policies can have on broader society, and do more to respond where needed to the extent of disadvantage in their communities. Methods such as lotteries or banding should also be considered to deal with over-subscription.
- There needs to be more development of how the increasing number of autonomous schools will be regulated and an exit strategy for failing schools or failing managements.
- Fragmentation of the system has its risks and there are issues that need close monitoring as a result of quasi-autonomous schools being incentivised to do things in their own interest, which do not necessarily correspond with the collective interest. Examples of issues where this might arise are pupil

exclusions, children with special educational needs, and provision of school places in the appropriate areas. It would be useful to have a clearer vision of the role of local government in this context.

Notes

1 Teddlie and Reynolds (2000); Todd and Wolpin (2007); Kramarz, Machin and Ouazad (2009).
2 See Dustmann *et al.* (2010) for gaps by ethnicity and Crawford *et al.* (2007) for gaps according to a child's month of birth.
3 Dobbie and Fryer (2011); Abdukadiroglu *et al.* (2011).
4 Gibbons (2012).
5 Dearden *et al.* (2011).
6 Hanushek (2008).
7 Angrist and Lavy (1999); Krueger (1999); Krueger and Whitmore (2001).
8 Gibbons and McNally (2013).
9 Levačić *et al.* (2005); Jenkins *et al.* (2006).
10 Machin *et al.* (2010).
11 Holmlund *et al.* (2010).
12 Gibbons *et al.* (2011).
13 Gibbons and McNally (2013).
14 Carpenter *et al.* (2013).
15 Allen and Burgess (2011).
16 Hastings and Weinstein (2008).
17 Leckie and Goldstein (2011).
18 Dearden and Vignoles (2011).
19 Hussain (2012).
20 Muriel and Smith (2011).
21 Hussain (2012); Allen and Burgess (2012).
22 For England, see Burgess *et al.* (2009); Gibbons and Machin (2003); Gibbons *et al.* (2009); Rosenthal (2003).
23 West and Pennell (1999).
24 Allen and Vignoles (2007).
25 Gibbons *et al.* (2008).
26 Bradley *et al.* (2001).
27 Gibbons *et al.* (2008).
28 Bagaria *et al.* (2013) give a good discussion of policy details and the evolution in the 'academy' movement over time.
29 www.gov.uk/government/publications/open-academies-and-academy-projects-in-development.
30 Machin and Vernoit (2011).
31 Machin and Silva (2013).
32 www.naht.org.uk/welcome/news-and-media/blogs/warwick-mansell/exclusive-sponsored-academies-seemingly-faring-poorly-in-inspections/.
33 Machin and Vernoit (2011).
34 Bohlmark and Lindahl (2008).
35 Hanushek *et al.* (2013).
36 Bagaria *et al.* (2013).
37 Hallinger and Heck (1998).
38 Marzano *et al.* (2005).
39 Manning and Pischke (2006).
40 Clark (2007).
41 Atkinson *et al.* (2006).
42 Aakvik *et al.* (2010) for Norway; Meghir and Palme (2005) for Sweden; Pekkala *et al.* (2013) for Finland.
43 Betts and Shkolnik (2000).
44 OECD (2009).
45 Green *et al.* (2008).
46 Green *et al.* (2012).

Bibliography

Aakvik, A., Salvanes, K.G. and Vaage, K. (2010) 'Measuring heterogeneity in the returns to education using educational reforms', *European Economic Review* 54(4): 483–500.

Abdukadiroglu, A., Angrist, J.D., Dynarksi, S.M., Kane, T.J. and Parthak, P. (2011) 'Accountability and flexibility in public schools: Evidence from Boston's charters and pilots', *Quarterly Journal of Economics* 126(2): 699–748.

Allen, R. and A. Vignoles. (2007) 'What should an index of school segregation measure?', *Oxford Review of Education* 33(5): 643–668.

Allen, R. and Burgess, S. (2011) 'Can school league tables help parents choose schools?' *Fiscal Studies* 32(2): 245–261.

Allen, R. and Burgess, S. (2012) *How Should We Treat Under-Performing Schools? A Regression Discontinuity Analysis of School Inspections in England.* Working Paper 12/87, Centre for Market and Public Organisation.

Angrist, J. and Lavy, V. (1999) 'Using Maimonides' rule to estimate the effect of class size on scholastic achievement', *Quarterly Journal of Economics* 114: 533–575.

Atkinson A., Gregg, P. and McConnell, B. (2006) *The Result of 11+ Selection: An Investigation into Opportunities and Outcomes for Pupils in Selective LEAs,* CMPO Working Paper no. 06/150, Bristol: Centre for Market and Public Organisation, University of Bristol.

Bagaria, N., Bottini, B. and Coelho, M. (2013) 'Human capital and growth: A focus on primary and secondary education in the UK'. In T. Besley and J. Van Reenen (eds) *Investing for Prosperity: A Manifesto for Growth,* London: London School of Economics and Political Science, pp. 91–151.

Betts, J. R. and Shkolnik, J.L. (2000) 'The effects of ability grouping on student achievement and resource allocation in secondary schools', *Economics of Education Review* 19: 1–15.

Bohlmark. A. and Lindahl, M. (2008) *Does School Privatisation Improve Educational Achievement? Evidence from Sweden's Voucher Reform,* IZA Discussion Paper no. 3691, Bonn: Institute for the Study of Labor.

Bradley, S., Johnes, G. and Millington, J. (2001) 'School choice, competition and the efficiency of secondary schools in England', *European Journal of Operational Research* 135: 527–544.

Burgess, S., Greaves, E., Vignoles, A. and Wilson, D. (2009) *Parental Choice of Primary School in England: What Type of School do Parents Choose?* Bristol, UK: The Centre for Market and Public Organisation 09/224, Department of Economics, University of Bristol.

Carpenter, H., Papps, I., Bragg, J., Dyson, A., Harris, D., Kerr, K., Todd, L. and Laing, K. (2013), *Evaluation of Pupil Premium Research Report,* London: Department for Education.

Clark, D. (2007) *Selective Schools and Academic Achievement.* IZA Discussion Paper 3182, Bonn: Institute for the Study of Labor.

Crawford, C., Dearden, L. and Meghir, C. (2007) *When You Are Born Matters: The Impact of Date of Birth on Child Cognitive Outcomes in England,* CEE Discussion Paper no. 93. London: Centre for the Economics of Education.

Dearden, L. and Vignoles, A. (2011) 'Schools, markets and league tables', *Fiscal Studies* 32(2): 179–186.

Dearden, L., Micklewright, J. and Vignoles, A. (2011) 'The effectiveness of English secondary schools for pupils of different ability levels', *Fiscal Studies* 32(2): 225–244.

Demie, F. (2005) 'Achievement of Black Caribbean pupils: Good practice in Lambeth schools', *British Educational Research Journal* 31(4): 481–508.

Demie, F. (2013) *Using Data to Raise Achievement: Good Practice in Schools,* London: Lambeth Council, Research and Statistics Unit.

Dobbie, W. and Fryer, R.G. (2011) 'Are high quality schools enough to close the achievement gap? Evidence from the Harlem Children's Zone', *American Economic Journal: Applied Economics* 3(3): 158–187.

Dustmann, C., Machin, S. and Schonberg, U. (2010) Educational achievement and ethnicity in compulsory schooling, *Economic Journal* 120(546): F272–F297.

Gibbons, S. (2012) 'Big ideas: valuing schooling through house prices', *Centrepiece* 17(2): 2–5.

Gibbons S. and Machin, S. (2003) 'Valuing English primary schools', *Journal of Urban Economics* 53: 197–219.

Gibbons, S. and McNally, S. (2013) *The Effects of Resources Across School Phases: A Summary of Recent Evidence,* CEP Discussion Papers, CEPDP1226, London: Centre for Economic Performance, London School of Economics and Political Science.

Gibbons, S., Machin, S. and Silva, O. (2008) 'Competition, choice and pupil achievement', *Journal of the European Economic Association* 6: 912–947.

Gibbons, S., Machin, S. and Silva, O. (2009) *Valuing School Quality Using Boundary Discontinuity Regressions*, SERC DP0018, London: London School of Economics.

Gibbons, S., McNally, S. and Viarengo, M. (2011) *Does Additional Spending Help Urban Schools? An Evaluation Using Boundary Discontinuities?* CEE Discussion Paper no. 128, London: London School of Economics.

Greaves, E., Macmillan, L. and Sibieta, L. (2014) *Lessons from London Schools For Attainment Gaps and Social Mobility*, report for the Social Mobility and Child Poverty Commission, London.

Green, F., Machin, S., Murphy, R. and Zhu, Y. (2008) 'Competition for private and state school teachers', *Journal of Education and Work* 21(5): 383–404.

Green, F., Machin, S., Murphy, R. and Zhu, Y. (2012) 'The changing economic advantage from private schools', *Economica* 79(316): 658–679.

Hallinger, P. and Heck, R.H. (1998) 'Exploring the principal's contribution to school effectiveness: 1980–1995', *School Effectiveness and School Improvement* 9: 157–191

Hanushek, E.A. (2008) 'Education production functions'. In S. Durlauf, and L. Blume (eds) *The New Palgrave Dictionary of Economics*, Basingstoke: Palgrave Macmillan.

Hanushek, E.A, Link, S. and Woessmann, L. (2013) 'Does school autonomy make sense everywhere? Panel estimates from PISA', *Journal of Development Economics* 104(C): 212–232.

Hastings, J. and Weinstein, J.M. (2008) 'Information, school choice and academic achievement: Evidence from two experiments', *Quarterly Journal of Economics* 123(4): 1373–1414.

Holmlund, H., McNally, S. and Viarengo, M. (2010) 'Does money matter for schools?' *Economics of Education Review* 29: 1154–1164.

Hussain, I. (2012) *Subjective Performance Evaluation in the Public Sector: Evidence from School Inspections*, CEE Discussion Paper no. 135, London: Centre for the Economics of Education.

Hutchings, M., Greenwood, C., Hollingworth, S., Mansaray, A., Rose, A., Minty, S. and Glass, K. (2012) *Evaluation of the City Challenge Programme*, Research Report DFE-RR215, London: Department for Education.

Jenkins, A., Levacic, R. and Vignoles, A. (2006) *Estimating the Relationship between School Resources and Pupil Attainment at GCSE*, Research Report RR727, London: Department for Education and Skills.

Kramarz, F., Machin, S. and Ouazad, A. (2009) *What Makes a Test Score? The Respective Contributions of Pupils, Schools and Peers in Achievement in English Primary Education*, CEE Discussion Paper no. 102, London: Centre for the Economics of Education.

Krueger, A. (1999) 'Experimental estimates of education production functions', *Quarterly Journal of Economics* 114: 497–532.

Krueger, A. and Whitmore, D. (2001) 'The effect of attending a small class in the early grades on college-test taking and middle school test results: Evidence from Project Star', *Economic Journal* 111: 1–28.

Leckie, G. and Goldstein, H. (2011) 'Understanding uncertainty in school league tables', *Fiscal Studies* 32(2): 207–224.

Levačić, R., Jenkins, A., Vignoles, A., Steele, F. and Allen, R. (2005) *Estimating the Relationship Between School Resources and Pupil Attainment at Key Stage 3*, Research Report RR679, London: Department for Education and Skills.

Machin, S. and McNally, S. (2008) 'The literacy hour', *Journal of Public Economics* 92: 1141–1462.

Machin, S. and Vernoit, J. (2011) *Changing School Autonomy: Academy Schools and Their Introduction to England's Education*, CEE Discussion Paper. no. 123, London: London School of Economics.

Machin, S. and Silva, O. (2013) *School Structure, School Autonomy and the Tail*, CEP Special Report, London: Centre for Economic Performance, London School of Economics.

Machin, S., McNally, S. and Meghir, C. (2010) Resources and standards in urban schools, *Journal of Human Capital* 4: 365–393.

Manning, A. and Pischke, J.S. (2006) *Comprehensive Versus Selective Schooling in England and Wales: What Do We Know?* IZA Discussion Paper no. 2072, Bonn: Institute for the Study of Labor.

Marzano, R.J., Waters J. and McNulty, B. (2005) *School Leadership that Works: From Research to Results*, Aurora, CO: ASCD & McREL.

Meghir, C. and Palme, M. (2005) 'Educational reform, ability and family backround', *American Economic Review* 95(1): 414–424.

Muriel, A. and Smith, J. (2011) 'On educational performance measures', *Fiscal Studies* 32(1): 187–206.

OECD (2009) *Education at a Glance*, Paris: OECD.

Pekkala, S., Pekkarinen, T. and Uusitalo, R. (2013) 'School tracking and development of cognitive skills', *Journal of Labor Economics* 31 (3): 577–602.

Rosenthal, L. (2003) 'The value of secondary school quality', *Oxford Bulletin of Economics and Statistics* 65: 329–355.

Teddlie, C. and Reynolds, D. (2000) *The International Handbook Of School Effectiveness Research*, London/New York: Falmer Press.

Todd, P. and Wolpin, K.I. (2007) 'The production of cognitive achievement in children: Home, school and racial score gaps', *Journal of Human Capital* 1(1): 91–136.

West, A. and Pennell, H. (1999) 'School admissions: Increasing equity, accountability and transparency', *British Journal of Education Studies* 46: 188–200.

Woods, D., Husbands, C. and Brown, C. (2013) *Transforming Education for All: The Tower Hamlets Story*, London: Tower Hamlets Council.

6

WHAT MAKES A GOOD TEACHER?

Robert Cassen

Introduction

This chapter reviews the evidence about teaching, looking at different methods of assessing teachers and various practices associated with teaching, such as formative assessment, personalised learning, setting and streaming, and the management of classroom behaviour. It then examines initial teacher training, including recruitment and the role of teachers' pay and incentives; continuing professional development; and the role of teachers' engagement with research.

Background

The problem

Most of the easily available information about teachers commonly says little about how good they are at their job. Pay, qualifications and certification often do not have much bearing on their pupils' outcomes. A teacher's length of experience does affect the quality of teaching, but mainly from the early years in the classroom: that is, it is 'learning by doing', but there seems to be less of such learning as time goes on.[1] Yet apart from a teacher's references these are often the criteria on the basis of which teachers are recruited. Research about what makes teachers effective seems to have a variable influence on teacher training – not nearly enough influence, according to some.[2]

   John Hattie, on the basis of a very large survey of research, concluded that about 50 per cent of the variation in student outcomes is due to students and their cognitive ability; the next largest source of variation is teaching, at about 30 per cent. If you are looking for things you can change to improve education, he makes a good case that this is where to go.[3] Home background (much of which is already accounted for by the student measure), schools, head teachers and peer effects, all contribute, but may be harder to change for the better. In a more recent study,[4] he distinguishes interestingly between teachers and teaching approaches, and comments on several of the latter, some of which are discussed here. It should be noted though that Hattie's derivation of effect sizes from meta-analyses is methodologically controversial, not least when average effect-sizes are calculated from numbers of meta-analyses of varying quality, time-periods and contexts. A further critique of the use of effect sizes so calculated can be found in Wiliam (2013b).

What makes good teachers has only relatively recently benefitted from really clarifying research in the UK, and improving teaching has not always been at the forefront of policy – perhaps, as some suggest, because of the sensitivity of the teaching profession. One might rather look to the dominance of the issue of *school effectiveness*.[5]

The latter has been the subject of very considerable research and debate, and improving schools has been virtually the key instrument of policy for improving education under recent governments. Reorganisation of school structures, competition between schools and so forth, have all been far more prominent in recent changes to the education system than efforts to improve teaching. Is this because it is easier to reorganise than solve fundamental problems about recruiting able people into teaching without paying them more? Certainly governments have given less attention in recent decades to the fact that so much variation in student performance is due to factors within schools and in particular to teachers. The topic has even acquired an acronym, WSV (within school variation).[6] Research suggests that variation within schools is *several times* greater than that between schools.[7] Who you are taught by matters much more than which school you go to.

We can often tell who the good teachers *are*; one – not perfectly reliable – way is by looking at their 'value-added', the difference they make to their pupils' outcomes, after allowing for everything else. We can then examine what the effect

AN EXTREME CASE

Michelle Rhee, appointed by the Mayor of Washington DC as Public Schools Chancellor in 2007, provoked a furore by her attempts to reform teaching. The district had the lowest student scores in America; she believed in the research about teaching quality, and set about improving it in a rather ham-fisted way, sacking hundreds of teachers and closing poorly performing schools with little consultation. DC's student outcomes improved radically, but Rhee aroused the ire of the teachers' union, which raised $1,000,000 to fight the Mayor's re-election. Michelle Rhee lost her job, and the Mayor lost the election.

Rhee went on to found StudentsFirst, an NGO dedicated to securing better outcomes for pupils.

Whitmire (2011)

of being a good teacher can be. Looking at student performance in America by individual teacher and allowing for other possible influences, well-known studies have said that a good teacher will deliver a year and a half of learning in a single academic year, while a poor one delivers half a year of learning;[8] and most of the variation in the quality of instruction occurred within schools – allowing for differences between schools did not change the estimate much. It is claimed that the effects of good teaching can outweigh the influence of disadvantaged backgrounds to a considerable extent:

> These estimates of teacher quality can also be related to the popular argument that family background is overwhelmingly important and that schools cannot be expected to make up for bad preparation from home. This perspective emanates from work that treats schools as monolithic institutions or equates quality with expenditure. The existence of substantial within-school variation in teacher quality . . . points to the fact that high quality teachers can offset a substantial portion of disadvantage related to family economic and social circumstances.[9]

The findings of research have obvious policy implications: to choose effective teachers, or to reward them for their performance, schools need to know how to collect and assess the evidence. Also, without further evidence, we would not know how to make teacher-training more effective, or what to look for in teacher certification.

One US study cites a number of estimates of teacher quality as measured by student value-added and their effects on schools and students.

> The magnitudes of these estimates support the beliefs that teacher quality is an important determinant of school quality and achievement. For example, the math results imply that having a teacher at the 25th percentile as compared to the 75th percentile of the quality distribution would mean a difference in learning gains [that] . . . would move a student at the middle of the achievement distribution to the 59th per centile. The magnitude of such an effect is large both relative to typical measures of black-white or income achievement gaps . . . and to methodologically compelling estimates of the effects of a ten student reduction in class size.[10]

Another US study found that 'value-added [VA] measures can successfully identify which teachers have the greatest ability to raise students' test scores'. But it cautioned that

> one cannot conclude from this result that teacher VA is a good measure of teacher quality . . . as test scores are not the ultimate outcome of interest. Do high VA teachers also improve students' long-term outcomes, or are they simply better at teaching to the test?[11]

It should also be noted that high-performing educational systems 'build their human resource systems by putting the energy up front, in attracting, training and supporting good teachers, rather than on the back end of reducing attrition and firing weak teachers'.[12] (See further in this chapter on teacher incentives.)

In fact there is not much openly available teacher value-added data for the UK; many schools create their own, but do not publish it, and there are no national figures. There is an exception, a study that measured teacher value-added for some 740 teachers and 7,300 pupils' exam results. It found effects similar to those quoted in the US studies already referred to; better teachers improved their pupils' exam results quite significantly.[13] But there are limits to the usefulness of teachers' value-added: if it were used as a principal and sole mechanism for selecting or promoting teachers, it could drive teachers to 'teach to the test'. Where results are studied over multiple years, they may be more reliable; but it is only possible to measure value-added where students are taught by the same teacher and their results are graded at suitable intervals. But how does one judge new teachers? Also some studies have found that the value-added measures can vary from year to year simply due to statistical variation. We will discuss other means of evaluating teaching performance later in this chapter.

Eric Hanushek claims a dramatic potential impact on student achievement, based on American data, just by replacing the worst teachers with average teachers.

> By this quality estimate, if a student had a good teacher as opposed to an average teacher for four or five years in a row, the increased learning would be sufficient to close entirely the average gap between a typical low-income student receiving a free or reduced-price lunch and the average student who is not receiving free or reduced-price lunches.[14]

Furthermore, he says, this is a lower-bound estimate. Estimates have been made for the UK too. One made in 2011 said that if just the bottom 10 per cent of teachers were as effective as the average teacher over a period of 10 years, the UK's position in OECD rankings would improve to fifth place in maths and third place in reading.[15] Most of the studies find that improvements in teaching are particularly effective for disadvantaged pupils.[16] However, any policy that aimed simply to *replace* ineffective teachers would face difficulties in evaluating teachers' performance, and could have deleterious effects on teachers' collaboration.

Classroom observation

Research using direct observation can permit a different idea of what matters in the classroom. A method pioneered by Robert Pianta and colleagues at the University of Virginia has been used in US and UK schools to help evaluate the quality of teaching. Teachers and children are observed in a classroom setting and detailed measurements are made of such things as teachers' sensitivity, respect for the students' perspective, attention to individual pupils, and so forth. Pianta showed an interviewer a good and a less good teacher on a video, and then said:

Two and a half minutes into the lesson – the length of time it took that subpar teacher to turn on the computer – [the good teacher] had already laid out the problem, checked in with nearly every student in the class, and was back at the blackboard, to take the lesson a step further.[17]

As noted above, only a few studies show a positive relationship between teachers' credentials and their students' outcomes. One such study, using very detailed longitudinal data on teachers and students in North Carolina, did find that teachers' credentials, especially their length of experience, showed positive effects on outcomes.[18] However, in general the evidence on the importance of credentials is mixed. One possible explanation is suggested by Pianta and his colleagues, who found that teachers' classroom styles were commonly defective, despite their solid credentials. The researchers used their methods to substantiate the claim that 'a focus on standards-based reform and teacher credentialing may lead to instruction that is overly broad and thin'.[19]

The Pianta framework is known as the Classroom Assessment Scoring System (CLASS). Assessors are given extensive training and can then evaluate teachers' performance under three main headings:

- *Emotional support* – includes the degree of 'warmth and connectedness' of the classroom climate; teachers' sensitivity to students' needs; and the ability to respond to students' autonomy and take advantage of peer interactions.
- *Classroom organisation* – includes teachers' behaviour and time management, and their ability to use varied methods in presenting their subjects.
- *Instructional support* – includes teachers' own conceptual understanding of their subjects; their ability to teach not just the subject but higher-order thinking skills involved in it; and the quality of feedback.

(This reflects 'CLASS-S' for secondary schools, but the method is similar for elementary teaching.) Following this scoring method, teachers can be assisted in improving their performance and crucially teachers who score higher on these assessments achieve greater gains in their students' outcomes, as tested in very large numbers of classroom situations.[20]

There is relatively little comparable research for the UK, though one such study found that the quality of teaching, as measured by the Pianta method, did indeed have significant positive effects on children's outcomes in primary school. It improved children's performance in reading and maths, and the effects were stronger than family disadvantage as measured by free school meals – though not stronger than the home-learning environment or mothers' educational qualifications. As is commonly found, the home environment was more important for reading, while teaching mattered more for maths.[21] Hence this evidence on the usefulness of the Pianta method might suggest one way to measure teacher effectiveness and avoid relying completely on value-added measures with their resulting dangers.

Formative assessment

A well-known book, *Inside the Black Box*, showed significant gains from the way teachers interact with their students.[22] Known more broadly as 'assessment for learning' or 'formative assessment', it is not about assessment in its usual meaning of grading and so forth, but rather a whole approach to teaching. One study found a 15 per cent improvement in outcomes in the classes where teachers used the techniques compared with those where they were not used.[23] What basically are the techniques of formative assessment? The main ones are: teachers' use of questioning; feedback; peer and self assessment by students; and formative use of tests. Of course all teachers make use of these things; it is *how* they do so that matters.

A key factor is moving away from 'transmission teaching', or simply 'delivering' the curriculum. Rather, teachers emphasise more their role in helping students to learn, and making more effort to get students to 'own' their learning. Often this means not seeing students as having fixed levels of ability, but helping them deal with things they find hard. It means starting from what students already know, and setting a learning goal that takes them to the next stage; teachers develop diagnostic 'probes' to identify what students need to learn. Class discussions play a part: everyone is expected to participate – this helps students to think more, rather than just accept what the teacher says. (While sensitivity to individual students, small-group discussions and the like, are all important, research also shows the value of whole-class teaching – not least for keeping everyone on task.[24])

There is no simple formula for adopting formative assessment; it is rather a matter of teachers finding out what works in their own schools and classrooms. But there is guidance available. Teachers have first to work on the kind of questions they ask. They should prepare questions in advance, and should not just ask questions with a right or wrong answer; rather, they should make them open-ended: 'What do you think about this?' instead of 'What is the answer?' And then follow it up with 'Why do you think that?' Or 'Can you go into more detail?' Gradually teaching becomes an exchange, not spoon-feeding by the teacher and hoped-for absorption by the pupil. An important discovery was that teachers waited too short a time for students to reply. Simply allowing more time helps students to think and work out answers, which makes a big difference, though teachers initially find that difficult; letting silences go on too long can seem like dead time.

Letting go in general is a part of the procedure. It involves getting students to participate more; they can be encouraged to discuss questions with their desk neighbours before offering their responses. They can take part in 'peer assessment' – that is, the teacher doesn't comment directly on an answer, but asks students to comment. Similarly students can look at each other's test answers or homework and make comments. The teacher uses the comments to make sure everyone understands what is going on, not just their ability to give the 'right' answer. The process of peer assessment encourages students to express themselves and to think.

These practices should guide the teacher with the all important ingredient of feedback. It helps the student very little to know that she has got something right or wrong as such; rather teachers should let students know what they have done well and where they need further work or help. All these features of good teaching are designed to let students feel they are progressing in their own learning and to help overcome unwillingness to speak out in case they get something wrong. Everyone is being encouraged to learn.

One further component of formative assessment is commenting on tests *without marks*. This too turns out to be difficult for teachers to initiate; but once they have done it, it proves to be helpful. Comments show the way forward; marks only encourage competition and discourage the weaker performers – and typically when there are comments *and* marks, the comments are ignored. Once students get used to the new system of assessment, they take to it.

These techniques were first intensively studied in a small number of representative schools and were shown to have positive outcomes in terms of students' progress, their reported contentment with their schooling, and the teachers' own satisfaction. They also showed gains in externally conducted tests such as GCSEs though the approach as a whole has not been evaluated at scale. This is partly because the elements of the approach are not at all easy to adopt and need leadership and support in schools for teachers willing to try new methods.[25] In fact observation later found that while *Inside the Black Box* sold over 100,000 copies and its suggestions were well received, and were also in line with advice from official education bodies, the methods were not widely adopted and led to an effort by the General Teaching Council of England to give teachers practical advice on how to put them into practice.[26]

Personalised learning

A number of issues arise from the straightforward observation that learners have different levels of ability and different styles of learning. How should teaching take account of that? One method might be to take direct and detailed account of learning styles – but research has shown that this is not particularly effective. This is because getting children working on their own with individualised attention from teachers is not effective as a main procedure, however valuable it might be in small doses.[27] It is the opposite of whole-class teaching, which has been found to be more effective. This does not mean though that individual differences cannot or should not be catered for.

Streaming by ability does not seem to be the way to do it. As already noted, ability is not fixed and unchanging in young people, and is in any case not the only factor in achievement. Lower streams may be given diminished curriculums and suffer from low teacher expectations. Where tried it has also been seen as inequitable, disadvantaged and ethnic minority pupils tending to be placed in lower streams and suffering accordingly.[28] *Setting*, which is essentially streaming by ability but in specific subjects, has a somewhat better press and is certainly widespread in secondary schools. But the results are mixed. Some of the same defects found with streaming, such as low teacher expectations and inequity, are also present in setting.

Results compared with mixed ability classes tend to be better for higher ability pupils (though not very much), and worse for those of low ability, who can learn from their higher ability peers. The results for average ability pupils are mixed. On the other hand setting makes teaching at the appropriate level easier for teachers, and can therefore benefit pupils. The research literature gives no unique guidance, and practice may depend on how wide the variation of ability is in particular schools, the size of the class and the resources at the teacher's disposal (including preparation time). If it is to be used, some of the disadvantages may perhaps be avoided by making setting flexible, with easy movement between sets; sets can also employ the 'zip method', grouping pupils by average ability but with each group having at least one higher ability pupil.[29]

There are, however, other ways to teach in a way that allows learners some freedom to follow their different learning styles. Some of these are described in Chapter 10 on information technology. But a potentially effective example is described by Marcella McCarthy, an Advanced Skills Teacher at the time of her writing.[30] She contrasts a traditional Year 7 lesson with a much more creative one. The subject is a poem by Tennyson. The traditional teacher announces the poem as the subject, and immediately loses half the class. She then goes on with typical tasks such as asking the students to find examples of alliteration and onomatopoeia and so forth, and ends up tired out with only the better students having achieved much. The more creative teacher seats the students in pairs who will work together and then announces her subject: 'Thinking like a poet'. She gets the students to ask how a poet chooses his words, gives them word cards, compares the students' own ideas about which words work best with the ones Tennyson used. The result is that the students are engaged, do most of the work, learn a lot in their own way (including the use of alliteration and onomatopoeia), and the teacher has had an enjoyable class. Many teachers no doubt do not need this example of how to be a good teacher, but where needed, approaches such as those in this article might help to reduce the prevalence of 'formulaic' lessons – see below.

Engagement

So far we have not examined the issue of student engagement, which of course underlies much of what teachers can achieve. There is plentiful evidence of a lack of educational aspirations among some pupils, particularly among the disadvantaged White British.[31] It has also been claimed that lack of aspirations is not the key problem so much as low self-belief.[32] But do learners enter school without a determination to succeed, or do schools or teachers fail to engage them? Pupils may be demotivated by lack of success. Certainly if they do not learn to read properly they may well become bored and unable to keep up – hence the critical importance of reading and the excessive extent of reading failure to which Chapter 7 draws attention. Not surprisingly, as a Canadian study noted, 'On average, schools with high levels of engagement tended to have high levels of literacy skills.'[33]

This is a complex area where many factors intermingle. Pupils may have aspirations to become pop singers, footballers or models and not see the relevance of education. Of course these are high-risk strategies, as a glance at the data will show: on average students who leave school unqualified will not enjoy well-paid jobs. But disengaged pupils will probably not be moved by statistical arguments. Whatever the source of lack of enthusiasm for learning, however, the question is what can be done to promote engagement among the disaffected?

Naturally good teaching is itself valuable for engagement, so are some forms of digital technology, referred to in Chapter 10. But wider approaches may well be needed. Particular claims are made for Learning Futures, a programme supported by the Paul Hamlyn Foundation, working to improve engagement and student outcomes with 40 Secondary schools.[34] The schools employ a share of project-based learning to complement normal pedagogy, with a curriculum that appeals to the disengaged; they encourage a range of adult supporters – mentors, carers, parents, business and community experts – to work with pupils as learning coaches, not least to bolster pupils' self-belief and resilience; they work with other schools, firms and community organisations; and they make efforts to design learning in cooperation between pupils and teachers. It was too early for systematic evaluation at the time of writing, but initial results appear positive.[35]

Classroom behaviour

All these teaching methods depend on a good atmosphere in the classroom, and the teacher being able to control unruly and disruptive behaviour. But of course the relationship is reciprocal – an engaging teacher is likely under most circumstances to encounter less disruptive behaviour. There is a range of resources available to teachers: how-to books that have been well accepted by expert reviewers and teachers,[36] or analysis and guidance from government, teaching union and other websites.[37]

There is far less robust evidence on what works in terms of behaviour management in class. It is inherently difficult to research classroom management and the bulk of research results come from the USA, few of them statistically robust and, given the complexity of the topic, not necessarily transferable to the UK. The most common form of 'challenging behaviour' in the UK is low-level class disruption, which occurs mainly at ages 8–9 and 12–15, the latter often associated with poor adjustment in the move from primary to secondary school. Of course there are other ages at which such behaviour occurs, including in early primary years, particularly with children coming to school 'ill-prepared socially and emotionally', often from troubled families or in care.[38] And there are worse cases of behaviour, sometimes violent.

Teachers should – but may not – acquire much of what they need to know during their initial teacher training (ITT). And effective classroom behaviour management does not rest with the individual teacher alone. Parents will commonly need to be involved; and support for appropriate parenting programmes from local authorities and others.[39] Guidance for schools with SEN and disabled students in particular is available through the *Achievement for All* programme, piloted by the DfE in the wake of the 2009 Lamb Inquiry, and run by a group of school leaders. Its overall objective is to assist the education of vulnerable pupils from 0–19.[40] (See further Chapters 3 and 8.) School leadership is often critical. When schools in similar circumstances face varying levels of behaviour difficulties, Ofsted at least has concluded it is often down to school management.[41]

The general tenor of advice is that prevention is better than cure. The features of school and classroom management that encourage better behaviour are well rehearsed in the literature. Schools need to recognise and analyse their behavioural issues and take active and pre-emptive steps to limit disruption. They are better able to do this if they foster a sense of community, enjoy collaboration among their teachers, and promote autonomy among their students to the extent possible.[42] A variety of features of classroom management are also relevant; they vary from the physical setting to the 'climate' teachers manage to establish.[43] When it comes to the individual teacher facing difficult behaviour, the advice is to be authoritative and not authoritarian; to respond rather than react; to employ positive reinforcement as much as possible rather than negative criticism; and to seek help from colleagues in analysing and coping with particular pupils. There is a great deal of available advice and 'best practice' in the literature. Clearly much must depend on the teacher's own personality; but the wealth of experience available can help even there – that experience includes advice for teachers to modify and adapt their own responsiveness and sensitivity. And of course pupils too can learn or be taught to control their own behaviour.

Improving teaching

There are about 440,000 teachers in UK state schools and some 37,000 new teachers are trained annually to replace those retiring or leaving, or to cope with demographic change. This means that efforts to improve recruitment and teacher training can act only slowly on teaching throughout our schools; any such efforts must be accompanied by action to enhance teaching – where necessary – among the large body of existing teachers. Both these aspects can be considered in the light of the evidence.

Improving recruitment and teacher training

In 2012 over 70 per cent of new teacher trainees had upper-second degrees or better, and 14 per cent had first-class degrees, in both cases an improvement over previous years. This still leaves a substantial minority without such qualifications, and several specific subjects in the teaching force as a whole, which are often taught by people with only modest qualifications in those subjects, such as mathematics. The Coalition Government in 2011 announced that only teachers with second-class degrees would be accepted for ITT; and only those with upper seconds would receive bursaries. In addition high bursaries – up to £20,000 – were to be offered to trainee teachers in shortage subjects, including maths, physics, chemistry and modern languages, the highest bursaries going to those with first-class degrees. Musset (2010) on the basis of international experience suggests alternative routes into teaching for subject specialists based on skills and qualifications obtained outside teaching, together with tailor-made teacher training. An internationally accepted new qualification for maths teachers, CMathTeach, may also help recruitment.[44]

The principle of raising the bar for entry to teaching has been questioned: if degree status and so forth do not predict teaching quality, perhaps we have got ITT the wrong way round. We should make it easier to enter ITT, but harder to qualify, by extending probationary periods and subjecting entrants to more rigorous quality control. At present most entrants to ITT qualify and poorly performing teachers are hard to dismiss.[45]

Many studies depict the desirable qualities of teachers: enthusiasm, commitment, ability to engage students, respect for others, communication skills, in addition to their knowledge and command of their subjects. Are good teachers born or made? And how far does teacher training follow the findings of research about what makes a good teacher?

Initial teacher training

There are several routes into ITT. By far the most common, nearly four-fifths of trainees in 2010–2011, was university-based entry. Achieving a Post-Graduate Certificate in Education (PGCE) takes 38 weeks, half of which is in school placements. Of the remainder, 16.6 per cent were in employment-based schemes (EBITTs), and 4.6 per cent in school-based programmes (SCITTs).[46] The schemes vary by entry requirements, whether salaried or not, but both EBITTs and SCITTs also offer a route to a PGCE. The would-be teacher will choose according to his or her preferences and qualifications. They can also apply under the recently created School Direct scheme (replacing the earlier Graduate Training Programme). It is led by schools, which can select the kind of trainee teacher they are looking for; the scheme aims to attract good graduates and can offer bursaries or salaried employment, with the prospect of employment in the school or group of schools where they train.

The Coalition Government's teaching White Paper (DfE 2010) called for wider use of school-based training, though on the whole the university-based scheme was higher rated by Smithers (2012) (even if only on some criteria), and also by Ofsted. The latter judged 47 per cent of university-based programmes to be outstanding in 2009/2010, compared with only 26 per cent of school-based routes.[47] Though it is notable that there is no research relating the training route taken by the teacher and the progress made by their students. Some also question whether ITT needs to be based so heavily on school experience, rather than programmes that could give intending teachers more exposure to the findings of research on effective teaching.

Research on teacher education practices is important because it has the potential to open up new ways of challenging the hegemonic status of arenas of practice (the school, the classroom) as the only places in which to acquire knowledge of teaching.[48]

The 2010 White Paper had various proposals for improving ITT, not least the rolling out of Teaching Schools. As they are so new there is no evidence about their effectiveness in the UK, though CfBT (2012) reviews the modest – and encouraging – evidence from elsewhere. There is considerable experience in the USA, with at least five universities cooperating with networks of schools in their areas.[49] The need will be to develop alliances of schools here, which will pool their experience on the selection and training of teachers.

Teach First

One initiative that is claimed to have helped to raise standards in teaching is Teach First. The programme is supported one-third by private donors and two-thirds by government. It recruits from 66 universities, and in 2012 was training 1,000 teachers a year. The trainees receive salaries and 6 weeks' initial training in addition to normal school-based teacher training – mainly for secondary schooling. They have a 2-year commitment to teach in disadvantaged schools. It is an attractive route into teaching, perhaps in part because of the moral challenge, and because it enables students to try teaching with no commitment to remaining in the profession longer than a few years unless they want to. Trainees can also expect to be treated favourably in later recruitment by top firms if they leave teaching. Application is over-subscribed, with seven applicants for every place, with a likely positive impact on the reputation of the scheme and the quality of those accepted.

The teachers are clearly well motivated and there is some (non-experimental) evidence that they have a positive effect on school outcomes. They receive continuing professional development from their original training institute, from Teach First headquarters, and in school. They can and many do take a Masters equipping them for school leadership roles. Teach First also has a mentoring programme, HEAPS, the Higher Education Access Programme for Schools, in which they encourage and help disadvantaged pupils to get through A-levels and apply for university places – the great majority of the students succeed. The Coalition government in 2012 announced a decision to double the number of Teach First trainees to 2000 by 2015. Altogether the programme has arguably had an impact on the status of teaching as a profession, and Teach First itself by 2013 had risen to be the largest single graduate employer, ahead of several well-known graduate employment agencies.[50]

There is a downside: a large proportion of Teach First teachers (60 per cent by 2012) were no longer in teaching after 5 years, though of course the intention of the scheme was that many graduates would move on to other jobs. Many in fact start out seeing the programme as a jumping-off point for other careers, and more

'My students are in the lowest percentiles for almost every socioeconomic indicator there is. I know the impact Teach First applicants can have in raising aspirations. Energetic, innovative, enthusiastic, resilient and wonderfully committed to the students, what parent wouldn't want their child taught by a teacher like that? What head teacher wouldn't want their school full of teachers like that? That's why Teach First is so important to me and my students.'

A head teacher in Bradford, quoted in Hill (2012)

stay on than originally thought they would. However, 'It is essentially 40 per cent gained for teaching rather than 60 per cent lost, but given Teach First's high profile and strong government backing it is not necessarily what people want to hear.'[51]

One of the lessons from Teach First is the assessments they adopt for selecting candidates to their programme. Teach First and similar programmes in Finland, Singapore and the USA regularly use criteria of aptitude, personality and resilience in choosing among their applicants. The UK version includes delivery by the candidate to assessors of a 7-minute lesson for Key Stage 3 students on their subject qualification, and detailed interviewing about required teaching skills.

There has been evaluation of Teach First; one study, while not conclusive even in the authors' own estimate, found that a large proportion of student GCSE performance was explained by a Teach First association in comparison with matched schools that had no Teach First teachers. [52] However, an alternative and arguably more robust approach found a far smaller effect.[53] In any case, whatever its benefits, this is a small programme relative to the size of the teaching force.

Good teaching comes in many forms. In 2013 the *Guardian* newspaper ran a 'My best lesson' series by teachers. The first one was a report by an English teacher. Determined to get his class, predicted to get Bs, up to A/A* standard, he started by getting them to cut up a shape with scissors and paper to represent a theme from a book they were reading, and explain it to their desk partner. Then they had to find quotes to prove their points. Then he danced alongside a rap video, about being 'picky'. The students joined in. Then he had them analysing their quotes, but writing on tables and windows with magic pens, getting a 'good word' bank, and finally turning all these images and words into a written A-grade exam answer. It worked because it was memorable and fun.

Guardian Education 19 February 2013

Future Leaders and Teaching Leaders

Future Leaders is a recent programme for teachers to enhance their management and leadership skills, and eventually assume headships in disadvantaged schools; it aims to bring better school experiences to pupils in these schools. Since 2013 it has recruited primary school trainees as well as secondary. It gives them initial training and continuing support and mentoring from senior leaders.[54] There has been one non-experimental evaluation of the programme, which found modest positive effects in terms of pupil outcomes in schools having Future Leaders participating, matched against comparison schools without them; but it was too early for there to have been enough Future Leaders in headship posts to examine their effects on schools.[55]

Teaching Leaders aims specifically at middle management in schools – heads of year or department, or of areas such as SEN or EAL. The ambition is to improve teaching and pupil outcomes by focussing on teaching at these levels, offering lesson observation, mentoring and so forth. The programme only began in 2008 and has not yet been evaluated, but by 2013 had already several hundred Fellows working in schools. It also has a licence from the National College for School Leadership to deliver the National Professional Qualification for Middle Leadership and offers it for schools in challenging contexts. It works with Future Leaders, both of them in association with the National College and the Ark Trust.[56]

In 2013 the Education Endowment Foundation and J.P. Morgan together granted nearly £3 million to fund Achieve Together, an initiative to be delivered by Teach First, Teaching Leaders and Future Leaders together, to help attract, retain and develop excellent teachers, middle leaders and heads to raise standards in schools in low-income communities. This evaluation is due to report in 2017, and will clearly be crucial in helping determine the role that such programmes can play in improving student performance.

Teachers' pay and incentives

At least one study for the UK has found a positive relationship between teachers' pay and student outcomes.[57] The researchers took advantage of the introduction of 'performance-related pay' (PRP) in 1999; this was a scheme under which experienced teachers could apply for pay bonuses, based on their performance. The study concluded that 'teachers do respond to incentives. In an incentive scheme strongly based on student outcomes, test scores improved'[58] – by about half a grade per student. But the authors note various limitations of the findings; and somewhat troublingly for the study, while the grade improvements were positive for English and science, they were non-existent for maths (perhaps reflecting differences between teachers of mathematics and teachers of other subjects). The authors could only conclude that pay incentives were a policy tool worth considering. But the majority of studies of the effect of pay incentives on teaching come from the USA. They hardly support the idea of effectiveness of performance pay.[59]

The Coalition Government re-introduced PRP in 2013 and gave guidance about how it was to be implemented. Pay progression would no longer be linked to length of service, but entirely related to performance, with each school determining its own performance criteria. Schools' senior leaderships were to ask teachers to submit appraisals of their performance, based on a number of criteria, including the progress of their pupils and wider contributions to the school and its objectives. Teachers could then make progress on the main pay scale, graduate to the upper pay scale, or progress on the leadership scale. They could also receive additional responsibility payments, including those for work with SEN pupils. The whole process was to be overseen by the head teacher and authorisation for pay progression given by the Governing Body.[60]

This is not very different from the PRP approach followed previously in the UK. We know something of how that actually worked. Schools could mostly provide data on individual teachers' value-added by looking at their pupils' performance at two separate intervals, so that their progress could be monitored by this criterion – though see earlier in this chapter on the unreliability of value-added estimates. Judgements were also made on other criteria for teachers' contributions. The processes were reasonably transparent, with teachers having a right of appeal. The vast majority of teachers applied for passing what was then called the 'threshold'; their self-evaluation was commonly accepted, and head teachers were reluctant to deny progress, so that most of those who applied succeeded.[61] It remains to be seen whether the lessons learned then will be followed in the new situation post-2013, but the new provisions are calibrated in greater detail. In addition, the qualification of Advanced Skills Teacher has been abolished and replaced by a category of 'leading practitioner' whose 'primary purpose is to model and lead the improvement of teaching skills'.[62]

In a wider perspective, however, it is clear that the pay and prestige of the teaching profession has significantly to do with the quality of teaching. In educationally well-performing countries, teaching is a highly valued and well-rewarded profession. In Finland, for example, which consistently ranks among the very highest performers in international educational comparisons, teachers are selected from the top university graduates and teaching is a highly competitive profession to get into.[63] Teachers' pay is good and they also enjoy more autonomy in classrooms and better working conditions than most of their opposite numbers elsewhere.[64] In Singapore, students the government wants to attract into teaching are selected from the higher tiers of secondary school graduating classes; they are given monthly bursaries while still in school, on condition that they commit to teaching for 3 years. The profession is monitored continuously to ensure salaries remain competitive with other professions, to maintain standards, and to select teachers for leadership and management training.[65] If the UK wanted to match these standards, it would take a substantial amount of time, direction and resources. It would also require a valuation of education and teaching in British society that seems, at present at least, quite implausible, however desirable.

Continuing professional development

The main means of improving teaching beyond ITT is Continuing Professional Development, or CPD. It happens countrywide, but in a somewhat fragmentary way, varying from place to place and involving some combination of local authorities, universities, or schools or groups of schools. There are merits in each combination, but it is not easy to come to conclusions about how well the overall system is working – if system it is.

There is some evidence of what 'works' in CPD in terms of teachers' learning and pupils' outcomes. One 'strong and pervasive success factor' was found to be 'the contribution of peer support to professional development'.[66] This is opposed to a view of CPD as something done to and for teachers – rather, it sees CPD in a largely school-based context, where external specialist help can be brought in, but mainly schools and school leaders work to learn from and support each other. 'School-based professional development, with judicious use of external support, proved to be the most effective means of improving staff's skills. In the schools where professional development was most successful, staff discussed and reflected on what they were learning. The leaders of these schools were prepared to create the time for this to happen.'[67] Indeed, one study[68] looked at five school leadership practices found to be associated with good student outcomes, and found by far the biggest effect came from 'promoting and participating in professional learning'. Philippa Cordingley, of the Centre for the Use of Research and Evidence in Education, says she explored this evidence with 2000 school leaders, only a few of whom were aware of the finding; she concluded that schools should pay greater attention to the learning environment for both teachers and pupils.[69]

To pursue CPD effectively, schools needed to use collaboration at all levels; collect and use evidence of what is working for teaching and for pupil outcomes; and be able to identify, evaluate and make use of specialist support from within and beyond the school. Very often a teacher has the skills that are necessary and can share them in the right environment. Some studies speak of the 'critical friend': another teacher, who is trusted and can facilitate the appropriate learning process effectively.[70] Similarly constructive partnerships can be formed between schools, local authorities and universities, if they are based on sympathetic mutual enquiry and learning.[71] Dylan Wiliam has persuasively argued that effective CPD requires time: he calls for 'at least 10 years of deliberate practice', to overcome the effect noted above that teachers' own learning falls off over time.[72]

A particular and potentially valuable, though as yet unevaluated, CPD measure is the online Self-Evaluation Form (SEF), which schools are now able, though not required, to use. With its help, school leaders can evaluate their schools under a variety of headings, and grade their schools in several aspects, which include learners' achievement and the quality of teaching and learning. In one detailed study of nine schools, the authors found staff development to be critical for the school improvement process in general. It proved essential to enlist staff and convince them that changes were both desirable and possible, but active support from school leadership teams was also necessary. The process commonly involved lesson observation and feedback. But there were common weaknesses, including insufficient attention to how learning outcomes improved as a result of the initiatives. The study advocated schools' moving to 'a more personalised approach to staff development', just as there is attention to students' personalised learning.[73]

An alternative to the SEF is for schools to design their own evaluation criteria. Many use DfE guidelines for what is now called Performance Appraisal (formerly Performance Management). In some schools teachers each have an appraiser from among the senior management team, and if they are found to need improvement, will receive follow-up advice and training. It can be a demanding process for schools with dozens of teachers – but an essential one. One author has strongly advocated combining three main methods of evaluation: value-added, classroom observation, and pupil surveys. Each has its weaknesses, but in combination they are likely to give a fair picture of how teachers are doing and assist the improvement of teaching.[74] Ofsted too does work on assessing the quality of teaching. The new Inspection Framework of 2011 indicated how this was to be done: essentially combining schools' and teachers' own evaluations with Ofsted inspectors' lesson observation and assessments, and examining such findings in the light of pupils' results.[75] We have not found any publications of data about teachers, but they have been used to indicate teaching quality in schools: this was found to be highly variable in the most deprived areas, for example in London, 77 per cent of secondary schools catering to those areas were judged to have good or outstanding teaching, the figure for the North East was 29 per cent.[76]

> CPD is the vehicle through which all new policies must work if change is to become embedded rather than cosmetic. The cumulative picture of positive outcomes for teachers and pupils emerging from . . . reviews suggests that collaborative CPD between teachers has the potential to play a critical role in interpreting and embedding all policy initiatives in practice. The complex combinations of sustained peer and specialist support, of in-class experimentation coupled with protected space for reflection and structured dialogue, and the role of collaboration in personalising goals, sustaining commitment and developing ownership, are all challenging. They sit at some distance from traditional conceptions of CPD and the current arrangements for organising and evaluating it in many schools. However, they reinforce the emerging consensus about the nature of a proactive, modern profession within which teachers are seen as an important resource for each other in supporting and sustaining the development of their own and their colleagues' practice. Policy-makers should consider reviewing both explicit and implicit assumptions about the ways in which new initiatives are implemented in schools and how these may be enhanced by an explicit commitment to sustained, collaborative CPD.[77]

In addition, teachers can access a very large variety of videos on good classroom practice made by Teachers TV. While the programme itself has been discontinued, the DfE has made the videos available free of charge through 12 independent websites; they can be found on the website www.education.gov.uk/schools/tools andinitiatives/teacherstv. Teachers appear to value them. But whether the provision of such materials really impacts on classroom practice in a widespread way, or indeed eventually impacts on student achievement, is unclear.

In general we have a clear idea of what makes for effective CPD. What we do not know is how widely the good practice is practised. Certainly the 2012 Ofsted Annual Report found much to be desired and called for school leaders to do more to improve teaching quality.

> Where a school is stuck in mediocrity and struggling to get to 'good', the head may be an effective manager, but is probably not exercising leadership on the central issue of raising standards through better teaching. As a result, Ofsted sees lessons that are too formulaic, with not enough thought given to what really works for young people – lessons where students are not fully engaged or stretched to reach their full potential.[78]

And the British Educational Research Association (BERA) still found in 2014 that 'in many settings teachers' experience of CPD is fragmented, occasional, and insufficiently informed by research'.[79]

Engaging with research

The latter comment brings us to the issue of teachers' engagement with research. It is a topic that has been around for decades, but was given new emphasis by a BERA-RSA inquiry published in 2014.[80] It called for 'a teaching force that is research-informed and research-inquisitive', which would only be achieved with 'a *research-rich* culture in our schools and colleges'.[81] The concern is for teachers' exposure to research as part of their ITT, and for involvement with it as part of their CPD.

This chapter has already noted the paucity of research on the effectiveness of different types of ITT; the growth of School Direct entry into the profession in particular has raised concerns about whether trainee teachers are sufficiently exposed to research findings during their training. But the main thrust of the BERA-RSA inquiry has been to look at the role of involvement with research in CPD, or as it also calls it, CPDL – Continuing Professional Development and Learning. The first thing to note is that studies have shown significant improvements in teaching and student results, with large effect sizes, from engagement with research.[82] The question is how it is to be carried out. There is no single best way, but rather a number of ways depending on schools, teachers and pupils. It is not suggested that schools and teachers engage in wide-scale academic research projects; rather they should be familiar with the findings of research, and examine their own practice – their teaching approaches and/or their students' results for example – using research methods, with the help of trained researchers if needed.

To these ends the BERA-RSA inquiry has made a number of recommendations for England, including: that the National College for Teaching and Leadership (NCTL) work with the emerging Teaching Schools to establish a national network of educational research leaders; that the DfE make research literacy a requirement of teacher qualification and progression to middle or senior leadership roles; and that Ofsted make the capacity of teachers to engage in research and enquiry a hallmark of 'outstanding' practice in ITT, schools and colleges. Comparable relevant recommendations are also made for Northern Ireland, Scotland and Wales. Under the Test and Learn programme managed by CUREE and the NCTL, grants are available for schools wishing to undertake research relevant to reducing the social gap.

Key findings

- The quality of teaching is responsible for a large proportion of school and student outcomes and may be more amenable to improvement than some of the other main factors such as the home environment.
- A variety of means is available for identifying the quality of teachers, including value-added, classroom observation and pupil surveys, probably best used in combination.
- Research has a great deal to say about what contributes to good teaching. 'Formative assessment' and feedback are high on the list of helpful approaches. Personalised learning, understood correctly, has an important part to play. Other advice is available for making teaching creative though it is less clear from the research what impact this will have on achievement. Streaming by ability does not come off well in research, but setting can be valuable depending on conditions in each school. Performance-related pay has been found to have a mixed record, only one or two studies showing positive effects. In its latest guise in England it is part of a set of measures for teacher evaluation and reward, and its impact remains to be judged.
- There is some evidence that Teach First has had a positive impact on student achievement. It may well also have influenced the reputation of teachers and teaching, to judge by the number of students wanting to pursue it. However the numbers are small relative to the size of the teaching profession.
- Classroom behaviour and management are obviously essential to teaching. A range of advice and support is available, though again more needs to be done to evaluate what is effective in this domain. The same is true of pupil engagement.

Key policies

- There are some potential problems with initial teacher training; concerns are expressed that it is too much based on school experience, with insufficient weight given to incorporating research findings in training. There are also suggestions that it should be made easier to enter teacher training, but harder to qualify, with longer probationary periods. Research is clearly needed to provide evidence, currently lacking, of the effectiveness of different routes into teaching.

• Upgrading the skills and effectiveness of the teaching force as a whole is the key policy for improving teaching and the main instrument for this is Continuing Professional Development (CPD). A great deal is known about how to do CPD effectively, though many individual programmes remain unevaluated. The key seems mainly to be to transmit skills within schools to those teachers who need improvement, with outside help when necessary, or with the collaboration of partnerships. Actual practice in pursuing CPD is highly variable across the school system, as is the quality of teaching, and this remains an important area for improvement.

• Engagement with research should become part of teacher training and practice in schools, following the recommendations of the BERA-RSA inquiry.

Notes

1 Hanushek and Rivkin (2006); Clotfelter *et al.* (2007).
2 Walsh (2006).
3 Hattie (2003).
4 Hattie (2009).
5 Muijs and Reynolds (2010); and see Chapter 4.
6 Reynolds (2007).
7 OECD (2009).
8 Hanushek (1992); and similarly Hanushek and Rivkin (2006: 18); Rivkin *et al.* (2005) show a more conservative but still strong effect.
9 Hanushek and Rivkin (2006: 19).
10 Hanushek and Rivkin (2010: 4–5).
11 Chetty *et al.* (2013: 41). In another paper the same authors find that there is a long-term effect: high value-added teachers improve students' pay modestly at age 28 (Chetty *et al.* (2011)).
12 Schleicher (2011: 14).
13 Slater *et al.* (2012).
14 Hanushek (2009: 6).
15 Murphy (2011).
16 See evidence given to House of Commons (2014). A helpful source for research on teaching in the USA is www.caldercenter.org/facts-behind-superman.cfm.
17 Gladwell (2008: 5).
18 Clotfelter *et al.* (2007).
19 Pianta *et al.* (2007: 2).
20 Allen *et al.* (2012).
21 Sammons *et al.* (2008). The study also used another method of classroom observation, and Ofsted reports of school quality; they were all in broad agreement.
22 Black and Wiliam (1998).
23 Black *et al.* (2003).
24 Muijs and Reynolds (2010).
25 See in general Black *et al.* (2003); Harrison (2013).
26 GTCE (2004).
27 See numerous references cited in Muijs and Reynolds (2010), Chapter 2.
28 See e.g. Ireson *et al.* (2002).

29 Muijs and Reynolds (2010), Chapter 17; for the zip method, see p. 235. See further West-Burnham and Coates (2005).
30 McCarthy (2009).
31 House of Commons (2014).
32 Carter-Wall and Whitfield (2012); Goodman and Gregg (2010).
33 Willms *et al.* (2009), p. 56.
34 www.learningfutures.org.
35 Price (2013).
36 For example Beadle and Murphy (2013); Cowley (2010); Rogers (2011).
37 E.g. Ofsted (2005); Watkins (2011); www.goodcpdguide.com; www.pivotaleducation.com; www.behaviourneeds.com; and listings on www.theguardian.com/teacher-network.
38 Ofsted (2005) p. 6.
39 Hallam *et al.* (2004).
40 See www.afa3as.org.uk and Blandford and Knowles (2013).
41 Ofsted (2005).
42 Watkins (2011).
43 See references cited in notes 27, 28 and 30.
44 See www.cmathteach.org.uk.
45 Allen and Burgess (2013); Slater *et al.* (2009).
46 Smithers *et al.* (2012).
47 Ofsted (2010c).
48 Murray (2011) p. 14. For further research see Auguste *et al.* (2010); Ingvarson *et al.* (2005); Menter (2010); Musset (2010); and OECD (2005).
49 They can be found on the website of the National Commission on Teaching and America's Future, www.nctaf.org.
50 Hill (2012); www.teachfirst.org.uk/TFNews/ThePrimeMinsterpupilsandteacherscelebrate TeachFirstsuccessasUKnumberonegraduateemployer37076.aspx.
51 Smithers *et al.* (2012) pp. 8–9. This is a useful source for all manner of data on teacher training, including evaluations of various routes into teaching.
52 Muijs *et al.* (2010). Teach First is descended from Teach for America. Information on the latter and its effects can be found in Xu *et al.* (2009).
53 Allen and Allnut (2013).
54 The website is www.futureleaders.org.uk.
55 Hayes and Morgan (2012).
56 See www.teachingleaders.org.uk.
57 Atkinson *et al.* (2004); their paper contains a further review of other research.
58 Ibid., p. 6.
59 Hanushek (2003). Of four US studies – Glazerman and Seifullah (2010), Goodman and Turner (2010), Springer *et al.* (2010), Winters *et al.* (2008) – the first three found no impact; the fourth found a positive impact, but is not a high-quality study.
60 DfE (2013).
61 Croxson and Atkinson (2001).
62 DfE (2013: 5).
63 'In 2010, over 6,600 applicants competed for 660 available slots' in primary school teacher training programmes. Ibid., Box 1.3, p. 17.
64 Ibid. See further Aho *et al.* (2006); Grubb *et al.* (2005); Malaty (2002); Ofsted (2010a), etc.
65 Schleicher (2011: 15).
66 Cordingley (2013a: 24). Some of the main comprehensive reviews are: Cordingley *et al.* (2005); Robinson *et al.* (2009); Stoll *et al.* (2006); Timperley *et al.* (2007).
67 Ofsted (2010b: 5).
68 Robinson *et al.* (2009).
69 Cordingley (2013a: 27–28).
70 Frost (2013).
71 Byers *et al.* (2013).
72 Wiliam (2013a), p. 55.
73 Bubb and Earley (2008).
74 Murphy (2013).

75 See 'Introduction to the New School Inspection Framework: the quality of teaching', Ofsted 18 November 2011, MP3 video, accessed from the Ofsted website on 29/10/2013.
76 Ofsted (2013).
77 Cordingley *et al.* (2005), no page numbers.
78 Ofsted (2012: 14).
79 BERA (2014a), p. 12.
80 BERA (2014a and b).
81 BERA (2014a) p. 12. Italics in original.
82 Bell *et al.* (2010); Timperley *et al.* (2007). (The latter paper reviews New Zealand but also international research.)

Bibliography

Aho, E., Pitkänen, K. and Sahlberg, P. (2006) 'Policy development and reform principles of basic and secondary education in Finland since 1968', *Education Working Paper Series* no. 2, Washington, DC: World Bank.

Allen, J., Gregory, A., Mikami, A., Lun, J., Hamre, B. and Pianta, R. (2012) *Predicting Adolescent Achievement with the CLASS(tm)S Observation Tool*, University of Virginia, VA: Center for Advanced Study of Teaching and Learning.

Allen, R. and Allnut, J. (2013) 'Matched panel data estimates of the impact of Teach First on school and departmental performance', DoQSS *Working Paper* no. 13–11, London: Institute of Education.

Allen, R. and Burgess, S. (2013) 'Reforming teacher training', *Research in Public Policy*, Winter 2012/13, 15: 11–13.

Atkinson, A., Burgess, S., Croxson, B., Gregg, P., Propper, C., Slater, H. and Wilson, D. (2004) 'Evaluating the impact of performance related pay for teachers in England', *Working Paper* no. 04/113, Bristol: CMPO, University of Bristol.

Auguste, B., Kihn, P. and Miller, M. (2010) *Closing the Talent Gap: Attracting and Retaining Top-Third Graduates to Careers in Teaching – An International and Market Research-Based Perspective*, Washington, DC: McKinsey & Co.

Beadle, P. and Murphy, M. (2013) *Why are You Shouting at Us? The Do's and Don'ts of Behaviour Management*, London: Bloomsbury Education.

Bell, M., Cordingley, P., Isham, C. and Davis, R. (2010) *Report of Professional Practitioner Use of Research Review: Practitioner Engagement in and/or with Research*, Coventry: CUREE, GTCE, LSIS & NTRP.

Bell, M., Cordingley, P., Crisp, P. and Hawkins, M. (2012) *Understanding What Enables High Quality Professional Learning: A Report on the Research Evidence*, London: Pearson School Improvement [online]. Available at: www.pearsonschoolmodel.co.uk/wp-content/uploads/2011/09/CUREE-Report.pdf (accessed 22 April 2013).

BERA (British Educational Research Association) (2014a) *Research and the Teaching Profession: Building The Capacity for a Self-Improving Education System*, London: British Educational Research Association with the Royal Society of Arts.

BERA (2014b) *The Role of Research in Teacher Education: Reviewing the Evidence*, London: British Educational Research Association with the Royal Society of Arts.

Black, P. and Wiliam, D. (1998) *Inside the Black Box: Raising Standards Through Classroom Assessment*, London: School of Education, King's College.

Black, P., Harrison, C., Lee, C., Marshall, B. and Wiliam, D. (2003) *Assessment for Learning: Putting it into Practice*, Maidenhead: Open University Press, 2003.

Blandford, S. and Knowles, K. (2013) *Achievement for All: Raising Aspirations, Access and Achievement*, London: Bloomsbury Education.

Bridges, D., Smeyers, P. and Smith, R. (eds) (2009) 'Evidence based policy: What evidence? What basis? Whose policy?' *Journal of Philosophy of Education*, Supplement 1, 42, August.

Brown, J., Jones, S., LaRusso, M. and Aber, J. (2010) 'Improving classroom quality: Teacher influences and experimental impacts of the 4Rs Program', *Journal of Educational Psychology* 102(1): 153–167.

Bubb, S. and Earley, P. (2008) *From Self-Evaluation to School Improvement: The Importance of Effective Staff Development*, Reading: CfBT Education Trust.

Byers, R., Scott, S. and Rosier, V. (2013) 'Creating reflexive communities of enquiry: experiences of professional development partnerships between schools, local authorities and a university'. In C. McLaughlin (ed.) *Teachers Learning: Professional Development and Education*, The Cambridge Teacher Series, Cambridge: Cambridge University Press.

Cadima, J., Leal, T. and Burchinal, M. (2010) 'The quality of teacher–student interactions: Associations with first graders' academic and behavioral outcomes', *American Journal of Education* 119(3):455–470.

Carter-Wall, C. and Whitfield, G. (2012) *The Role of Aspirations, Attitudes and Behaviour in Closing the Educational Attainment Gap*, York: Joseph Rowntree Foundation.

CfBT (2012) *School2School: How to Make Teaching Schools a Success*, Reading: CfBT Education Trust.

Chetty, R., Friedman, J. and Rockoff, J. (2011) 'The long-term impacts of teachers: Teacher value-added and student outcomes in adulthood', National Bureau of Economic Research, *Working Papers* 17699. Available at: www.nber.org/papers/w17699 (accessed 22 April 2013).

Chetty, R., Friedman, J. and Rockoff, J. (2013) 'Measuring the impacts of teachers I: Evaluating bias in teacher value-added estimates', National Bureau of Economic Research, *Working Papers* 19423. Available at: www.nber.org/papers/w19423 (accessed 22 April 2013).

Clifton, J. and Cook, W. (2012) *A Long Division: Closing the Attainment Gap in England's Secondary Schools*, London: Institute for Public Policy Research. Available at: www.ippr.org/publication/55/9585/a-long-division-closing-the-attainment-gap-in-englands-secondary-schools (accessed 22 April 2013).

Clotfelter, C., Ladd, H. and Vigdor, J. (2007) 'How and why do teacher credentials matter for student achievement?' *Working Paper no.* 2, Washington DC: Urban Institute.

Cordingley, P. (2013a) 'The role of professional learning in determining the profession's future'. In C. McLaughlin (ed.) *Teachers Learning: Professional Development and Education*, The Cambridge Teacher Series, Cambridge: Cambridge University Press, pp. 21–31.

Cordingley, P. (2013b) 'The contribution of research to teachers' professional learning and development', *Research and Teacher Education: the BERA-RSA Inquiry*. Available at: www.bera.ac.uk (accessed 22 April 2013).

Cordingley, P., Bell, M., Evans, D., Firth, A. (2005) *The Impact of Collaborative CPD on Classroom Teaching and Learning. Review: What do Teacher Impact Data Tell Us About Collaborative CPD?* In: *Research Evidence in Education Library*, London: EPPI-Centre, Social Science Research Unit, Institute of Education, University of London. Available at: http://eppi.ioe.ac.uk/cms/Default.aspx?tabid=395 (accessed 29 March 2013).

Cowley, S. (2010) *Getting the Buggers to Behave*, 4th edn, London: Continuum.

Creemers, B. (2012) *Improving Quality in Education: Dynamic Approaches to School Improvement*, London: Routledge.

Creemers, B., Kyriakides, L. and Sammons, P. (eds) (2010) *Methodological Advances in Educational Effectiveness Research*, London: Routledge/Taylor & Francis.

Croxson, B. and Atkinson, A. (2001) 'The implementation of the performance threshold in UK secondary schools', *Working Paper* no. 01/44, Bristol: CMPO, University of Bristol.

CUREE (Centre for the Use of Research Evidence in Education) (2012) *Understanding What Enables High Quality Professional Learning: A report on the research evidence*, London: Centre for the Use of Research Evidence in Education.

DfE (Department for Education) (2010) *The Importance of Teaching*, London: Department for Education.

DfE (2013) *Departmental Advice: Reviewing and Revising Your School's Approach to Teachers' Pay*, London: Department for Education.

Earley, P. and Porritt, V. (eds) (2009) *Effective Practices in Continuing Professional Development: Lessons from Schools*, London: Institute of Education.

Frost, D. (2013) 'Developing teachers, schools and systems: partnership approaches'. In C. McLaughlin (ed.) *Teachers Learning: Professional Development and Education*, The Cambridge Teacher Series, Cambridge: Cambridge University Press, pp. 52–69.

Gladwell, M. (2008) 'Most likely to succeed: How do we hire when we can't tell who's right for the job?' *The New Yorker*, 15 December.

Glazerman, S. and Seifullah, A. (2010) *An Evaluation of the Teacher Advancement Program (TAP) in Chicago: Year Two Impact Report* (ref. no. 6319–520). Washington, DC: Mathematica Policy Research.

Goodman, A. and Gregg, P. (2010) *Poorer Children's Educational Attainment: How Important are Attitudes and Behaviour?* York: Joseph Rowntree Foundation.

Goodman, S.F. and Turner, L.J. (2010) *Teacher Incentive Pay and Educational Outcomes: Evidence from the New York City Bonus Program.* New York: Columbia University.

Grigg, R. (2010) *Becoming an Outstanding Primary School Teacher,* Harlow: Longman.

Grossman, P., Hammerness, K. and McDonald, M. (2009) 'Redefining teaching, re-imagining teacher education', *Teachers and Teaching: Theory and Practice* 15(2): 273–289.

Grossman, P., Loeb, S., Cohen, J., Hammerness, K., Wyckoff, J., Boyd, D. and Lankford, H. (2010) 'Measure for measure: The relationship between measures of instructional practice in middle school English Language Arts and teachers' value-added scores', *NBER Working Paper,* no. 16015.

Grubb, N., Jahr, H., Neumuller, J. and Field, S. (2005) *Equity in Education: Thematic Review of Finland,* Paris: OECD.

GTCE (2004) *Assessment For Learning: Putting it into Practice.* Available at: www.gtce.org.uk (accessed 29 January 2012).

Hallam, S., Rogers, L. and Shaw, J. (2004) *Improving Children's Behaviour and Attendance through the Use of Parenting Programmes: An Examination of Good Practice,* RR-585, London: Department for Education and Skills.

Hanushek, E. (1992) 'The trade-off between child quantity and quality', *Journal of Political Economy* 100(1): 84–117.

Hanushek, E. (2003) 'The failure of input-based schooling policies', *Economic Journal* 113: F64–F98.

Hanushek, E. (2009) 'Teacher deselection'. In D. Goldhaber, D. and Hannaway, J. (eds) *Creating a New Teaching Profession,* Washington, DC: Urban Institute Press, pp. 165–180.

Hanushek, E. (2010) 'The economic value of higher teacher quality', *Working Paper* no. 56, Washington, DC: Urban Institute.

Hanushek, E. and Rivkin, S. (2004) 'How to improve the supply of high quality teachers'. In D. Ravitch (ed.) *Brookings Papers on Education Policy,* Washington DC: Brookings Institution.

Hanushek, E. and Rivkin, S. (2006) 'Teacher quality'. In E. Hanushek and F. Welch (eds) *Handbook of the Economics of Education 2,* Amsterdam: Elsevier, pp. 1051–1078.

Hanushek, E. and Rivkin, S. (2010) 'Generalizations about using value-added measures of teacher quality', Paper presented at the annual meetings of the American Economic Association, Atlanta, GA, January 3–5.

Harlen, W. and Deakin Crick, R. (2002) *A Systematic Review of the Impact of Summative Assessment and Tests on Students' Motivation for Learning,* EPPI-Centre Review, version 1.1, *Research Evidence in Education Library.* Issue 1, London: EPPI-Centre, Social Science Research Unit, Institute of Education, University of London.

Harrison, C. (2013) 'Testing times: Reforming classroom teaching through assessment'. In IPPR (Institute of Public Policy Research) (2013) *Excellence and Equity: Tackling Educational Disadvantage in England's Secondary Schools,* London: Institute of Public Policy Research.

Hattie, J. (2003) 'Teachers make a difference', Australian Council for Education Research. Available at: www.acer.edu.au/documents/RC2003_Hattie_TeachersMakeADifference.pdf (accessed 4 March 2012).

Hattie, J. (2009) *Visible Learning: A Synthesis of Over 800 Meta-Analyses Relating to Achievement,* London: Routledge.

Hayes, S. and Morgan, A. (2012) *An Evaluation of the Future Leaders Programme 2010/11,* Reading: Learning Plus UK.

Hill, R. (2012) *Teach First: Ten Years of Impact,* Teach First. Available at: www.teachfirst.org.uk (accessed 26 February 2013).

House of Commons (2014) *Underachievement in Education by White Working Class Children,* First Report of Session 2014–15, London: House of Commons Select Committee on Education.

Ingvarson, L. and Hattie, J. (2008) *Assessing Teachers for Professional Certification: The First Decade of the National Board for Professional Teaching Standards,* Amsterdam: Elsevier.

Ingvarson, L., Meiers, M. and Beavis, A. (2005) 'Factors affecting the impact of professional development programs on teachers' knowledge, practice, student outcomes and efficacy'. In S. Dorn (ed.) *Education Policy Analysis Archives* 13(10): 1–28.

IPPR (Institute of Public Policy Research) (2013) *Excellence and Equity: Tackling Educational*

Disadvantage in England's Secondary Schools, London: Institute of Public Policy Research.

Ireson, J., Hallam, S., Hack, S., Clark, J. and Plewis, I. (2002) 'Ability grouping in English secondary schools: Effects on attainment in English, Mathematics and Science', *Educational Research and Evaluation* 8(3): 299–318.

James, C., Connolly, M., Dunning, G. and Elliot, T. (2005) 'The characteristics of high attainment primary schools in disadvantaged settings', Paper submitted to the *British Journal of Educational Studies*, September.

Kington, A., Regan, E., Sammons, P. and Day, C. (2011) *Effective Classroom Practice in Primary and Secondary Schools: A Research Digest*, Nottingham: Jubilee Press.

Kington, A., Day, C., Sammons, P., Regan, E., Brown, E. and Gunraj, J. (2011) 'What makes teachers effective?: Profiles of innovative classroom practice'. In C. Day, (ed.) *The Routledge International Handbook of Teacher and School Development*, London: Routledge, pp. 319–334.

McCarthy, M. (2009) 'How to make every lesson outstanding', *Professional Development Today* 12(3): 22–28.

McLaughlin, C. (ed.) (2013) *Teachers Learning: Professional Development and Education*, The Cambridge Teacher Series, Cambridge: Cambridge University Press.

Malaty, G. (2002) 'What are the reasons behind the success of Finland in PISA?' Available at: www.cimt.plymouth.ac.uk/journal/malaty.pdf (accessed 20 April 2013).

Menter, I. (2010) *Teachers: Formation, Training and Identity: A Literature Review*, Newcastle: Creativity, Culture and Education.

Ministry of Education Publications (2008) *PISA06 Finland: Analyses, Reflections and Explanations*, FI-00023 Government, Helsinki: Helsinki University Press.

Muijs, D. and Reynolds, D. (2010) *Effective Teaching: Evidence and Practice*, 3rd edn, London: Sage.

Muijs, D., Chapman, C., Collins, A. and Armstrong, P. (2010) *Maximum Impact Evaluation: The Impact of Teach First Teachers in Schools*, Maximum Impact Programme for Teach First Final Report, Manchester: University of Manchester.

Murphy, R. (2011) *Improving the Impact of Teachers on Pupil Achievement in the UK – Interim Findings*, London: The Sutton Trust.

Murphy, R. (2013) *Testing Teachers: What Works Best for Teacher Evaluation and Appraisal*, London: The Sutton Trust.

Murray, J. (2011) 'Teacher education research in England: Present realities, future possibilities?', *Research Intelligence (BERA)* 116: 14–16.

Musset, P. (2010) 'Initial teacher education and continuing training policies in a comparative perspective: Current practices in OECD countries and a literature review on potential effects', *OECD Education Working Papers*, no. 48, Paris: OECD.

NCTQ (National Council on Teacher Quality) (2011) *State of the States: Trends and Early Lessons on Teacher Evaluation and Effectiveness Policies*, Washington, DC: National Council on Teacher Quality.

Nye, B., Konstantopoulus, S. and Hedges, L.V. (2004) 'How large are teacher effects?' *Educational Evaluation and Policy Analysis* 26(3): 237–257.

OECD (Organisation for Economic Cooperation and Development) (2005) *Teachers Matter: Attracting, Developing and Retaining Effective Teachers*, Paris: OECD.

OECD (2009) *PISA 2009 Volume II: Overcoming Social Background: Equity in Learning Opportunities and Outcomes*, Paris: OECD.

Ofsted (2005) *Managing Challenging Behaviour*, HMI-2363, London: Ofsted.

Ofsted (2010a) *Finnish Pupils' Success in Mathematics: Factors that Contribute to Finnish Pupils' Success in Mathematics*, Manchester: Ofsted.

Ofsted (2010b) *Good Professional Development in Schools*, Manchester: Ofsted.

Ofsted (2010c) *The Annual Report of Her Majesty's Chief Inspector of Education, Children's Services and Skills 2009/10*, London: The Stationery Office.

Ofsted (2012) *The Annual Report of Her Majesty's Chief Inspector of Education, Children's Services and Skills 2011/12*, London: The Stationery Office.

Ofsted (2013) *Unseen Children: Access and Achievement 20 Years On*, London: The Stationery Office.

Pianta, R.C., Belsky, J., Houts, R. and Morrison, F. (2007) 'Teaching: Opportunities to learn in America's elementary classrooms', *Science* 315(5820): 1795.

Pianta, R.C., Belsky, J., Vandergrift, N., Houts, R. and Morrison, F.J. (2008) 'Classroom effects on children's achievement trajectories in elementary school', *American Educational Research Journal*

45(2): 365–397.

Pickering, J., Daly, C. and Pachler, N. (eds) (2007) *New Designs for Teachers' Professional Learning*, Bedford Way Papers, London: Institute of Education.

Price, D. (2013) 'Tackling pupil disengagement: Making the curriculum more engaging'. In IPPR (Institute of Public Policy Research) (2013) *Excellence and Equity: Tackling Educational Disadvantage in England's Secondary Schools*, London: Institute of Public Policy Research.

Reynolds, D. (2007) *Schools Learning From their Best: The Within School Variation (WSV) Project*, Nottingham: National College for School Leadership.

Rivkin, S., Hanushek, E. and Kain, J. (2005) 'Teachers, schools, and academic achievement', *Econometrica* 73(2): 417–458.

Robinson, V., Hohepa, M. and Lloyd, C. (2009) *School Leadership and Student Outcomes: Identifying What Works and Why*, Wellington, NZ: University of Auckland.

Rockoff, J. (2004) 'The impact of individual teachers on student achievement: Evidence from panel data', *American Economic Review* 94(2): 247–252.

Rogers, B. (2011) *Classroom Behaviour*, 3rd edn, London: Sage.

Rowe, N., Wilkin, A. and Wilson, R. (2012) *Mapping of Seminal Reports on Good Teaching*, NFER Research Programme: Developing the Education Workforce, Slough: National Foundation for Educational Research.

Sammons, P. (2010) 'Equity and educational effectiveness'. In P. Peterson, E. Baker and B. McGaw (eds) *International Encyclopedia of Education*, vol. 5, Oxford: Elsevier, pp. 51–57.

Sammons, P. (2010) 'The contribution of mixed methods to recent research on educational effectiveness'. In A. Tashakkori and C. Teddlie (eds) *Handbook of Mixed Methods Research*, 2nd edn, London: Sage, pp. 697–723.

Sammons, P., Sylva, K., Melhuish, E., Siraj-Blatchford, I., Taggart, B., Barreau, S. and Grabbe, Y. (2008) *The Influence of School and Teaching Quality on Children's Progress in Primary School*, Effective Pre-school and Primary Education 3–11 Project, DCSF RR028.

Schleicher, A. (2011) *Building a High-Quality Teaching Profession: Lessons from Around the World*, Paris: OECD.

Simmons, J. (ed.) (2006) *Breaking Through: Transforming Urban School Districts*, New York: Teachers College Press.

Slater, H., Davies, N. and Burgess, S. (2009) 'Do teachers matter? Measuring the variation in teacher effectiveness in England, CMPO *Working Paper* no. 09/212, Bristol: University of Bristol, Centre for Market and Public Organisation.

Slater, H., Davies, N. and Burgess, S. (2012) 'Do teachers matter? Measuring the variation in teacher effectiveness in England', *Oxford Bulletin of Economics and Statistics* 74(5): 629–645.

Smithers, A., Robinson, P. and Coughlan, M.D. (2012) *The Good Teacher Training Guide 2012*, Buckingham: University of Buckingham, Centre for Education and Employment Research.

Springer, M. G., Ballou, D., Hamilton, L., Le, V., Lockwood, J. R., McCaffrey, D., Pepper, M. and Stecher, B. (2010) *Teacher Pay For Performance: Experimental Evidence From the Project on Incentives in Teaching*. Nashville, TN: National Center on Performance Incentives at Vanderbilt University.

Staiger, D. and Rockoff, J. (2010) 'Searching for effective teachers with imperfect information', *Journal of Economic Perspectives* 24(3): 97–118.

Stoll, L., Bolam, R., McMahon, A., Wallace, M. and Thomas, S. (2006) 'Professional learning communities: A review of the literature', *Journal of Educational Change* 7(4): 221–258.

Sylva, K., Melhuish, E., Sammons, P., Siraj-Blatchford, I. and Taggart, B. (eds) (2010) *Early Childhood Matters: Evidence from the Effective Pre-school and Primary Education Project*, Abingdon: Routledge.

Teaching Agency (2012) *Initial Teacher Training Census 2012 Summary*, London: Department of Education.

Teddlie, C. and Sammons, P. (2010) 'Applications of mixed methods to the field of educational effectiveness research'. In B. Creemers, L. Kyriakides and P. Sammons (eds) *Methodological Advances in Educational Effectiveness Research*, London: Routledge/Taylor & Francis, pp. 115–152.

Timperley, H., Wilson, A., Barrar, H. and Fung, I. (2007) *Teacher Professional Learning and Development: Best Evidence Synthesis Iteration (BES)* Wellington, NZ: Ministry of Education. Available at: www.oecd.org/edu/preschoolandschool/48727127.pdf (accessed 6 December 2013).

Walsh, K. (2006) 'Teacher education: Coming up empty', *Fwd* 3(1): 1–6.

Watkins, C. (2011) *Managing Classroom Behaviour*, London: Association of Teachers and Lecturers.

West-Burnham, J. and Coates, M. (2005) *Personalizing Learning: Transforming Education For Every Child*, Stafford: Network Educational Press.

Whitmire, R. (2011) *The Bee Eater: Michelle Rhee Takes on the Nation's Worst School District*, San Francisco, CA: Jossey-Bass.

Wiliam, D. (2013a) 'The importance of teaching'. In IPPR (Institute of Public Policy Research) (2013) *Excellence and Equity: Tackling Educational Disadvantage in England's Secondary Schools*, London: Institute of Public Policy Research.

Wiliam, D. (2013b) 'The formative evaluation of teaching performance', Seminar Paper. Available at: www.dylanwiliam.org/Dylan_Wiliams_website/Papers.html (accessed 6 December 2013).

Willms J., Milton, P. and Friesen, S. (2009) *What Did You Do in School Today?*, Toronto, ON: Canadian Education Association.

Winters, M., Greene, J.P., Ritter, G. and Marsh, R. (2008) 'The effect of performance-pay in Little Rock, Arkansas on student achievement', *Working Paper*, no. 2008–02, Nashville, TN: Vanderbilt University, National Center on Performance Incentives.

Xu, Z., Hannaway, J. and Taylor, C. 'Making a difference? The effects of Teach for America in high school', CALDER *Working Paper* no. 17, Washington DC: The Urban Institute.

7

READING AND WRITING

Robert Cassen

Introduction

This chapter considers the evidence on the teaching of reading and writing. It observes a substantial 'tail' of learners leaving primary school with poor levels of both, a bigger tail than would be left if best practice were followed, especially in reading. The sources of poor reading are examined, and the key measures to improve reading, under the main headings of phonics-plus, focussed attention, technology, and reading engagement; also covered are the specific problems of boys' reading, and the teaching of reading beyond primary school.

Writing has been much less studied, but again performance leaves a lot to be desired. With less research to go by, the chapter is only able to address some measures, which have and have not been found helpful. A strong association with reading is a recurrent theme.

Reading

Where we are

Reading is obviously crucial to children's education, and much more besides. Those who fail to learn to read properly by age 11 commonly have poor educational outcomes at age 16 and often suffer from a variety of social setbacks in later life.[1] Literacy skills are critical for earnings in the labour market.[2] Writing also matters, but the longer-term consequences of writing failure have been less studied.

The proportion of children reaching the key official UK target for reading – Level 4 at age 11 – was 86 per cent in 2013, or 83 per cent of boys and 88 per cent of girls, actually a modest decline relative to 2012. That may still sound quite good – but it means that one boy in 6 did not reach the target, and one girl in 10, or about 75,000 pupils in all. Some 30,000 children are entering secondary school each year with a reading age of 7.[3] These figures for what is essentially reading failure should be nowhere near that high, as we will see.

A small part of the 'problem' is the numbers of children whose first language is not English. They do not always have difficulty in secondary school, as they frequently recover from a slow start in English and do well by the time they reach 16. But the proportion of children in primary schools with 'EAL' (English as an additional language) has risen steadily in recent years, as a result of immigration and higher than average fertility among immigrant families. That proportion was nearly 8 per cent in 1997, and over 17 per cent in 2012. This rise may have contributed somewhat to the stagnation in reading performance at age 11; but it neither explains nor excuses it. Though there are significant differences at the local level, nationally at least in 2011 the proportion of EAL pupils in England getting Level 4 in reading was only three percentage points below that of children whose first language is English.[4] (Perhaps this just indicates how badly many home English speakers have been doing!) London has a disproportionately large share of the increase in EAL children − 40 per cent of London children have EAL − and yet London school results have improved more than elsewhere; their Level 4 results in 2011 were one percentage point better than the national average for both boys and girls.[5]

We can go back and see the Key Stage 2 (age 11) reading data from 1997 up to 2013. In 1997 the situation looked fairly dire, with only a little over 60 per cent of boys and less than 80 per cent of girls reaching the Level 4 target. But 1998 saw the introduction of the National Literacy Strategy and then to 2000 there was considerable progress in reading scores.[6] With the Strategy came the Literacy Hour, which was found to have positive effects.[7] Seeing the figures rise made the government of the day feel it was doing well; but the figures stayed level and the government did little until 2005, when Every Child a Reader was launched; in December 2006 the Chancellor's pre-budget statement announced that it would be extended nationally. It would provide help to some 30,000 children by 2010. But initially it was only to be extended to 4,000 children in 18 local authorities. While the situation has gradually improved, the proportions not reaching Level 4

TABLE 7.1 Percentage of children getting Level 4 in reading

Year	Boys	Girls	All
1997	63	79	67
1998	64	82	71
1999	75	86	78
2000	80	85	83
2001	78	83	82
2002	77	84	80
2003	78	87	81
2004	79	87	83
2005	82	87	84

TABLE 7.2 Percentage of children getting Level 4 in reading

Year	Boys	Girls	All
2006	79	87	83
2007	81	87	84
2008	83	90	87
2009	82	89	86
2010	80	87	83
2011	80	87	84
2012	84	90	87
2013	83	88	86

Source: DfE data

were, as noted, still unacceptably high in 2013. Every Child a Reader is still operating – but the Coalition Government that took office in 2010 removed its ring-fenced funding before the target of 30,000 was reached.

Why so many failures – what is the problem?

When we say that the figures for poor reading at age 11 should not be so high, we do have evidence. Of course there are such things as reading disability and other special needs affecting reading, but a carefully monitored project in the United States found that with appropriate remedial help for those who needed it, poor reading was reduced to 1.5 per cent of the population studied – as the study put it, 'a far cry from the 10 per cent to 15 per cent figures that have emerged as estimates of the incidence of reading disability in the relevant literature'.[8] In 2010 Ofsted looked at 12 outstanding primary schools in a range of communities and social and economic backgrounds; they were teaching 'virtually every child to read, regardless of the social and economic circumstances of their neighbour-hoods, the ethnicity of their pupils, the language spoken at home and most special educational needs or disabilities', in this case getting children to the target level at Key Stage 1.[9]

Reading disability is often misunderstood. We need first to unscramble the underlying conditions. Some children are simply late in learning to read, others have physiological problems that may need addressing. Often everything is put together under the heading of 'dyslexia', but this may not be helpful. Children can have a neurological problem and still learn to read, or vice versa – they may find reading difficult without an underlying neurological condition. Since the remedy is the same in most cases, apart from the most acute physiological problems, some have concluded we would be better off without the term dyslexia at all, though it is at the very least socially helpful – a child may well feel better if she is termed 'dyslexic', rather than have her poor reading skill put down to low intelligence or some form of disability. A recent book has made the case for leaving behind the term 'dyslexia',[10] though of course some defend it, not least the Dyslexia Association.

Learning to read is quite complex: the child has to master the association between letters, sounds and meaning. There is some evidence that the process is harder in English than in other languages, because of the variety of different spellings for the same sound and different sounds for the same spelling.[11] Many nevertheless do grasp the reading process easily. When they don't, it is usually a question of identifying where precisely the child is having difficulty.

There appears to be something of a genetic connection with reading disability in some cases, but as so often, there is really an interaction between genes and environment, or as one study put it, many people are not born with dyslexia, but rather have a 'susceptibility that requires more intense instruction'.[12] The proportions with a physiological condition that needs remediation are very low and with or without it the 'treatment' is mostly the same: individual-specific help, more or less regardless of the origin of the problem, except in the most severe cases or for those with clearly physiological difficulties, which can be identified by testing.[13]

The most basic and most common cause of problems in learning to read is a lack of facility in identifying words, which in turn requires a basic ability to decode print and its relation to speech sounds. That, in turn, depends on 'phonological awareness', the ability to recognise the speech sounds and combinations of sounds that make up words. Hulme and Snowling (2012) point to two key skills that underlie reading: phoneme awareness and letter knowledge.[14] They report studies that showed how teaching phoneme awareness and letter-sound knowledge side by side with direct reading instruction produced significantly better results than in a control group receiving an oral language intervention, and that the effect was lasting.

So where lateness in learning to read is present, the key remedy is not diagnosing the 'cause', but finding out what the individual is having difficulty with and giving appropriate help. In sum, the lack of progress in reading at primary level has only a little to do with neurological issues or disability. It is mainly to do with learners not getting the teaching and support they need.

What can be done?

A great deal has been learned about the teaching of reading in recent times. As with most things in education, much is due to home background. Poor reading is often associated with a lack of books in the home, with uneducated parents or indeed parents themselves lacking literacy, or failing to read to their children or interest them in reading. There are many ways to address these home and parenting issues; as far as pre-school is concerned the research has been reviewed in Chapter 3 on early years. Parents can help pre-school children with 'code-focussed' activities, i.e. teaching children the relationships between letters and sounds and how to recognise printed words; and 'meaning-focussed' activities such as reading stories and discussing them, which improves language and reading comprehension.[15] Public and voluntary programmes can also help in their own centres and with parenting; Sure Start is the major public programme.

But schools also play a major part. One study suggested that 'up until age 5, the family is the main environmental determinant of a child's development, but . . . by age 10 this has grown to include – and to a certain point been replaced by – the school environment.'[16] For primary teaching, the three key areas of concentration might be called phonics *plus*, focussed attention and reading engagement.

Phonics plus

It is widely agreed that teaching phonics, or 'synthetic phonics', is an effective and important part of the teaching of reading. But there is debate about whether it is adequate by itself, or how it needs supplementing. Official enthusiasm for synthetic phonics owes much to findings in Clackmannanshire, where a detailed study showed children taught with the method doing much better than others taught differently. The study was, though, based on only 300 pupils in 8 schools. Subsequent research has suggested a range of potential reasons for the strong result, not least the highly trained teachers and effective support by the head teacher. The method had less successful results in other Scottish authorities and West Dunbartonshire – poorer than Clackmannanshire – 'designed possibly the most successful intervention and based it on a "literacy for all" agenda'.[17]

Despite what should have been reservations such as these, the Clackmannanshire results powerfully influenced the 'Rose Review' of 2006,[18] a government-commissioned report on early reading teaching, and continued to be cited in support of the Coalition Government's endorsement of synthetic phonics. There have been other questions raised about the unique use of phonics. The UK Literary Association, for example, has criticised excessive concentration on phonics in official instructions to schools.[19] Even more controversial has been the Phonics Screening Check, taken by 6-year-olds for the first time in 2012. They have to pronounce both real and made-up (i.e. nonsense) words and syllables. Since only 69 per cent of children (three-quarters of girls and two-thirds of boys) passed the test in 2013, one must indeed wonder what its virtues are, given that a much higher proportion of pupils have been learning to read well without taking such a test. It has been widely criticised by teachers' unions. The DfE claimed that it has helped teachers identify pupils with difficulties that they would otherwise not have found, but teachers and their associations commonly say they do not need it. Indeed teachers have found a large proportion of competent readers fail the test.[20]

Such strictures were born out by a 2014 evaluation of the check[21]:

> Responses from teachers . . . revealed that almost all schools are committed to teaching phonics to some degree and that, within literacy teaching, considerable emphasis is placed on phonics as a method of teaching children to learn to decode. However, the findings indicate that most teachers do not see a commitment to systematic synthetic phonics as incompatible with the teaching of other decoding strategies.[22]

Furthermore,

> attainment in reading and writing more broadly appears unaffected by the school's enthusiasm, or not, for systematic synthetic phonics and the check, and by their approach to the teaching of phonics. [23]

But a key issue is the *plus* in phonics *plus*. Phonics can indeed instruct children well to learn words from text. But to go beyond that in comprehension and taking pleasure in reading requires something further. Children need in particular to have their reading interests extended by exposure to a wide variety of texts, not least books. The National Literacy Strategy was criticised for its concentration on isolated texts; enthusiasts for books claim that texts alone do not generate the emotional involvement that can come from a book. Two somewhat similar strategies or programmes, among others, are designed to help this: Power of Reading, and Building Communities of Readers – see further in this chapter.[24] The Progress in International Reading Literacy Study (PIRLS) of 2011, based on tests of 10-year-olds in 40 countries, showed only 26 per cent of English pupils at that age actually liked reading.[25]

Focussed attention

Individual attention is likely to be important for every child learning to read. It is simply a mark of good teaching, as the chapter on teaching quality makes clear: a good teacher identifies any problems a particular child is having with his lessons and responds as necessary. Teachers commonly know how to discover what their pupils need individually and if their classes are not too large, can often provide whatever is wanted.

For those with more than modest reading difficulties, however, individual attention may be essential and requires skills that ordinary teaching and teacher training do not provide. An important one-on-one approach for children who are late in learning to read is Reading Recovery, provided within Every Child a Reader (ECaR). Many schools are achieving satisfactory results without such a programme. But where there are large numbers of children struggling with their reading, ECaR is a tested way to make improvements.[26] It provides three 'waves' of teaching in the first 2 years of primary school. The first wave combines systematic phonics with word recognition and language comprehension; the second is a supportive programme including oral language and independent reading; the third is Reading Recovery aimed at the lowest 5 per cent in reading achievement, as discussed below.

The evidence suggests that it should be started early, as early as Year 1 of primary school; prolonged poor reading can lead to deficiencies that are hard or impossible to surmount.[27] Reading Recovery (RR) has been assessed in a controlled study of a group of the most disadvantaged children in the most disadvantaged schools in some of London's most disadvantaged boroughs. It was found to have positive and significant results for children and better results than for those receiving other interventions.[28] Some of the specific findings are impressive: for example,

> More than half of the lowest [achieving] children in schools without RR were considered by their teachers to have made none or marginal growth across Year 1 in reading comprehension, whereas 87 per cent of children who had received RR were considered to have made average to exceptional progress in reading comprehension.[29]

Another study found that with RR the proportion reaching Level 1 – the target level – in Year 1 was 26 percentage points higher than in the matched comparison group.[30] ECaR has also been found to have positive school-wide effects, and positive influences on parents' engagement with their children's literacy.

Training to become an RR teacher takes a year part-time. The cost per pupil of ECaR has been estimated at some £2,600 in the long term (running costs only), £3,100 in the short term (that is, including start-up costs). These are large sums, when multiplied by the number of pupils who need it, but the benefits are found to be positive and considerable.[31] The costs of *not* providing it are much greater, in terms of blighted lives, wasted education, and the prospect of unemployment or a life on the wrong side of the law – all too common destinations of those who do not learn to read.

A further study has examined a range of programmes for 'struggling readers', including several in the USA and other countries.[32] It gives high marks to Reading Recovery, and highest of all to the US programme Success for All, which is similar to Reading Recovery in some ways but includes teaching beyond the first years – such teaching is also found to be important to convert the gains from Reading Recovery into longer-lasting effects. The study further finds that programmes incorporating phonics teaching are considerably more effective than those without it. Children are also found to be better served by fully qualified teachers than 'para-professionals', though the latter can be valuable. Also small-group teaching can be effective, but may not save much of the teacher's time. Cooperative study with pupils working in pairs can be effective too.[33] Success for All was introduced in

---

'The needs of a young dyslexic are seldom adequately catered for. This results in huge numbers of them becoming bewildered, disengaged and failing in the classroom by the age of 8, 9 or 10. Without effective support, the dyslexic child might become obstructive, and dismissive of educational goals . . . Many drop out, truant, and follow a depressingly familiar downward path that leads them into the courts.'

J. Hewitt-Main, special needs tutor at Chelmsford Prison, *Education Guardian*, 23 January 2007

England in 1997, and is followed in more than 100 schools. A study of 18 schools found it to be effective in improving word-level and decoding skills, compared with a carefully matched group of control schools.[34] Response to Intervention: Breakthroughs in Literacy, a CUREE programme, has also had some success in a controlled trial with disadvantaged pupils in Year 6, and was being further trialled at the time of writing.[35]

It is also worth recalling the *Evening Standard*'s Get London Reading, a programme of training and employing reading-teacher volunteers in deprived areas, partly funded by the Mayor's 'Inspiring Reading' initiative. It was a laudable approach and appeared to be having some success as the box below shows. The question is, why was it left to the *Evening Standard*? Surely the government should have been doing it years ago, and not just in London.

'We sent St Mary's an army of reading volunteers trained by our literacy campaign partner Volunteer Reading Help (since renamed Beanstalk) and in 6 months, increased their Sats scores from 52 to 91 per cent.'
David Cohen, *Evening Standard* 11 December 2012

Beanstalk by 2014 had helped over 7,300 pupils in over 1,100 schools, and claimed significant improvement in reading compared with pupils not receiving support. www.beanstalkcharity.org.uk.

Technology

There are a number of IT programmes designed to assist the learning of basic reading. Read Write Inc. is a widely used phonics-based programme.[36] Another that emerges fairly well in a What Works Clearinghouse comparison is Lexia Reading.[37] This programme allows pupils to work at home or in school and also allows teachers to see where pupils are doing well or need support. The What Works site in fact lists more than 20 such programmes, several of them even more highly rated.[38]

For those with specific types of reading disability, there are a variety of 'assistive' technologies. An example is the resources available on www.altformat.org/mytext book/, developed by Dolphin Technologies. This is a programme designed for pupils with print recognition difficulties and its basic contribution is to turn print – textbooks for example – into speech. It has been evaluated and found to have positive effects.[39]

A programme to help every teacher and learner is Accelerated Reader, developed by Renaissance Learning. It finds out each pupil's reading age and can grade the books in the school library for reading age as well. It is a laptop-based programme run interactively between teacher and pupils. The child does reading exercises on screen, the laptop grades them, and the teacher can see what each child is doing well or needs help with. The child's reading age is assessed at the

'I have to say what I loved this afternoon was watching the students, the faces, the sheer excitement that they have about something they can use. J and L are two of our most severe dyslexic students. Both are statemented and find it really hard to access material and have done so throughout their whole time here. J just said, "I can read this", and it was wonderful. To see a child who really does experience difficulty across the curriculum finding something that allows success is great.'

Teacher, on using Dolphin text-to-speech
programme, cited in DfE (2011a)

same time. The programme has also already scanned over 20,000 books and coded their age appropriateness – the child can go to the school library and pick out books by their colour code, knowing it is at her level.

It should also be noted that others have found IT programmes to have relatively modest effects compared with good teaching, though these did not include the most recent programmes.[40] One salutary study showed a frequently used, but also older, programme to be expensive and not very effective.[41] Clearly schools should be careful, and take claims of programme suppliers with a pinch of salt.

Reading engagement

Both programmes discussed here are based on the finding that teachers may have limited knowledge of contemporary children's books, often relying on texts that were popular in their own childhood; whereas there is today a wide range of books developed to capture the interest and enthusiasm of today's readers. Building Communities of Readers quotes a survey reporting that 20 per cent of teachers found a single book had turned a reluctant or refusing reader in their classes into an avid one. Both this programme and Power of Reading offer to help teachers become acquainted with appropriate books, and to assist them in teaching reading with their use. Power of Reading has been evaluated, with positive findings.[42] Children do differ widely in their interests and reading habits, so finding the right literature is part of the key to engagement.

Another effective means is collaborative story writing. This can be and is tried by teachers, but again there is a well-liked teacher-led (free) programme that can assist it. It is called BoomWriter.[43] Under the programme, each child is given a start for a story, which can come from the teacher or elsewhere. The child then writes his own story and submits it; all the writers then vote for a story (they can't vote for their own, and they don't know who has written the others); and the winner gets 'published'. Story writing and oral storytelling are valuable in their own right and also assist with reading. There are many links between reading and writing, as we discuss further below.

INNOVATIVE IDEAS

An imaginative library was created in Rosendale Primary School in North London; children were asked how they liked to read, and not one said 'at a desk'. So the school converted a double-decker bus into a library, and put it in a corner of the playground. It proved hugely popular, attracting children who had shown little interest in reading in the classroom.

'Re-imagining the classroom', *The Guardian* 14 May 2013

A variety of other IT resources for classroom teaching may be helpful, such as the American digital learning platform Time to Know.[44] This is another interactive laptop-based programme, designed for English and maths teaching, in the first instance for 9- to 11-year-olds. The teacher monitors her pupils as they go through exercises contained in the programme and again it helps the teacher assess pupils' individual needs. As well as improving English, the programme has also been found to improve engagement. The main evaluation was done with fourth and fifth graders in Texas.[45]

It is worth recalling that while several of the twelve schools examined in Ofsted (2010) used Read Write Inc. as the basis of their phonics teaching, several did not use specific software. In every case though, the ingredients of success included a commitment to get every child reading; leadership from the head teacher and, usually, a literacy coordinator; beginning reading in nursery classes where present; involving parents when necessary; not letting any child fall behind, and giving intensive catch-up support when needed; and employing teachers trained for effective delivery of phonics plus a variety of oral and print-based reading activities. There are many further aids to the latter, such as 'Rooted in Reading passports'.[46]

Boys

As already seen in the data, there is a particular problem with boys' reading. It is well known that boys are frequently later learning to read than girls, are harder to engage in reading, and when they do read, often have reading tastes very different from girls'. A well-known story in the literature is of a boy going home from school with books under his t-shirt – he didn't want other boys to see him. Boys may regard reading as a 'girly' thing. Ofsted (2004) identified a wide range of practice in better- and worse-performing primary schools. Good practice ranged from whole-school policies with what might be called boy-friendly features, to special activities that encourage boys' reading and a literary culture. All the measures referred to above have particular significance for boys.[47] The fact that special educational needs are more prevalent among boys than girls, as noted in the SEN chapter, Chapter 9, is also very much relevant to the reading question.

Beyond Key Stage 2

At present many pupils start secondary schooling behind in their reading: as noted, there were 75,000 pupils in 2013 not getting Level 4 at Key Stage 2. Schools may receive intakes with 30–50 per cent of pupils below their expected reading age, often far below. Successful schools will take measures to bring them up to scratch. Some have literacy specialist teachers; many have activities designed to help older children with reading, including literacy breakfasts, involving parents – not least helping parents to read if they need reading help – and most of the measures outlined above for primary teaching but at an age-appropriate level. One secondary school[48] visited by one of the present authors had a literacy specialist deputy head teacher and appointed an extra English teacher out of its own budget to take pupils out of their classes in small groups to give them whatever English help they needed, all the way from basic skills to whatever high-fliers required. It was part of the ethos of the school that every child would be pushed to achieve and in particular become successful readers who enjoyed reading. As with the primary schools in Ofsted (2010), it was a matter of leadership and commitment at every level.[49]

Further schemes found to be beneficial include *Reading Connects*, developed by the National Literacy Trust and supported by the then Department for Children, Schools and Families (DCSF).[50] This proposed a range of activities – whole school, reading promotion, library-based, reading events and reading groups, and family and community involvement. It offered schools a complete strategy to improve reading. *Everyone's Reading*, from the School Library Association, also supported originally by the DCSF, provides a comprehensive guide to books and reading materials for a variety of readers.[51] *Rooted in Reading* may also be used in secondary schools.

In 2014 the Educational Endowment Foundation (EEF) published an evidence brief listing programmes that had proved effective – to varying degrees – for struggling readers in secondary school. It emphasised that efforts were required to establish what it is that students are struggling with, whether word recognition, vocabulary, or reading comprehension, and choose appropriate methods to address their specific problems. Several of the programmes had been tested with RCTs, albeit often on a small scale, and were costed as well.[52]

As of 2014 the government has offered a 'literacy and numeracy catch-up premium' of £500 to assist pupils not reaching Level 4. The EEF brief has clear suggestions for what might prove cost-effective, and can help to guide schools in their approach, which may vary from one-on-one or small group tuition to broader reading interventions. One-on-one tuition such as Switch-on Reading appeared to have the strongest results, but was also expensive.

Writing

Where we are

Writing scores in terms of national tests at Key Stages 1 and 2 fall below expected standards by more than in reading, maths and science. In 2012, 83 per cent of children reached Level 2 at Key Stage 1, though only 70 per cent of FSM children, and 46 per cent of children with SEN. At Key Stage 2, 81 per cent of pupils achieved Level 4. At both Key Stage 1 and Key Stage 2 there was a considerable gender gap, with 76 per cent of boys achieving the expected level at Key Stage 2 compared with 87 per cent of girls. Achievement gaps of each kind are also higher for writing than for the other main subjects. Basically one fifth of all pupils and one quarter of boys are not writing as well as they should be by age 11.[53]

It does matter; research suggests that controlling for other factors, not getting Level 4 in writing at age 11 is quite strongly related to outcomes at age 16, not as strong as reading, but more than half as strong as being on free school meals, controlling for other factors.[54] It is true that students can now use word-processing programmes. But as long as classroom work and examinations require handwriting, it will continue to be important for educational outcomes and it is in any case an obviously necessary skill for many aspects of life beyond school. Poor handwriting has been found to affect pupils' compositional ability.[55] Writing and reading are inter-related in the learning process too.[56] Writing is referred to in the literature not just as putting handwriting on the page; it is also the ability to create an account of a topic and develop an argument. As such it is part of the foundation of intellectual activity and self-expression.

What can be done

It is not easy to summarise good practice in the teaching of writing. The Department of Education's *Research Evidence on Writing* lists some 25 principles for good teaching[57] and a further 20 for teaching boys specifically,[58] taken from a variety of sources. The Department also publishes its own curriculum guidance for teaching writing, at various Key Stage levels.

One factor is allocating specific time to writing. The transformative head teacher of George Eliot Primary School, chosen as 'School of the Year 2013' by the *Times Educational Supplement*, attributed part of her success to starting off the school day with a writing period; it 'focuses pupils' minds on work and learning', she said, 'it's a very constructive start'.[59] The research supports this, provided that the teaching follows other good-practice principles. These particularly include teaching how to use writing for a variety of purposes, and strategies for using every component of the writing process until the pupils become independent writers.[60] Other major factors are the teacher's enthusiasm for writing and the presentation of good writing models, as well as the more mundane features of writing such as sentence construction, grammar and punctuation, and drafting and revising.

One approach that does not come out very well in the research is Every Child a Writer. The quantitative research does not find very significant results at the school or individual pupil level, compared with other methods. Qualitatively however teachers report fairly favourably on the programme, and so do pupils who receive individual support.[61] Every Child a Reader, on the other hand, has been found to have positive effects on writing, improving writing attainment by 4 to 6 percentage points in the second and third years of operation.[62] This is not surprising, given the focus of much reading teaching on stories and narrative and relating oral to written work.

One study has examined the teaching of non-fiction writing.[63] It follows the kinds of advice on writing teaching already outlined, but adds the specific dimension of *argument* writing, designed to persuade or rebut. It can and should, the authors say, be taught at ages 7–11 as well as 11–14. This is now embodied in the National Curriculum, but the authors suggest that further spelling-out of detailed advice is needed. They advocate teaching of a writing process model, a degree of cognitive reasoning training, peer collaboration, and teacher modelling of argumentative writing, among other approaches.

The research on teaching boys' writing is somewhat older.[64] Its findings are akin to those for boys' reading. Given the association with reading, it is important that teaching is based on literature that appeals to boys. Active learning tasks including 'drama strategies' are recommended, as are tightly structured lessons with clear learning goals. Enlisting older male pupils as reading and writing 'buddies' is also suggested, and selective publication of their work as writing models. 'Talk for writing' time should be included in lessons so that pupils can talk about their text before they start to write.

Also as with reading, there is specific advice for teaching struggling writers and pupils with SEN.[65] A significant approach is Self-Regulated Strategy Development (SRSD), a comprehensive method that supports students in the several essential stages of writing, from composing to revising. It has been found effective with students with learning disabilities and ADHD. SRSD is suitable for primary and secondary school pupils.[66] Specific forms of help with sentence and paragraph construction are described in another study; they are more effective when adopted from a wide range of examples.[67] Finally, a range of measures can be found under the Achievement for All programme. Not surprisingly, they emphasise high expectations on the part of teachers, and encouraging enjoyment in the learning process, as well as providing practical advice for teachers and parents.[68]

The way ahead

There is no single measure to improve reading and writing; but a great deal is known about how to do better, especially to reduce the high number of those not learning to read and write well in primary school. Much of it is covered in the research referred to above; and it is also well summarised in Ofsted's *Moving English Forward* and reflected too in the 2014 *Inspection Handbook*.[69] The essential combination of policies would include in particular better quality of early years provision, and heightened emphasis in reception year and Year 1 to make early progress and identify reading problems as soon as possible and then address them. The latter might mean better leadership in some schools and better subject-knowledge where it is missing; perhaps above all a more single-minded concentration on improving reading by age 11. Ofsted also emphasises the need to improve use of information in the transition between Key Stage 2 and Key Stage 3. First and foremost policy should be informed by the knowledge that if young people do not achieve good reading ability and reading enjoyment, their education and quite possibly their lives will suffer.

Key findings

- Far too many children are not learning to read to an adequate standard in primary school – one boy in six and one girl in ten.
- This places a burden on secondary schools and often limits children throughout their education and beyond.
- Low-achieving children are mostly from disadvantaged families, though early disadvantage is by no means an insuperable obstacle. Even in disadvantaged households parental help can, or can be assisted to, improve reading.
- The principal problem in schools is the lack of appropriate teaching or, when needed, adequate individual support. With that teaching and support, the number not learning to read properly could be brought down to a fraction of where it is at present.
- Individual support can be expensive, but the social and educational costs of not learning to read far exceed any costs of good reading teaching.
- A variety of programmes and information technology, detailed in the chapter, is available to assist young people in learning to read and reading for pleasure.
- One fifth of all pupils, and one quarter of boys, are not writing properly at age 11.
- The consequences of not learning to write well are less researched than for reading, but the evidence suggests they are considerable.
- As with reading, measures to improve writing are known, but practice in pursuing them is highly variable.

Key policies

- Families should be supported at home with better quality pre-school education and parental involvement; and struggling children in primary school should receive proven methods of teaching, plus specific group or individual attention such as Reading Recovery where needed.
- Phonics teaching is now widely practised, properly so, but the evidence supports different means of teaching it; and it needs to be combined with programmes that encourage and help reading engagement such as Building Communities of Readers or Power of Reading.
- There are parallel policies for teaching writing, including Self-Regulated Strategy Development, a programme specifically designed for SEN pupils.
- Boys figure more commonly than girls as poor readers and writers; their issues should be addressed with measures specific to them.

- Secondary schools are faced with considerable numbers of insufficiently prepared learners and must first diagnose their particular reading difficulties, then address them following evidence-based good practice methods.

Notes

1 See Cassen and Kingdon (2007) and Burroughs-Lange (2008) and numerous references cited there.
2 Hansen and Vignoles (2005); see also McIntosh and Vignoles (2001). The problems faced by schools do of course depend to a degree on the size and composition of their EAL intake.
3 DfE (2012a).
4 Figures from www.naldic.org.uk.
5 Ibid. One or two London boroughs had over 70 per cent EAL children. Advice on the teaching of EAL children can be found in Sood and Mistry (2011).
6 Though some doubted whether the improvement was real – see Wyse (2003); Tymms (2004).
7 Machin and McNally (2004).
8 Cited in Vellutino et al. (2004). See further, on the US evidence, NICHD (2000).
9 Ofsted (2010); the quote is from p. 5.
10 Elliott and Grigorenko (2014).
11 '[S]everal studies now show that the developmental progress of children learning to read in transparent orthographies such as German or Italian is generally faster than that of children learning written English . . . Such children also show correspondingly faster development of phoneme awareness.' Vellutino et al. (2004), p. 16. See also Seymour (2005).
12 Ibid. See also Pennington and Olson (2005).
13 For example, there is a specific print-recognition disability, such as problems in seeing black letters on a white background, which may be correctable with tinted spectacles.
14 They discuss a third skill, rapid automatised naming, or RAN, which seems to be important and associated with reading ability; but it cannot be taught – and it is no more or less important in English than in other languages with more regular spelling.
15 Hulme and Snowling (2013); Senechal and LeFevre (2002).
16 Parsons et al. (2011).
17 Ellis (2007), p. 294.
18 DfES (2006).
19 UKLA (2010).
20 Richardson (2012), reporting a range of opinions.
21 DfE (2014).
22 Ibid., p. 70
23 Ibid., p. 72.
24 The former is produced by the Centre for Literacy in Primary Education, see www.clpe.co.uk; for the latter, Cremin et al. (2008). See further Ofsted (2004).
25 Mortimore (2013), p. 146, citing http://timssandpirls.bc.edu/pirls2011.
26 For the research, see DfE (2011b); also DfES (2006).
27 Alakeson (2005).
28 Burroughs-Lange (2008); DfE (2011b).
29 Ibid., p. 22.
30 DfE (2011b), p. 162.
31 Figures of costs and benefits are in DfE (2011b), p. 177. The cost-effectiveness measure was £15–25,000 for bringing a child to the expected level at Key Stage 1. See also KPMG (2006); Lochner (2011).
32 Slavin et al. (2009).
33 The most comprehensive source for Reading Recovery is Burroughs-Lange and Ince (2013).
34 Tracey et al. (2013).
35 See www.curee.co.uk/node/3146#breakthroughs.
36 www.oup.com/oxed/primary/rwi/.
37 www.lexialearning.com/effectiveness/research.
38 http://ies.ed.gov/ncee/wwc/findwhatworks.aspx.
39 DfE (2011a).

40 Slavin *et al.* (2009).
41 Rouse and Krueger (2004).
42 O'Sullivan and McGonigle (2010).
43 www.boomwriter.com.
44 www.timetoknow.com.
45 For the evaluation research, see Rosen and Beck-Hill (2012).
46 Willshaw (2012).
47 See also Frater (2000); Safford *et al.* (2004).
48 Preston Manor High School in Brent.
49 See further Frater (1997).
50 See NLT (2008) and www.readingconnects.org.uk.
51 SLA (2009).
52 Higgins *et al.* (2014).
53 Data from DfE (2012b).
54 Kingdon and Cassen (2007).
55 Medwell *et al.* (2009).
56 Burroughs-Lange and Ince (2013), p. 89ff.
57 DfE (2012b), pp. 6–7.
58 Ibid., pp. 11–12.
59 *Evening Standard*, 10 July 2013, p. 25. The school had been rated as inadequate by Ofsted in 2006.
60 What Works Clearinghouse (2012) p. 12ff.
61 Fisher and Twist (2011).
62 DfE (2011b).
63 Andrews *et al.* (2009).
64 Daly (2003); Ofsted (2005a). The latter is a detailed manual for a training course for teachers.
65 Santangelo and Olinghouse (2009); DfE (2012b).
66 Mason *et al.* (2011) describe the method in detail.
67 Santangelo and Olinghouse (2009).
68 Humphrey and Squires (2011).
69 Ofsted (2012, 2014).

Bibliography

Alakeson, V. (2005) *Too Much, Too Late: Life Chances and Spending on Education and Training*, London: Social Market Foundation.

Alexander, R., Armstrong, M., Flutter, J., Hargreaves, L., Harrison, D., Harlen, W., Hartley-Brewer, E., Kershner, R., MacBeath, J., Mayall, B., Northen, G., Pugh, G., Richards, C. and Utting, D. (2010) *Cambridge Primary Review: Children, their World, their Education*, London: Routledge.

Andrews, R., Torgerson, C., Low, G. and McGuinn, N. (2009) *Teaching Argument Writing to 7- to 14-Year-Olds: An International Review of the Evidence of Successful Practice*, EPPI-Centre Report, London: Institute of Education.

Burroughs-Lange, S. (2006) *Evaluation of Reading Recovery in London Schools: Every Child a Reader 2005–2006*, London: Institute of Education.

Burroughs-Lange, S. (2008) *Comparison of Literacy Progress of Young Children in London Schools: A Reading Recovery Follow up Study*, London: University of London Institute of Education.

Burroughs-Lange, S. and Ince, A. (eds) (2013) *Reading Recovery and Every Child a Reader: History, Policies and Practice*, London: Institute of Education Press.

Cassen, R. and Kingdon, G. (2007) *Tackling Low Educational Achievement*, Report to the Joseph Rowntree Foundation, York: Joseph Rowntree Foundation.

Clark, C. with Burke, D. (2012) *Boys' Reading Commission. A Review of Existing Research to Underpin the Commission*, London: National Literacy Trust.

Cremin, T., Mottram, M., Collins, F. and Powell, S. (2008) *Building Communities of Readers*, Leicester: University of Leicester UKLA.

Daly, C. (2003) *Literature Search on Improving Boys' Writing*, London: Ofsted.

Dede, C. and Richards, J. (eds) (2012) *Digital Teaching Platforms: Customizing Classroom Learning for Each Student*, New York: Teachers College Press.

DfE (2011a) *Accessible Resources Pilot Project: Final Report, Dolphin Inclusive Team*, London: Department for Education.

DfE (2011b) *Evaluation of Every Child a Reader (ECaR)*, Research Report DFE-RR114, London: Department for Education.

DfE (2012a) 'National Curriculum assessments at Key Stage 2'. Available at: www.education. gov.uk/researchandstatistics/statistics/announcements/a00211650/statistical-release-national-curriculum-assessment-ks2.

DfE (2012b) *The Research Evidence on Writing*, Research Report DFE-RR636, London: Department for Education.

DfE (2014) *Phonics Screening Check Evaluation*, Research Report DFE-RR339, London: Department for Education.

DfES (2004) *English Department Training 2004: Improving Writing*, London: DfES.

DfES (2006) *Independent Review of the Teaching of Early Reading (The 'Rose Report')*, Final Report, London: Department for Education and Skills.

Elliott, J. and Grigorenko, E. (2014) *The Dyslexia Debate*, Cambridge: Cambridge University Press.

Ellis, S. (2007) 'Policy and research: Lessons from the Clackmannanshire Synthetic Phonics initiative', *Journal of Early Childhood Literacy* 7(3): 281–297.

Fisher, R. and Twist, L. (2011) *Evaluation of Every Child a Writer Report 1*, DfE RR108a, Exeter: University of Exeter and National Foundation for Educational Research.

Frater, G. (1997) *Improving Boys' Literacy: A Survey of Effective Practice in Secondary Schools*, London: Basic Skills Agency.

Frater, G. (2000) *Securing Boys' Literacy: A Survey of Effective Practice in Primary Schools*, London: Basic Skills Agency.

Gillespie, A. and Graham, S. (2010) *Evidence-Based Practices for Teaching Writing*, Baltimore, MD: Johns Hopkins University School of Education, New Horizon for Learning.

Graham S. (2010) 'Teaching writing'. In D. Crystal (ed.) *Cambridge Encyclopedia of Language, 3rd edition*, Cambridge: Cambridge University Press.

Hansen, K. and Vignoles, A. (2005) 'The United Kingdom education system in a comparative context'. In S. Machin and A. Vignoles (eds) *What's the Good of Education? The Economics of Education in the United Kingdom*, Princeton, NJ: Princeton University Press, pp. 13–35.

Higgins, S., Katsipataki, M. and Coleman, R. (2014) *Reading at the Transition: Interim Evidence Brief*, London: Education Endowment Foundation.

Hulme, C. and Snowling (2013) 'Learning to read: What we know and what we need to understand better', *Child Development Perspectives* 7(1): 1–55.

Humphrey, N. and Squires, G. (2011) *Achievement for All National Evaluation: Final Report*, DfE RR176, London: Department for Education.

House of Commons (2005) *Teaching Children to Read, Eighth Report of Session 2004–2005*, London: House of Commons, Education and Skills Committee.

Kingdon, G. and Cassen, R. (2007) *Understanding Low Achievement in English Schools*, CASE Paper 118, London: London School of Economics, Centre for Analysis of Social Exclusion.

KPMG (2006) *The Long Term Costs of Literacy Difficulties*, London: KPMG Foundation.

Lochner, L. (2011) *Non-Production Benefits of Education: Crime, Health, and Good Citizenship*, NBER Working Paper no. 16722, Cambridge, MA: National Bureau of Economic Research.

Machin, S. and McNally, S. (2004) *The Literacy Hour*, CEE Discussion Paper 0043,

London: London School of Economics, Centre for the Economics of Education.

McIntosh, S. and Vignoles, A. (2001) 'Measuring and assessing the impact of basic skills on labour market outcomes', *Oxford Economic Papers* 53(3): 453–481.

Mason, L., Harris, K. and Graham, S. (2011) 'Self-regulated strategy development for students with writing difficulties', *Theory and Practice* 50(1): 20–27.

Medwell, J., Strand, S. and Wray, D. (2009) 'The links between handwriting and composing for Y6 children'. *Cambridge Journal of Education* 39(3): 329–344.

Mortimore, P. (2013) *Education Under Siege: Why There is a Better Alternative*, Bristol: Policy Press.

NICHD (National Institute of Child Health and Human Development) (2000) *Report of the National Reading Panel: Teaching Children to Read: An Evidence-Based Assessment of the Scientific Research Literature on Reading and its Implications for Reading Instruction* (NIH Publication no. 00_4769), Washington, DC: U.S. National Institute of Child Health and Human Development.

NLT (National Literacy Trust) (2008) *Reading Connects Handbook*, London: National Literacy Trust.

NLT (2012) *Boys' Reading Commission: The report of the All-Party Parliamentary Literacy Group Commission*, London: National Literacy Trust.

Ofsted (2003) The *Education of Six-Year-Olds in England, Denmark and Finland*, London: Ofsted.

Ofsted (2004) *Reading for Purpose and Pleasure: An Evaluation of the Teaching of Reading in Primary Schools*, HMI 2393, London: Ofsted.

Ofsted (2005a) *Informing Practice in English: A Review of Recent Research in Literacy and the Teaching of English*, London: Ofsted.

Ofsted (2005b) *The National Literacy and Numeracy Strategies and the Primary Curriculum*, London: Ofsted.

Ofsted (2010) *Reading by Six: How the Best Schools do it*, ref. no. 100197, London: Ofsted.

Ofsted (2011) *Promoting Reading in a Secondary School: Don Valley School and Performing Arts College*, ref. no. 210126, London: Ofsted.

Ofsted (2012) *Moving English Forward*, ref. no. 110118, London: Ofsted.

Ofsted (2014) *Inspection Handbook*, ref. no. 120101, London: Ofsted.

O'Sullivan, O. and McGonigle, S. (2010) 'Transforming readers: teachers and children in the Centre for Literacy in Primary Education Power of Reading project', *Literacy* 44(2): 51–59.

Parsons, S., Schoon, I., Rush, R. and Law, J. (2011) 'Long-term outcomes for children with early language problems: beating the odds', *Children and Society* 25(3): 202–214.

Pennington, B. and Olson, R. (2005) 'Genetics of dyslexia'. In M. Snowling and C. Hulme (eds) *The Science of Reading: A Handbook*, Oxford: Blackwell, pp. 453–472.

Richardson, H. (2012) 'New phonics test failed by four out of 10 pupils', BBC News Sept. 27.

Rosen, Y. and Beck-Hill, D. (2012) 'Intertwining digital content and a one-to-one laptop environment in teaching and learning: Lessons from the Time To Know program', *Journal of Research on Technology in Education* 44(3): 225–241.

Rouse, C. and Krueger, A. (2004) 'Putting computerised instruction to the test: A randomised evaluation of a "scientifically based" reading program', *Economics of Education Review* 23: 323–338.

Safford, K., O'Sullivan, O. and Barrs, M. (2004) *Boys on the Margin*, London: Centre for Literacy in Primary Education.

Santangelo, T. and Olinghouse, N. (2009) 'Effective writing instruction for students who have writing difficulties', *Focus on Exceptional Children* 42(4): 1–21.

Senechal, M. and LeFevre, J. (2002) 'Parental involvement in the development of children's reading skill: A 5-year longitudinal study', *Child Development* 73: 445–460.

Seymour, P. (2005) 'Early reading development in European orthographies'. In M. Snowling and C. Hulme (eds) *The Science of Reading: A Handbook*, Oxford: Blackwell, pp. 296–315.

SLA (School Library Association) (2009) *Riveting Reads Plus: Everyone's Reading*. Swindon: School Library Association.

Slavin, R., Lake, C., Davis, S. and Madden, N. (2009) *Effective Programs for Struggling Readers: A Best-Evidence Synthesis, Best Evidence Encyclopedia*, Baltimore, MD: Johns Hopkins University.

Sood, K. and Mistry, N. (2011) 'English as an Additional Language: Is there a need to embed cultural values and beliefs in institutional practice?' *Education 3–13* 39(2): 203–215.

Tracey, L., Chambers, B., Slavin, R., Hanley, P. and Cheung, A. (2013) *Success for All in England: Results From the Third Year of a National Evaluation*, York: University of York, Institute for Effective Education.

Tymms, P. (2004) 'Are standards rising in English primary schools?' *British Educational Research Journal* 30(4): 477–494.

UKLA (United Kingdom Literacy Association) (2005) *Submission to the Review of Best Practice in the Teaching of Early Reading*, Royston: United Kingdom Literacy Association.

UKLA (2006) *Response from the UKLA to the 'Independent Review of the Teaching of Early Reading'* Final Report. Available at: www.ukla.org. (accessed 22 April 2013).

UKLA (2010) *Teaching Reading: What the Evidence Says*, Leicester: University of Leicester, United Kingdom Literacy Association.

Vellutino, F.R., Fletcher, J.M., Snowling, M.J. and Scanlon, D.M. (2004) 'Specific reading disability (dyslexia): What have we learned in the past four decades?', *Journal of Child Psychology and Psychiatry* 45(1): 2–40.

What Works Clearinghouse (2012) *Teaching Elementary School Students to be Effective Writers*, NCE 2012–4058, Washington DC: US Department of Education. Available at: http://ies.ed.gov/ncee/wwc/pdf/practice_guides/writing_pg_062612.pdf (accessed 18 July 2013).

Willshaw, S. (2012) *Rooted in Reading Passports: Are they an Effective Way of Promoting Reading?* London: CfBT Education Trust.

Wyse, D. (2003) 'The National Literacy Strategy: A critical review of empirical evidence', *British Educational Research Journal*, 29(6): 903–916.

Younger, M. and Warrington, M. (2005) *Raising Boys' Achievement*, London: HMSO.

8

NUMERACY AND MATHEMATICS

Sandra McNally

Introduction

In this chapter, we discuss how maths attainment has evolved in the UK in recent years – as measured by national and international measures. We then discuss what we know (and don't know) about how to improve performance in maths.

At the most basic level, people need an adequate level of numeracy to cope with everyday situations, like shopping and household budgeting. While most people in the UK have acquired this level of numeracy by the time they complete their formal education, a significant minority of people have not. In fact 22 per cent of 16- to 19-year-olds in England were found to be 'functionally innumerate' – from a review of data in a 2010 study.[1] This means their numeracy levels are at or below that of an 11-year-old. Furthermore, there is a higher rate of innumeracy in the UK compared with many other industrialised countries. The 2012 'Skills for Life' survey (designed to measure basic skills in the English population aged between 16 and 69) found there to be a significant decline in numeracy skills among the youngest age group over the last 10 years or so, with little change in literacy skills.[2]

Unsurprisingly, studies show an association between basic skills in maths and future earnings. For example, an adult earns more than 30 per cent with 'level 1' numeracy (i.e. the skills of an 11-year-old) compared with those with even lower levels of numeracy.[3] An adult with level 2 numeracy earns about 16 per cent more than those with 'level 1'. Of course, these associations become lower when other factors are taken into account – but they are suggestive that numeracy has an important role for influencing how much a person can earn. There is also a strong association between basic levels of numeracy and literacy and the probability that a person is able to find a job. Other research shows there is a return for numeracy skills at the upper end of the distribution. People who have a maths A-level earn about 10 per cent more than those without such a qualification – even when taking account of GCSE performance, their highest qualification and their degree subject.[4]

There have been studies that have looked at the wage premium for numeracy skills for the 'average' learner.[5] Not only is this premium large, but it has also increased over time (between the early 1990s and the mid-2000s in one study). This suggests that although more people had good numeracy skills in the intervening period, the demand for such skills among employers increased by even more (i.e. they were willing to pay an even larger wage premium for numeracy skills when there were more people in the population with the relevant skills). One of the main explanations for this is known as 'skilled bias technological change'. This refers to the introduction of new technologies that are biased in favour of skilled workers. It comes from the hypothesis that employers' demand for skilled workers has been shaped by the kinds of technologies that are permeating into modern workplaces. In this changing environment, employers will be willing to pay more to workers who are skilled enough to operate these new technologies whereas less skilled workers will be less valued – and this will be reflected both in wages and in the employment probability. There is good evidence for the importance of skill biased technical change internationally.[6]

When we think of the whole economy, there is a strong relationship between maths and science skills and economic growth across countries,[7] although this will also reflect the impact of other skills (such as literacy).

How do we perform?

In international tests, the maths scores of 10- and 14-year-olds are measured by the TIMSS study and those of 15-year-olds in the PISA study.[8] Although one needs to be careful about reading too much into international leagues tables,[9] tests for recent years (2007 for TIMSS; 2009 for PISA) show that England and Scotland performed at about the OECD average for 14- and 15- year-olds. With regard to 10-year-olds, pupils in England performed at well above the average for countries taking part, whereas Scottish pupils fell just below the average. All parts of the UK participated in the most recent PISA study and did about the same (apart from Wales, which scores about 5 per cent below other parts of the UK). One might therefore conclude that the UK is about average for OECD countries when it comes to attainment in maths.

Because of methodological problems, it can be difficult to measure change over time from international surveys. TIMSS suggests that England has improved in the 2000s, but not much changed in PISA (comparing 2006 and 2009).

When it comes to national data, there is a longer time series to consider. Figures 8.1 and 8.2 show the percentage of students achieving a key indicator at age 11 and age 16 respectively. The former is the percentage of students achieving 'level 4' or above (i.e. the standard deemed 'expected' at age 11, according to the National Curriculum). The latter is the percentage of students achieving a grade A*–C (considered 'good' grades) in GCSE maths or equivalent. Both figures suggest modest progress over time (with the exception of the early-late 1990s for the age 11 tests). It is difficult to disentangle a genuine improvement in standards from

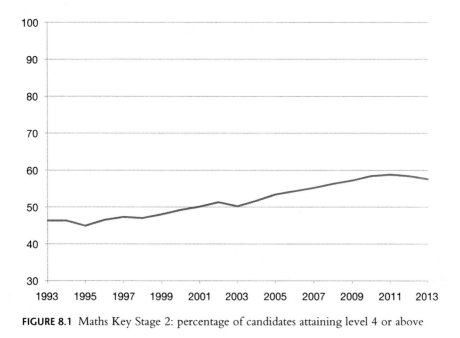

FIGURE 8.1 Maths Key Stage 2: percentage of candidates attaining level 4 or above

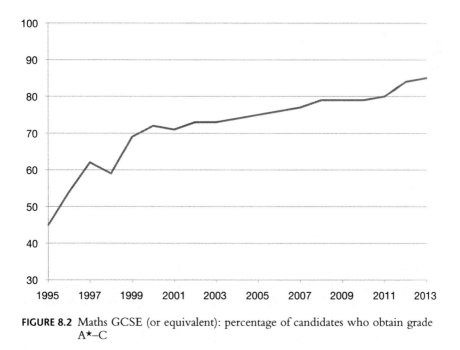

FIGURE 8.2 Maths GCSE (or equivalent): percentage of candidates who obtain grade
A★–C

better training for the examination (because of reasons such as 'teaching to the test' or any 'dumbing down' of exams), especially since schools face strong incentives to concentrate on those students who are close to these target indicators. These are indicators that contribute to a school's position in the performance tables (or 'league tables') of schools. However one interprets the level of these indicators and the change over time, it is striking just how many candidates taking maths at age 16 (almost everyone) do not achieve at least a grade C. Almost 40 per cent of candidates get a grade of D or below.

How to improve performance: what do we know?

In many respects, improving attainment in maths requires the same sort of policies that have been discussed in other chapters. For example 'very effective' teachers have been shown to be important for achievement in maths. One study finds that a 'very effective' teacher improves a pupil's maths performance by the equivalent of 25–45 per cent of an average school year.[10] Effects are even higher for pupils from disadvantaged backgrounds.[11] While there is no evidence that teacher qualifications are important for pupil achievement, it might nonetheless be an indication of teacher quality that only about half of maths teachers in the UK have a maths degree.[12] Furthermore, analysis of recruits to teacher training show that trainee maths teachers are less likely to have a 'good' degree than those teaching subjects like English or history.[13] Both these facts are illustrative of recruitment difficulties in maths (similar issues arise for subjects like science and foreign languages). One of the reasons for this is the high premium in the private sector for graduates with high numeracy skills (discussed above). Up to now, salary profiles within education have been relatively flat. A potential impact of recent pay reforms is that there will be more scope to increase the flexibility of pay. If this allows for higher salaries in hard-to-recruit subjects, this may help with the recruitment and retention of maths graduates in teaching.

Within the classroom, 'time on task' matters. In a cross-country study of instructional time, it was found that the effects of an extra hour per week devoted to maths, science or languages had effects that were modest to large – and more likely to be large for girls, those from lower socio-economic backgrounds and for immigrants.[14] This latter finding is particularly important given the development of a large National Curriculum in England that is compulsory (for community schools). If we need to find more time for maths or other particular subjects then we will clearly need to have less time for other subjects and this is likely to prove controversial among teachers, parents, and students.

Improvement in maths is not independent of improvement in literacy. For example, in a study looking at factors that contribute to Finnish pupils' success in maths, the authors note: 'it quickly became apparent that pupils' good skills in literacy enabled them to concentrate on the mathematics in written problems without being hampered by difficulties in reading and making sense of the context'.[15] Furthermore, an evaluation of the effects of 'the literacy hour' in England found that it had effects on attainment in maths as well as English in primary school.[16] These findings are important because they suggest that tackling low levels of achievement in maths might best be approached as part of a wider initiative to address low levels of achievement in literacy.

Like other subjects, maths teaching in England and Wales has been shaped by the National Curriculum (introduced in 1989) and national testing (starting in the early 1990s for pupils aged 7, 11 and 14 – and now only taking place for 11-year-olds). The National Curriculum was introduced to standardise content and the time spent on each subject. The content of this curriculum is hugely contested in education by a range of key stakeholders, though interestingly there is perhaps more consensus in mathematics than in some other subject areas.

The National Numeracy Strategy

In 1999, the National Numeracy Strategy was introduced to English primary schools in an effort to raise standards in mathematics. This followed the National Literacy Strategy, which was introduced in 1998. A key feature of these strategies was the introduction of a daily hour in numeracy and literacy respectively. As the amount of time given to these subjects was already stipulated in the National Curriculum, neither strategy represented an increase in the overall time allotted to teaching these subjects. But both represented a dramatic change in how these subjects were taught.[17] According to the Schools Inspectorate, the National Numeracy Strategy brought about radical, much needed change in the way mathematics was taught in English primary schools:

> It has provided teachers with the tools and confidence to regain control of the teaching of mathematics, rather than relying, as happened too often in the past, on pupils working their way through textbooks and worksheets. They are more prepared to interact with the whole class through direct teaching and to extend this to their work with small groups. The strategy's impact on the quality of teaching has been good.[18]

One can look at the effectiveness of the National Numeracy Strategy by examining the impact of the de-facto pilot ('the National Numeracy Project') that was introduced in just a handful of local authorities. One can evaluate effectiveness by comparing schools that had the opportunity to participate in this 'pilot' with other similar schools. It has been shown that the strategy was effective in these schools.[19] Another way to consider possible effects is to compare the experience in England with that in Wales (which did not insist that schools adopt this strategy). The divergent trends in attainment at Key Stage 2 maths during the late 1990s between England and Wales are consistent with the 'numeracy hour' having been effective in English schools.[20]

The per-pupil cost of the National Literacy and Numeracy Strategies was very low – because they mainly consisted of a very limited amount of teacher training.

They were also generally found to be effective in raising standards. Nonetheless, the numeracy and literacy strategies no longer have to be implemented by schools (from 2011). This does not mean that all schools have stopped implementing some of the successful approaches embedded in the National Strategies. However, there is likely to be greater variation in schools' approaches to numeracy (and indeed literacy) since schools have been free to adopt their own methods. Schools are also now encouraged to work together to find local solutions to improve their pupils' basic skills. Of course, this requires that schools have good information about the relative merits of different approaches and, as we review in this chapter, there is relatively limited, robust, evidence on effective pedagogies in mathematics.

Reviews of research and practice

There are a number of reports to draw on about what works to improve maths. Academic reports bring together a review that draws on studies meeting certain quality criteria.[21] A recent review of 189 studies (mainly from the US) gives no evidence that different mathematics curricula make a difference to achievement. The same review also found only limited evidence that technology is effective in mathematics teaching. However, the review found good evidence that use of effective teaching strategies matters – such as changing the way that children work together. For example, there was good evidence to support the efficacy of 'co-operative learning', where pupils work in pairs or small groups to help each other. Programmes that focused on classroom management and motivation were also found to generate positive effects. The authors point out that the debate about mathematics reforms has focused primarily on curriculum and not on professional development or instruction. Yet the review of maths programmes (for all levels of education) suggests that curriculum differences seem to be much less important than instructional differences in terms of their effects on maths achievement.

The authors of the above review of US studies comment that there are fewer large, high-quality studies than one would wish for. Furthermore, one cannot assume that the findings of US studies would hold true in a very different educational context. We don't know that much about the effectiveness of curricula, textbooks and teacher strategies that are being used in the UK today, although some research-based resources have been developed for teachers in the UK.[22] Relevant IT strategies that are increasingly being used in mathematics teaching are reviewed in Chapter 10 and some programmes appear to have had a positive effect (see box below for an example of a pedagogic approach that is currently being trialled in the UK (epiSTEMe)).

A background paper to this research notes the lack of relevant British studies and that most of the directly relevant research comes from the US.[23] Important aspects of this US research are about the effectiveness of a pedagogical model organised around carefully crafted problem situations, designed to appeal to students' wider life experience, to inculcate ideas of acting as mathematicians/scientists and to develop key disciplinary ideas. Material is developed in lessons that cycle

---

UNDER TRIAL IN ENGLAND: *epiSTEMe*

One example of a pedagogic approach currently being trialled in English schools is *'epiSTEMe'*. This involves organisation of lessons around carefully crafted problem situations which appeal to shared student experiences and interests. Tasks are framed and approached in ways that build students' ability to think as mathematicians and scientists and support key conceptual advances in a topic. In particular, many tasks have been designed to trigger critical examination of common forms of fallacious reasoning. A distinctive feature of the *epiSTEMe* approach is its use of dialogue – in small student groups and the whole class – to elicit and examine differing points of view on problem situations.

The evidence from a randomised field trial involving around 80 participating Year 7 classes and their teachers in 25 schools is currently being analysed.

www.educ.cam.ac.uk/research/projects/episteme/

---

through whole-class introduction by teachers, collaborative problem solving in small groups, whole-class synthesis by teachers and individual practice and consolidation by students.

The Schools Inspectorate has produced reports on the quality of maths teaching in schools, based on visits to schools and observation of lessons, though not generally drawing on evidence of impact on measurable outcomes such as test scores. The most recent report makes a number of interesting points.[24] It highlights the fact that children have varying pre-school experiences of maths and for many, this gap widens during schooling (particularly among those from poor backgrounds – as measured by eligibility to receive free school meals). They also found the quality of teaching to be highly variable. One aspect of this is differences between primary and secondary school, where teaching is rated more highly in the former. In primary schools, intervention is regarded as focused and timely in helping pupils overcome difficulties, whereas most secondary schools are focused on exam performance. This, the study suggested, encourages short-termism in teaching and a lack of attention to how the least able are getting on. The best teaching develops pupils' conceptual understanding, fluent recall of knowledge and confidence and problem solving. In many secondary schools, the study found that there is too much of a focus on the 'acquisition of disparate skills' that help with passing exams but do not equip the pupils with the next stage of their education. Although secondary schools receive more criticism than primary schools in this review, the report also says that in *each phase* of education, the students nearest to external assessments receive the better teaching. Less experienced, temporary and non-specialist teachers are more likely to teach the lower sets or younger pupils. Equally, the same study found that at the other end of the ability spectrum, more able pupils at all stages of education are not being sufficiently challenged. According to this report, the most common strategies to improve attainment focus on the use of assessment data to track pupils' progress in order to intervene to support pupils at risk of underachievement. It also places much emphasis on developing the expertise of staff both in initial teaching training and in professional development. An earlier report suggests that in more effective schools, collaboration between staff supports professional development but found that in general opportunities for teachers to improve their subject knowledge and subject-specific pedagogy were infrequent.[25]

Very low attainers

The 'Every Child Counts' (ECC) programme was developed because of a recommendation by the Williams Review (2008), which explored poor mathematical performance of the lowest achieving children. The concern is about pupils who are very low achievers by the end of primary school (i.e. the bottom 5–6 per cent of pupils).

The ECC initiative develops mathematics interventions for Year 2 children within the following three waves: Wave 1 – quality classroom teaching for all children; Wave 2 – small group additional intervention for children just below national expectations; Wave 3 – individual or very small group intervention with a trained and supported teaching assistant for children who are struggling, and additional intervention on an individual and/or very small group basis with a trained specialist teacher. This initiative has been evaluated, with a focus on the part of the initiative known as 'Numbers Count'.[26] This provides intensive one-to-one interventions for those children identified as the lowest achievers. It consists of daily 30-minute one-to-one sessions with specially trained Numbers Count teachers.

The researchers did a very convincing evaluation of the short-term impact of being part of the 'Numbers Count' initiative. The evaluators found that those children who were randomly assigned to the 'Numbers Count' intervention improved by a considerable amount after 12 weeks. However, because of how the experiment was set up, we do not have convincing evidence on whether the programme had lasting effects. This is, of course, a great shame and although the early impact from this programme gives reason for hope, we do need to determine whether such initiatives make a long term difference to pupils. Although the 'Numbers Count' initiative is quite expensive (£1,353 per child in this study), the cost reduces substantially if the teacher–pupil ratio increases to 2:1 or 3:1 (although there was inconclusive evidence on whether this made a difference to the effectiveness of the programme). However, at a minimum this mathematics intervention shows that (at least in the short term) it is possible to make a big difference to the performance of 'low achievers'. For most people, being bad at maths is not an immutable personality trait, something that we need to make far clearer in public discourse to dispel the notion that there are people who 'just can't do maths'!

However, a small minority of people are affected by a condition known as 'developmental dyscalculia' (about 5–7 per cent of the population). This is a severe disability in learning arithmetic and can affect learners with normal intelligence, although it may also occur with other developmental disorders. Those affected have difficulty with even very simple tasks and limited available evidence suggests it persists into adulthood. The effects of early and appropriate intervention have yet to be investigated.[27] In view of the importance of numeracy both for individuals and society in general, it would appear that the lack of attention paid to dyscalculia (in comparison with dyslexia) is misguided and should be redressed.

Key findings

- There is convincing evidence that numeracy and mathematics is important for people of all abilities in terms of their labour market employment and earnings. Of most concern in the UK is the large number of people with very low skills in these areas. Even on the GCSE (or equivalent) measure – which many people think is affected by 'grade inflation' – 40 per cent of candidates still get a grade of D or below.
- Many of the remedies are similar to those in other areas of education (i.e. better teaching). While there has been research on 'what works' in other countries, there are not many studies of comparable quality in the UK. However, there are specific interventions (such as those embedded in the National Numeracy Strategy) that show evidence of an impact. So far it has only been possible to look at the short-term impact.
- We need more long-run evaluations to determine the impact of particular pedagogical approaches on outcomes in maths.
- Certainly there is evidence that mathematical ability can be improved with the right kind of intervention. Therefore there is a clear need to change our cultural attitudes towards mathematics and our notion of mathematical skill being immutable.

Key policies

- Increased recognition that it might be hard to recruit and retain maths graduates into teaching because of lucrative outside options. This may need to be reflected in salary profiles (and not just the initial starting wage or incentives for teacher training).
- US research suggests that instructional methods matter more than curriculum for test scores in maths. There needs to be more UK-based research to help inform teaching practice here.

Notes

1 Rashid and Brooks (2010).
2 BIS (2012).
3 Layard *et al.* (2002).
4 Dolton and Vignoles (2002).
5 McIntosh and Vignoles (2001); Vignoles *et al.* (2011).
6 Berman *et al.* (1998), Machin and Van Reenen (1998).
7 Hanushek and Woessman (2012).
8 www.oecd.org/pisa/; http://timssandpirls.bc.edu/.
9 Jerrim (2013).
10 Aaronson *et al.* (2007).
11 For a review, see Murphy (2011).
12 www.education.gov.uk/get-into-teaching/faqs/becoming-a-teacher/teachers-degrees.
13 Smithers *et al.* (2012).
14 Lavy (2010).
15 Ofsted (2010).
16 Machin and McNally (2008).
17 See Machin and McNally (2008) with respect to the literacy hour.
18 Ofsted (2002).
19 Machin and McNally (2005).
20 This is discussed in McNally (2011).
21 Slavin *et al.* (2009).
22 www.nuffieldfoundation.org/key-ideas-teaching-mathematics.
23 Ruthven *et al.* (2010).
24 The most recent is Ofsted (2012).
25 Ofsted (2008).
26 Torgerson *et al.* (2010).
27 Butterworth *et al.* (2011).

Bibliography

Aaronson, D., Barrow, L. and Sander, W. (2007) 'Teachers and student achievement in the Chicago public high schools', *Journal of Labor Economics* 25(1): 95–135.

Berman, E., Bound. J. and Machin, S. (1998) 'Implications of skill-biased technological change: International evidence,' *Quarterly Journal of Economics* 113: 1245–1280.

BIS (Department for Business, Innovation and Skills) (2012) *The 2011 Skills for Life Survey: A Survey of Literacy, Numeracy and ICT Levels in England*, BIS Research Paper Number 81, London: Department for Business, Innovation and Skills.

Brown, M., Millett, A., Bibby, T. and Johnson, D.C. (2000) 'Turning our attention from the what to the how: The national numeracy strategy', *British Educational Research Journal* 26(4): 457–471.

Butterworth, B., Varma S. and Laurillard D. (2011) 'Dyscalculia: From brain to education', *Science* 332(6033): 1049–1053.

Dolton, P. and Vignoles, A. (2002) 'The return to post-compulsory school mathematics study', *Economica* 69(273): 113–142.

Hanushek, E. and Woessmann, L. (2012) 'Do better schools lead to more growth? Cognitive skills, economic outcomes and causation', *Journal of Economic Growth* 17(4): 267–321.

Jerrim, J. (2013) 'The reliability of trends over time in international education test scores: is the performance of England's secondary school pupils really in relative decline?', *Journal of Social Policy* 42(2): 259–279.

Jones, D.V. (2002) 'National numeracy initiatives in England and Wales: A comparative study of policy', *Curriculum Journal* 13: 5–23.

Lavy, V. (2010) *Do Differences in School's Instruction Time Explain International Achievement Gaps in Maths, Science and Language? Evidence from Developed and Developing Countries*, CEE Discussion Paper 118, London: London School of Economics.

Layard, R., McIntosh, S. and Vignoles, A. (2002) *Britain's Record on Skills*, CEE Discussion Paper 23, London: London School of Economics.

Machin, S. and Van Reenen, J. (1998) 'Technology and changes in skill structure: Evidence from seven OECD countries', *Quarterly Journal of Economics* 113: 1215–1244.

Machin, S. and McNally, S. (2005) 'Gender and educational attainment in the UK', *Oxford Review of Economic Policy* 21(3): 357–372.

Machin, S. and McNally, S. (2008) 'The literacy hour', *Journal of Public Economics* 92: 1141–1462.

Machin, S., McNally, S. and Wyness, G. (2012) *Educational Attainment Across the UK: Performance, Inequality and Evidence*, Program on Education Policy and Governance Working Papers Series, Cambridge, MA: Harvard University.

McIntosh, S. and Vignoles, A. (2001) 'Measuring and assessing the impact of basic skills on labour market outcomes', *Oxford Economic Paper* 53(3): 453–481.

McNally, S. (2011) 'Have reforms to the school system improved educational outcomes?' In P. Gregg and J. Wadsworth (eds) *The Labour Market in Winter: The State of Working Britain*. Oxford University Press, pp. 203–219.

Murphy, R. (2011) *Improving the Impact of Teachers on Pupil Achievement in the UK – Interim Findings*, Report to the Sutton Trust, London.

Ofsted (2002) *The National Numeracy Strategy: The First Three Years 1999–2000*, London: Ofsted.

Ofsted (2008) *Mathematics: Understanding the Score*, Report ref. no. 070063, London: Ofsted.

Ofsted (2010) *Finnish Pupils' Success in Mathematics*, Report ref. no. 100105, London: Ofsted.

Ofsted (2012) *Mathematics: Made to Measure: Messages from Inspection Evidence*, Report ref. no. 110159, London: Ofsted.

Rashid, S. and Brooks, G. (2010) *The Levels of Attainment in Literacy and Numeracy of 13- to 19-Year-Olds in England, 1948–2009*, London: National Research and Development Centre for Adult Literacy and Numeracy.

Ruthven, K., Howe, C., Mercer, N., Taber, K., Luthman, S., Hofmann, R. and Riga, F. (2010) 'Effecting principled improvement in STEM education: Research-based pedagogical development for student engagement and learning in early secondary-school physical sciences and mathematics', *Proceedings of the British Society for Research into Learning Mathematics* 30(1): 191–198.

Slavin, R.E., Lake, C. and Groff, C. (2009) *What Works in Teaching Maths?* Report summary, York: Institute for Effective Education, University of York.

Smithers, I., Robinson, P. and Coughlan, M. (2012) *The Good Teacher Training Guide 2012*, Centre for Education and Employment Research. University of Buckingham.

Torgerson, C.J., Wiggins, A., Torgerson, D.J., Ainsworth, H., Barmby, P., Hewitt, C., Jones, K., Hendry, V., Askew, M., Bland, M., Coe, R., Higgins, S., Hodgen, J., Hulme, C. and Tymms, P. (2010) *Every Child Counts: The Independent Evaluation* Technical Report, Research Report DFE-RR091a. Available at: www.education.gov.uk/publications/eOrderingDownload/DFE-RR091A.pdf (accessed 9 January 2015).

Vignoles, A., De Coulon, A. and Marcenaro-Guiterrez, O. (2011) 'The value of basic skills in the British labour market', *Oxford Economic Papers* 63(1): 27–48.

9

SPECIAL EDUCATIONAL NEEDS

Anna Vignoles

Introduction

In England, currently around one in five children are identified as having special educational needs (SEN). These children have been recognised as needing extra help and support if they are to make sufficient progress in school. Of course within this group of children who have some kind of SEN, there are those who need far more help than others. The challenge is to devise a system that allows for this considerable diversity of need. Further, our views on how we can best help our most needy children have also changed over time. The 'inclusion' agenda has led to a gradual reduction in the proportion of children being educated separately in special schools and an expectation that the vast majority of students can be educated in mainstream schools. Therefore currently only around 1 per cent of pupils in England are educated in special schools, while just fewer than one in five pupils have special educational needs that are, theoretically at least, being catered for in mainstream schools.[1] The challenge for educators and parents alike is to determine how the child's educational needs can best be met by the system as a whole, how their needs can be resourced on a 'fair' basis and what can be done to improve their learning and achievement.

In this chapter we start by considering how the issue of children having special educational needs is viewed in public discourse, before moving on to discuss in detail the current English special educational needs system, its strengths, weaknesses and evolution over time. We then consider the great diversity of needs that children have, recognising that designing a system that can help children with such a variety of needs is particularly challenging. We go on to describe the characteristics of children who have special educational needs, to gain a better understanding of which types of families are most likely to have children with SEN. We then review the evidence on the effectiveness of the system as a whole and of some specific policies and programmes to support children with SEN. We end with a discussion of how SEN policy is likely to develop in future.

How is the issue of children with special educational needs currently viewed?

There is a backdrop of public concern about the 'problem of special needs'. The popular belief is that the proportion of children with special educational needs has increased quite substantially in recent decades and that many of these children have behaviour problems or particular educational needs that can be disruptive to others. In fact the story is more complex than that. In the post-war period following the 1944 Education Act, special educational needs were defined in medical terms and hence only a very small proportion of (medically disabled) children were identified as having need of specialist education facilities. By 1978 however, the Warnock Report had acknowledged the need for a far wider definition of special educational needs and concluded that around 2 per cent of pupils required very specialist and separate kinds of education provision and that a further 18 per cent of children might benefit from some kind of additional support in mainstream schools. In other words, taking a long run historical perspective, the estimated proportion of children who may have some degree of special educational need has changed very little over the last 30 years and remains at one in five.

That said, those who claim that the proportion of children with special needs has been rising are not entirely wrong: it depends which period you are making comparisons with. The proportion of children identified as having SEN has increased significantly since the mid 1990s, following a period when a relatively smaller proportion of children were formally identified as having SEN. This is more than an exercise in statistics. The trends clearly illustrate a crucially important point in the debate: SEN is a fluid concept. The meaning of what constitutes a special educational need changes over time, not least with the political and economic cycle and in response to changes in attitudes and the resources available.

So why then is there a perception that the proportion of children having SEN is a growing problem in England? The first reason is the widespread belief that there are trends in society producing a genuine increase in the number of children who require additional help at school. If this were true, it would clearly be an issue of great concern to parents and educators alike. Further, a wide range of environmental factors, from the increasing incidence of premature birth, poor parenting, poor diet and new family structures, have all been cited as potential explanations for the 'growing problem' of children who struggle to make progress in school. A second opposing concern is that we are perhaps being too quick to label a child as having special needs. If 20 per cent of the cohort is identified as having 'special needs', perhaps the term has lost its true meaning? Certainly in England, the school regulator has taken this latter view.[2] Ofsted has questioned both whether too many children are being identified as having special educational needs and whether the system can and does provide sufficient support for those who genuinely need it. Such concerns have prompted the Government to reform the system, as we discuss further below.

How do we provide for children with special educational needs in the English education system?

In England, the system that has been set up to support children with special educational needs is both complex and dynamic. It aims both to identify those in need of additional help and to provide the necessary additional support to enable them to succeed at school. It is far from straightforward to design a system that is consistent, such that children with similar needs receive similar levels of help across the country as a whole, not least because all children (and their needs) are different and hence 'standard' levels of support are difficult to define. Further, schools often use slow academic progress as the major indicator for having SEN.[3] This does have an unfortunate consequence. How well a child is doing is generally judged in relation to their peers in the classroom and hence a child who is doing badly in a school with lots of higher achieving pupils is more likely to get identified as having special educational needs than a child doing equally badly in a school with lower achieving pupils.[4] Indeed it is this inconsistency in the system that results in children with similar underlying needs getting very different levels of support across different schools and local authorities that is precisely the criticism regularly levied by parents.[5] Ofsted, and a recent influential review of the special educational needs system in England,[6] have confirmed that this inconsistency is a major feature of the system.

The problem of consistency is in part caused by the fact that resources are always scarce in a state education system. Providing extra support for children with special needs takes additional resources that are then not available for other children. This inevitably leads to conflict between parents (who understandably want the best support possible for their child) and the state (which has to ration what it spends on each child). The conflict has ensured that the issue of how to organise and fund special needs systems remains hotly contested, with much criticism from parents of the English system. This is one of the major reasons behind the recent reforms. However, before we discuss these reforms and whether they really overcome the problem, it is useful to consider first the weaknesses in the SEN system prior to the recent changes.

In 2012 in England in most local authorities there were three levels of SEN support available for a child. Those with more major special educational needs were given a *statement*, which formally and legally identified their needs and clearly specified what the child was entitled to in the way of additional support. Local authorities were responsible for assessing applications for these statements and determining the resources needed by the child. At the same time local authorities were also responsible for providing the funding for these children. Needless to say this provided a clear incentive for local authorities to under-identify and under-resource the needs of statemented SEN pupils.[7] Schools under this system were, by contrast, likely to be very supportive of applications for statements since they brought additional resources into the school to help support the child. This produced yet another source of conflict in the system, this time between parents and the school on the one hand and the local authority on the other.

For students who had lower levels of need, and hence who did not need statements, there were two distinct categories of provision: 'school action' (11.4 per cent of pupils in 2010) and 'school action plus' (6.2 per cent of pupils in 2010). For both these categories of student, the school was supposed to identify their needs and provide the support the child required. Schools had to find the resources for this from within their existing budgets, which did include a specific component for SEN provision. 'School action' implied that the student needed relatively little support, e.g. some additional help from the teacher. 'School action plus' suggested that the child was likely to need additional help from outside the school (e.g. from an educational psychologist).

Since support for children with school-action and school-action-plus levels of SEN was funded from within school resources, there was an incentive for schools from a financial perspective to be somewhat reluctant to identify pupils as having these levels of special educational need, or at least a reluctance to provide them with specific additional support. Further, the money that was allocated to schools for lower levels of SEN did not necessarily have to be spent on particular pupils and so the link between this budget and the resources received by a particular child was unclear. Certainly schools were able to spend money allocated for SEN on other things. Again this meant that many parents were concerned that their child's needs were not being adequately met by the school.[8] The system was failing to satisfy parents. It was also arguably not meeting the needs of all children, despite the high proportion of children identified as having SEN and the more than £5 billion spent annually on SEN, with just under half of that funding going to mainstream schools directly.[9]

In response to these concerns, the Coalition Government reformed the system with the Children and Families Bill 2013. They wanted to reverse the trend towards what they and others viewed as 'over identification' of SEN. As mentioned earlier, there has been an increase in the proportion of children with SEN since the 1990s and this to many seems to be symptomatic of the tendency for parents and schools to want to identify a child as having SEN to secure additional resources. Although the White Paper that introduced the reforms did not explicitly call for a reduction in the number of children with the SEN label, the proposals did indicate that the Government thought there was confusion between pupils who may be simply learning more slowly if at all, and those who have specific SEN. The Government argued that this confusion had the unfortunate consequence that expectations were being lowered for students who did not necessarily have SEN but who were not making good progress.

The reforms were therefore designed to minimise or overcome these various problems with the system. The most radical aspect is that the Government has abolished the categories of 'school action' and 'school action plus' and replaced them with one category of school-based SEN that is more focused on attainment. For these children, their needs will be met entirely by the school and from within the school budget. Most significantly, the White Paper clearly sets out the Government's expectations that the low achievement of these children will be dealt with by schools using programmes that are targeted at improving achievement, rather than via the special educational needs system per se. Here the White Paper emphasises the importance of various programmes that provide group and one-to-one support for children who are struggling academically, particularly with basic and crucial skills such as literacy and numeracy. This is clearly an attempt to get schools to recognise that for many children who are currently identified as having SEN, their problem is primarily one of low achievement. Indeed the Government has gone further by changing the performance table information that is published in the media and on the Department's website to give parents better information about the academic progress made by the lowest achieving children in a school, with the intention of prompting schools to pay more attention to this group.

The pupil premium that provides additional resources to schools with more deprived students can also be seen as a way of getting schools additional resources to help low achieving children. About a third of children eligible for free school meals, and hence who attract a pupil-funding premium, are also currently identified as having SEN. The pupil premium is a substantial additional resource for many schools, and was just over £600 per FSM pupil in 2012/2013. Further, the Government has widened eligibility criteria to include children who have ever been eligible for FSM (in the last 6 years) so the premium now covers just under one third of the school population. It is too early to judge the effectiveness of the pupil premium and its impact on attainment. However, a recent Department for Education (2013) report does indicate that whether or not a child has special educational needs is a key criterion used to determine whether a child should benefit from activities funded by the pupil premium. Hence it will be particularly important in the longer term to see the impact of this additional resource on children with SEN.

So these reforms suggest an intention, on the part of the Government at least, to get schools to reduce the number of pupils identified as having SEN and instead pay greater attention to the learning of the lowest achieving children. The reforms do, however, recognise that pupils with more significant needs (who would have had a statement under the old system) clearly need more, or at least more streamlined, support. The intention is for the reforms to reduce the bureaucracy and conflict associated with the SEN statement process and minimise the tendency for children to 'fall between the cracks', with parents, local authorities, health authorities and schools unable to agree how to meet the needs of the child (and fund them). Specifically the Government have introduced a new single assessment process, in the form of an Education, Health and Care (EHC) plan, that will consider the child's education and health needs simultaneously in what the Government claim will be a more timely and efficient manner. Parents will be involved in this process to a greater extent than previously and the combined education and health plan for that child will continue up to age 25, to avoid cliff edges when support for individuals ceases suddenly at the age of 18. Further, local authorities and other relevant bodies will be required to update the EHC plan, the intention being to keep it relevant to a child's current needs. Additionally, parents and young people will also have greater choice in schooling options, including options for those aged over 16. For example, they will be able to choose from a wider range of institutions, including academies, sixth-form colleges, independent special schools and independent special colleges. This represents a shift away from the previous system of promoting inclusion even against the express wishes of the parent.

In the long run, the aims of the reforms are even more ambitious. The Government is proposing to give more autonomy to parents who want it – recognising that a huge amount of time and energy is spent by parents trying to get local authorities to fund particular types of support for their child. The Parents will be provided with budgets to meet their child's needs and eventually the plan is that parents will be able to spend the money available in ways they judge best to suit their child.

At the time of going to press, it is unclear how quickly these new reforms will be adopted, though there have been consultations on a proposed new Code of Practice for SEN.[10] An integrated care plan will require the co-operation of a number of different government agencies and that is clearly a challenge. There also remain concerns from parents and practitioners about how disabled children who do not have particular special educational needs might be included in this new integrated system. However, the big problem is actually how this new system will resolve the inevitable conflicts that will continue to arise when parents feel their child requires more support than he or she is given. While schools and local authorities will be required to be transparent about what their 'local offer' is, i.e. what they can normally provide for children with different types of SEN, at the moment there are no plans for specified national minimum standards of provision. Even if such standards existed this would not prevent conflicts between what parents feel their children need and what schools and local authorities feel they can offer. The reforms do include provision for compulsory mediation before parents could take their case to a tribunal, but this has had a mixed reception. In any case it is perhaps inevitable that the new system will continue to have the same conflicts between parents and the state in a world where resources are scarce and the state has to balance the needs of many children.

How diverse are children's special educational needs?

One reason for the complexity of the SEN system and indeed the conflicts that arise between parents and schools and local authorities is that the needs of pupils who have SEN are very diverse, as has been mentioned. Some children with particular medical and genetic conditions have quite major special educational needs, requiring a range of facilities and support. Other children may require minimal support beyond a recognition that they require longer to complete a task for example. We can get some understanding of this diversity of need by considering the specific types of SEN that children have. Administrative data in the English system records the type of need that a child has if their needs are more major,[11] though we must be mindful that the administrative record of a particular child's need may not fully reflect the views of parents, physicians or educational psychologists on the underlying problems faced by the child. Parents and the state often disagree on whether a child has special educational needs. Indeed, as we have discussed, some parents take the state to court in their attempts to ensure that their child is recognised as having SEN. Interestingly however, while such cases do occur, survey evidence suggests that it is more often the case that the school identifies that the pupil has special educational needs, while the parents do not report that their child has SEN.[12]

It is the students who have special needs linked to behaviour that have received the most attention in the media, with reports of badly behaved and out of control children. It is actually quite difficult to determine the proportion of children who have significant behaviour problems. We know a lot about pupils who have moderate or severe SEN because these are students who would have needed a statement or 'school action plus' under the old system, and there are administrative records of their particular needs. Unfortunately however, the administrative data cannot tell us the proportion of children with lower levels of special educational need (i.e. the old 'school action' category) who have behaviour problems. There is some evidence that children with lower levels of SEN are much more likely to have behavioural difficulties[13] and so this group of children are undoubtedly of particular policy and parental concern.

Though we may be worried about the numbers of pupils having behavioural difficulties, in fact only a very small proportion of such children have sufficiently severe behavioural needs that they get a full statement. Other types of SEN on the other hand are much more likely to lead to a statement. More than 90 per cent of children with profound and multiple learning difficulty have a statement, perhaps unsurprisingly. Further, while most pupils with special educational needs attend mainstream schools, this varies according to the type of SEN that the pupil has. For example, although only around 1 per cent of pupils attend special schools in England, around one quarter of pupils with identified Autistic Spectrum Disorder attend special schools and more than three quarters of those with profound and multiple learning difficulty (PMLD) do so. The challenge of designing a system to account for the full range of different needs that children have and provide an equally diverse set of support mechanisms to meet such needs is great indeed.

Who has special educational needs?

To meet the needs of children with SEN and indeed to start to understand the root causes of special needs, it is important that we understand who is most likely to have SEN. For example, boys are much more likely than girls to have SEN. There are also particular categories of SEN in which boys are very much more likely to be over represented. For instance, boys are much more likely than girls to have communication problems. Just under 90 per cent of those with Autistic Spectrum Disorder are boys and two thirds of those with speech, language and communication needs or indeed behavioural problems are boys. In general boys are around 2.5 times more likely than girls to have SEN in the English education system.[14] This raises interesting questions about how boys' needs, particularly the needs of those with SEN, can be better accommodated within the school system and whether indeed we may in fact be pathologising boys' behaviour.

What is particularly striking is that children from more disadvantaged families are much more likely to have special educational needs. This is actually part of a broader problem in England, namely the strong relationship between the social class of the parent and the educational achievement of the child. In England social class and academic achievement are arguably more strongly linked than in many other countries.[15] One way in which this strong link between family background and pupil achievement manifests itself is via poorer children being disproportionately more likely to be identified as having SEN. This is perhaps unsurprising given what we have said about schools using low achievement as a key indicator for a child having SEN, and the fact that poorer children on average are lower achieving. In general being poor and being male are greater influences on the likelihood of a child having special educational needs than any other factors, such as ethnicity.[16]

While poorer children are much more likely to have special educational needs, partially reflecting the deprivation in their early life experiences, what is interesting is that *if* a more advantaged pupil has special educational needs they are more likely to end up with a statement. Keslair and McNally (2012) conclude from this that wealthier parents may be better at ensuring that their child's needs are recognised and securing a statement and the resources that follow. Thus there may be some inequalities in how the system operates, over and above the fact that being poor makes a pupil far more likely to have special needs in the first place. In fact further analysis by Keslair and McNally (2012) suggested that even poorer children were more likely to get a statement if they lived in a wealthier area. In other words, because local authorities have limited resources, a child with special educational needs in a richer area where fewer children have SEN is likely to secure more resources and additional support than a poor child in a poorer area, where the demands on the SEN budget are greater. This problem is of course part of the motivation behind the reforms described earlier and a cause of much consternation among parents who perceive the system as resulting in a 'postcode lottery' of support for their children.

One interesting and potentially positive development however, is that minority ethnic group students are now actually under-represented in the SEN group as compared with White British students.[17] Historically in the UK there has been concern at the *over* representation of minority ethnic children with SEN.[18] Certainly in the US commentators have long worried about the disproportionately high number of minority ethnic students identified as having SEN, with Black Americans being far more likely to be identified as having cognitive disabilities and emotional and behavioural problems.[19] It is of course encouraging that not only are minority ethnic group children now making more progress academically than White children in the UK education system as discussed elsewhere in this book, so too they are less likely to be identified as having SEN. Some have argued, however, that since having a statement of SEN provides additional resources for the child, it may be that minority ethnic children are not having their needs fully recognised and are being under-resourced compared with White children. Further there is diversity across different ethnic minority groups. For instance, Black Caribbean pupils are disproportionately more likely to have behavioural problems than other ethnic minority groups. Black African pupils are disproportionately likely to have speech and communication problems. Pakistani pupils are disproportionately likely to have vision and hearing problems. This suggests that ethnicity and special needs are inter-related to some degree, even if on average ethnic minority children are now no more likely to have SEN than are White children.

Lastly, children who have English as an Additional Language are somewhat more likely to be identified as having SEN. Research has suggested that there may be some confusion in identifying children whose needs are related to their language problems and those who have English as an Additional Language. This issue of confusion between language needs and speech and communication problems is one that the US literature has also identified and is indicative of the general problem that in many cases children who make very slow progress or who are behind at school will be labelled as having SEN.

How effective is the current English SEN system?

Two recent reports commissioned by the UK government – the 2010 *Lamb Inquiry into Special Educational Needs and Parental Confidence* and the 2010 Ofsted *Special Educational Needs and Disability Review* – both stressed the need to better monitor the progress of pupils with SEN and in particular to avoid low expectations of the academic achievement of these children. Clearly with a significant amount of resources dedicated to providing additional support for children with special educational needs, it is crucial that we understand whether this support is having the desired effect.

On the face of it the achievement of children with SEN appears worryingly weak. In England, nearly two thirds of those who do not achieve 5 A*–C grades at GCSE (a target standard of achievement at age 16) have been identified as having SEN. Children who have SEN are also twice as likely to be absent from school and more than eight times more likely to be permanently excluded from school.[20] While we should not necessarily have lower expectations of children with SEN, it is also true that some pupils who have particular special needs may be expected to make slower progress at school even with additional support. Determining whether the SEN system does help such pupils achieve their potential therefore turns out to be a much harder question to answer than one might think, as it is not clear what their progress might have been without the system of SEN. Making a fair comparison to determine whether children who have SEN make sufficient progress and more specifically whether their progress is improved by the additional support they receive is difficult and hence the evidence is limited.[21]

Certainly children who have SEN tend to be low achievers. More specific-ally, children who have moderate or severe learning difficulties and those with behavioural and emotional difficulties are particularly likely to have low achieve-ment. Further, it turns out that those children who have non-statemented SEN are more likely to be lower achievers than those with statements. This might seem counter-intuitive but actually reflects the fact that many children who have non-statemented SEN have behavioural problems that are associated with weak learning and low achievement. Indeed a 2007 Rowntree report by Cassen and Kingdon indicated that nearly two thirds of low achievers who had no GCSE passes above a grade D were students with SEN. Further, students with many types of SEN, particularly behavioural or emotional needs, are more likely to be absent from school and to truant. So low achievement, disengagement with school and SEN certainly are inter-linked.

Knowing that children with SEN have lower achievement does not however, tell you about the effectiveness of SEN provision. For that you need to know what similar children who did not get identified as having SEN achieve. In a recent study Keslair, Maurin and McNally (2012) use statistical methods to determine the impact of being identified as having SEN in England on the attainment of these children at the end of primary school. They conclude that SEN programmes are not particularly effective on average, though clearly there are some students that may well benefit from the additional support they receive. This rather bleak view of the SEN system is reinforced by some research by Crawford and Vignoles (2010) that also examines the impact of receiving SEN support in primary school on pupils' achievement. This research focuses largely on pupils with behaviour problems and those without statements and concludes that pupils identified as having special educa-tional needs do not do any better than children who were equally low achieving and who also appeared to have behaviour problems but who had *not* been identified as having SEN. One might conclude from this evidence that at the very least, it is far from clear that the additional support SEN status is supposed to provide for pupils produces better academic achievement. Keslair and McNally were however, slightly more optimistic about the progress made by students with SEN in secondary school, suggesting that their progress is not dissimilar to their peers.

In general, academic research from both England and the US has struggled to show that children who are identified as having a special educational need do better than they otherwise would have.[22] In other words, taking the system as a whole, it does not appear that it necessarily helps children with SEN achieve more. Now we are not of course suggesting that if you were to remove the SEN system completely that children would do better. Certainly the very small proportion of children who have severe needs (i.e. children who would have received a statement under the old system) do clearly need additional resources and a range of support mechanisms in order to make progress in the education system, or indeed to access education at all. Further, removing support for some children may result in a negative impact on the other children around them if behaviour and disruption becomes worse. However, it is worrying that with one in five children identified as having some kind of special educational need, we can find no convincing evidence that the system as a whole helps them make more progress.

Part of the problem is that up to now, careful monitoring of the achievement of children with SEN was limited. Another issue is the school accountability system, which relied until recently on value added measures of school performance. This approach might have let schools off the hook since it potentially reduced the expected level of achievement for children with SEN. Again the recent government reform of the SEN system sought to change this by ensuring that children with special educational needs are expected to achieve as much progress as children without. While clearly this may not happen in practice as some of these children face considerable barriers to learning, what is to be welcomed is that the reforms have removed any incentive for schools to respond to the problem of lower achieving pupils by simply identifying them as having SEN. By making more public how the lowest achieving pupils in every school are doing academically, this has limited the ability of schools to improve their position in the value added league tables without actually helping these children achieve more. Clearly we are not suggesting that schools deliberately ignore or under-resource their lowest achieving children. However, the league table system did encourage schools to focus heavily on children on the border of the D/C GCSE grade border, potentially at the expense of those further down the achievement scale. Going forward one might therefore expect schools to focus more on the achievement of lower achieving children, including those with SEN.

What policies to support children with SEN are effective?

We have highlighted the great diversity of special educational needs that exist in the population and the question is of course: What are the ways we can improve the educational outcomes of these children? While we have considered the effectiveness of the SEN system as a whole, clearly very specific interventions and programmes are needed to help children experiencing such a wide variety of conditions and having very different needs. We cannot review all the interventions that have been developed for every condition but instead provide some overarching findings of relevance to the mainstream school system. In any case, despite the numerous interventions and treatments devised for different special educational needs, determining what programmes are effective is quite difficult. First, though we can monitor the progress of children with SEN in the school system, our data systems do not record in sufficient detail what types of help each child gets and what kinds of programmes schools run to help children with particular needs. Clearly within each school the special needs co-ordinator (SENCO) will be aware of what support each child receives but without sufficiently detailed information and national evaluation of what schools do to support these children we cannot systematise good practice nor draw lessons from across the school system.

We do know that by far the most common intervention used to help children with SEN in schools is to provide additional staff, normally in the form of learner support or teaching assistants (TAs). The number of such staff used in schools has increased by more than 60 per cent since the early 2000s. In fact the growth in teaching assistants has been so great that teachers now only constitute about half of the workforce employed by schools.[23] Teaching and learner support assistants are clearly not teachers; they are supposed to provide additional support for the teacher and for students, rather than replace teachers. However, some research has suggested that children with SEN do spend disproportionate time with teaching assistants and that this approach is ineffective. Children who spend more time with a teaching assistant have also been shown to make significantly less progress at school.[24] There is therefore a growing recognition that the deployment of teaching assistants has to be done carefully with good co-ordination between the TA and the teacher and that it should not be the case that children with SEN are being disproportionately taught by staff who are not qualified teachers. Alongside concern about the use of teaching assistants, there is also some evidence that children with SEN are taught by the weakest teachers.[25] Clearly if the students who need the most help are taught by the weakest teachers, this too may explain the relatively low achievement of children with SEN, especially given our discussion elsewhere in this book about the importance of teacher quality in promoting high achievement among students. Certainly there is a widespread belief among parents that children with SEN are viewed as inevitably lower achieving and that schools consequently do not focus on these children to the same extent as higher achieving children who may help the school improve their league table position.[26]

In response to these issues that were raised by Lamb in his review, the Government introduced a programme called Achievement for All. This programme is designed to encourage schools to focus on all pupils, particularly low achieving students with SEN and disabled students. This programme was piloted in 2009–2011 and, with its emphasis on monitoring student performance, greater parent engagement and a real focus on improving outcomes, it appears to have produced some positive results.[27] Specifically students on the programme made more progress in English and mathematics and showed improvements in behaviour and attendance. Though the programme was not evaluated using a randomised controlled trial, which would have been ideal to prove its effectiveness, the emerging evidence from this programme is encouraging.

A number of specific education based programmes have also been developed to support children with specific types of SEN, particularly for conditions that have either increased over time (e.g. Autistic Spectrum Disorder, Attention Deficit Hyperactivity Disorder (ADHD)) or that appear to be linked to environmental factors (e.g. ADHD, conduct disorder and emotional disorder). Such programmes are potentially very valuable since many of these specific conditions and disorders have major negative impacts on pupils' longer run academic achievement. For instance, ADHD and antisocial behaviour have been linked with reading difficulties, as have emotional disorders.[28] Conduct disorder also impacts on achievement when it is accompanied by attention problems, as in the case of ADHD. There is some evidence of the positive impact of pharmacological interventions for pupils with ADHD but much less good evidence on other interventions based on changing parenting techniques, using structured classroom teaching, etc.[29]

AUTISTIC SPECTRUM DISORDER: SOME FACTS

- Autistic Spectrum Disorder (ASD) covers a range of developmental disorders associated with social interaction problems, communication difficulties, obsessive or repetitive behaviours and sometimes delayed cognitive development.
- Girls are much less likely than boys to have ASD. Nearly 90 per cent of those with ASD are boys.
- Children with special educational needs are generally more likely to come from socio-economically disadvantaged families. However, pupils with ASD are no more likely to come from poor families than are students with no special educational needs.
- Seventy per cent of students with ASD have a statement even though only around 3 per cent of children have a statement overall.
- Around a quarter of those with ASD attend a special school. Only 1 per cent of pupils overall attend a special school.
- Children with ASD have similar levels of absence and truancy to those of children with no special educational needs.
- Children with ASD currently make slower progress through secondary school than otherwise similar children who have no special educational needs.
- During secondary school a declining proportion of children are identified as having ASD, perhaps because they no longer require additional support.

Some programmes for pupils with Autistic Spectrum Disorder (ASD) have limited evidence supporting their effectiveness. For example, Strain and Bovey (2011) conducted a RCT to evaluate the Learning Experiences and Alternative Program for Pre-schoolers and their Parents (LEAP). This is a programme for children with ASD based on the principle that children with ASD will learn most effectively in small groups alongside children who do not have ASD and with specific teacher training to support their social learning. Involving nearly 300 children randomly assigned to the programme or otherwise, the results from the RCT suggested that children on the programme made more progress in terms of both their cognitive and their social skills. Burgoyne et al. (2012) conducted a RCT to evaluate a programme called the Reading and Language Intervention for Children with Down syndrome (RLI), which was designed to improve reading. They found it had a positive impact on children's reading compared with pupils who experienced normal classroom teaching.

Beyond these specific interventions for particular conditions, a number of more general approaches to SEN have been evaluated. Approaches to teaching reading that have been robustly evaluated for use with disabled students are: small group instruction, pairing students and peer mentoring. All these methods of instruction do appear to be more successful than a conventional whole class approach for students with a range of learning needs and disabilities. Specifically these alternative class groupings appear to have produced better reading outcomes for students.[30]

Some, but by no means all, behaviour management strategies can be effective. For example, an approach called 'positive behaviours strategies' has been found to not only reduce poor behaviour but also to improve academic achievement. This strategic approach to behaviour management encourages educators to think about the systems and processes that are in place in schools that may encourage poor behaviour and to remove any inadvertent reward for poor behaviour.[31]

We also know that many children who have behavioural special needs have specific mental health problems, including emotional disorders. These mental health problems are treatable with psychiatric interventions.[32] Knapp *et al.* (2013) provide a review of the evidence on the costs of specific childhood mental health disorders, their implications for the public purse and the costs and benefits of potential treatments. A number of studies summarised by Knapp and Evans-Lacko (Evans-Lacko *et al.*, 2013) suggest that child mental health problems cost their families and indeed the state a great deal even in the short run. For example, Snell *et al.* (2013) show that in addition to the large direct costs of care associated with child mental health problems, there is a particularly large financial impact from such disorders on the education system. Leaving such conditions untreated clearly has very serious implications, with research suggesting that children with a persistent mental disorder are three and a half times more likely to leave full-time education by age 15 or 16 and twice as likely to have no qualifications. Later in life the costs of such disorders are higher still and may well fall on the criminal justice system. Better diagnosis and treatment would clearly help some of these children with large potential cost savings in the long run.

We also know that children with parents who have an unstable relationship, children with divorced or separated parents, those who have parents with mental health problems and those experiencing abuse and neglect are more likely to have mental health problems.[33] The fact that family factors play such a large role in putting children at risk of some kinds of special educational needs implies that we need to focus as much on how we can help families as on how schools should assist these children. There are a number of family based interventions that have been found to be particularly effective in improving parenting practices in at risk families and that help improve the development of children in socio-economically deprived families.[34] These are reviewed in Chapter 4 of this book.

One specific evaluation that is of interest is a randomised controlled trial in which children who are at risk of having conduct disorder are allocated to either a SPOKEs reading programme, to a parenting programme called Incredible Years (discussed in Chapter 4), to a combination of these programmes or to a control group.[35] Although the trial is ongoing, the initial evidence suggests that the short run outcomes are good. Parents of children who were allocated to the Incredible Years programme, the reading programme or the combined approach report that their children have fewer problems and that their reading also improved. Parents also appear to be more confident in dealing with their child's behaviour.

We have only been able to consider a limited range of the evidence base relating to children with SEN. There is a large medical literature on the costs and effectiveness of childhood medical conditions and treatments. Many of these conditions, such as ADHD, have educational implications and so even if these treatments have not been evaluated in terms of their impact on children's educational outcomes, such studies may still be informative. There is also an important evidence base on the effectiveness of early years programmes on children's outcomes, including outcomes for children who develop or might have developed SEN (see Chapter 3) and studies on parenting and parenting programmes (see Chapter 4). There is also a broader educational literature on issues relating to teaching children with SEN – one such example is a systematic review of the effectiveness of pedagogical approaches to teaching children with SEN in mainstream classes.[36] However, most of the educational studies in this field do not rely on experimental or quasi experimental evaluation methods and hence proving that these approaches are effective at scale is not possible. This means our understanding of the impact of different ways of teaching children with SEN is still quite limited. Certainly Rix *et al.* (2009) argue strongly that there is a clear need for more rigorous studies in this area.

How is policy likely to develop going forward?

The notion of special educational needs is, we have argued, to some extent fluid. To have special educational needs means different things at different times and in different contexts. This is why a child with a particular set of needs could be identified as having SEN in one school but not in another. One clear recommendation from the Lamb Review and our own reading of the evidence is that we need to do far more to level the playing field, so that children with particular needs in different parts of the country receive similar levels of support. The Government reforms to the system that we discussed above, and in particular the increased transparency in terms of what local authorities and schools can offer students in the way of support, should help with this.

We also concluded in this chapter that while specific programmes may well be effective in helping students with SEN, there is little evidence that the complex, and indeed costly, system of special educational needs in England helps children with SEN achieve more. Again this does not mean that all children with SEN fail to achieve within the system, nor indeed that the system is ineffective for all. Rather it does imply that we, along with many other countries, spend a lot of resources identifying children who are failing to achieve for whatever reason but we are still, on average, not able to help them catch up with their more advantaged counterparts. Further, the Lamb Inquiry has highlighted the very strong concerns expressed by many parents about the ineffectiveness of the system in meeting the needs of their children. Many parents feel that they constantly have to battle against the system in order to secure sufficient help for their child and, even more strikingly, they claim that the system has lower expectations of their child because of their special educational needs. In this regard we welcome the renewed emphasis on monitoring the progress of children with SEN and increased expectations about what they can achieve. Delivering this at school level will be key.

However, even if progress can be made so that children receive similar levels of support around the country and if schools raise their expectations of children with SEN, we do still need to recognise that some students are more likely to have SEN than others. Children with special educational needs are disproportionately male and disproportionately poor. Thus special educational needs provision is inextricably linked to a range of social problems that affect children's achievement at school. This does not of course detract from the point that children with very significant special needs (statements) can come from a range of socio-economic backgrounds and quite clearly do need substantial additional resources for them to access education. It does, however, indicate that solutions will need to come from outside the school system too. Parents matter and to enable them to be fully engaged with their children's education and to support their children, we need to improve their economic position. We would therefore urge continued efforts be made to reduce the proportion of children living in poverty as one element in a strategy to improve the achievement of children with SEN.

We are optimistic about the proposed changes to the SEN system. In response to the Lamb Inquiry, the recent government reforms in England have been based on the premise that in fact many children with SEN should be receiving the help they need from their school as a matter of course. Policy-makers want to shift away from a system that tended to encourage schools to identify a large number of children as having special educational needs but that did not put sufficient emphasis on ensuring that these children then succeeded in the education system. They want to move to a more personalised system, where children's needs, unless they are very major, are met fully by their schools and that the expectation will be that these children will achieve the highest levels of achievement possible.

While this is a noble aspiration, there has to be greater recognition that in times of austerity the pot of resources for education is fixed. If it is more costly to help some children who have particular special needs then clearly resources will need to be diverted away from other children to help the lowest achievers. Not only will this always produce some tension in the system, between schools trying to manage their resources fairly and parents trying to secure the best support possible for their child, it may also lead to inefficiencies. In all the discussion about special needs there is remarkably little discussion about how, with no additional resources, we can ensure that children with special needs achieve more without jeopardising standards over all. The pupil premium is perhaps one response to this problem but clearly we will also require better ways of working and more efficient use of existing resources. Certainly this is the educational challenge going forward and we would urge greater transparency in what schools do to help children with SEN.

Our account of the effectiveness of our SEN provision is perhaps somewhat negative. This is not meant in any way to undermine the excellent work going on in schools around the country with many dedicated professionals helping children with SEN. What is lacking, however, is robust evaluation evidence on what those dedicated people should be doing. What is needed is more research into the ways that the education system can best support pupils with specific conditions that lead to SEN. To really understand what policies are effective in this domain, as in many other areas of education, randomised controlled trials would potentially be very desirable. However, there are perhaps even more concerns about the ethics of random trials in the context of children with special needs. We would argue, however, that without a solid evidence base we will continue to be unable to help these children in the best way possible.

Key findings

- The current system of special educational needs in England does not always ensure that children who have similar needs receive similar levels of support across the country and it is for this reason, among others, that the Government has introduced radical reform to the SEN system.
- While the current SEN system helps many children, it is also complex and costly and there is little evidence that it has an overall positive impact on the achievement of pupils with SEN, though of course it may help teachers manage in the classroom and produce benefits for pupils without SEN.
- Many parents of children with SEN feel that the system fails to meet their children's needs.
- Although children with major disabilities and needs can come from a range of socio-economic backgrounds, more generally SEN is inextricably linked to social disadvantage. Certainly poorer students are far more likely to have SEN.

Key policies

- Reducing the proportion of children living in poverty and tackling socio-economic disadvantage is likely to be an important element in any strategy to improve the achievement of children with SEN.
- The SEN system is facing major change. The reforms attempt to ensure that most children's needs are to be met by their school (unless those needs are very major) and to encourage schools to have high expectations of these students, in terms of their academic achievement. Delivering this within a limited budget will be a major challenge.
- Greater efforts are needed to identify the specific special need a child may have in order that appropriate treatment or support may be given. Low attainment should not by itself be a criterion of SEN, even if it is an indicator that support is required.
- It is important that we have greater transparency and better data on the needs that children have and what support schools and local authorities are providing

for different children. This will help achieve greater consistency in provision across the country.
- A particular challenge is that we have only limited information on the school based interventions that are effective. We certainly need more robust evidence on what practices and programmes are effective for specific SEN conditions in a school setting.

Notes

1 Ofsted (2010).
2 Ibid.
3 Keslair et al. (2012); Ofsted (2010).
4 Keslair et al. (2012).
5 Peacey et al. (2009).
6 Lamb (2010).
7 Ibid.
8 Ibid.
9 Audit Commission (2010), www.sen-aen.audit-commission.gov.uk/static.aspx?page=intro1b.
10 www.education.gov.uk/consultations/downloadableDocs/Draft%20SEN%20Code%20of %20Practice.pdf.
11 Those in the old categories of school action plus and statemented.
12 Keslair and McNally (2009); Beckett et al. (2010).
13 Keslair and McNally (2012).
14 Strand and Lindsay (2009).
15 Hansen and Vignoles (2005).
16 Strand and Lindsay (2009).
17 Ibid.
18 Dunn (1968); Coard (1971).
19 Donovan and Cross (2002).
20 Lamb (2010).
21 Knapp et al. (2008).
22 Hanushek et al. (2002); Keslair et al. (2012); Crawford and Vignoles (2011).
23 Audit Commission (2011).
24 Blatchford et al. (2009).
25 Ofsted (2006).
26 Lamb (2010).
27 Humphrey and Squires (2011).
28 Rutter et al. (1970); Rapport et al. (2001).
29 Cassen et al. (2008).
30 Elbaum et al. (2000).
31 Chitiyo et al. (2011).
32 Cassen et al. (2008); Meltzer et al. (2003).
33 Rutter et al. (1998).
34 Olds et al. (2007).
35 Beckett et al. (2010).
36 Rix et al. (2009).

Bibliography

Audit Commission (2002) *Special Educational Needs: A Mainstream Issue*, London: Audit Commission.
Audit Commission (2010) *Against the Odds: Targeted Briefing – Young People with Special Educational Needs*. Available at: http://archive.audit-commission.gov.uk/auditcommission/SiteCollection Documents/Downloads/201008neetssen.pdf (accessed 10 January 2015).
Audit Commission (2011) *The Wider School Workforce: Better Value for Money in Schools*, London: Audit Commission.

Barnett, W.S. (2000) 'Economics of early childhood intervention'. In J.P. Shonkoff and S.J. Meisels (eds) *Handbook of Early Childhood intervention*, 2nd edn, Cambridge: Cambridge University Press, pp. 510–548.

Beckett, C., Kallitsoglou, A., Doolan, M., Ford, T. and Scott, S. (2010) *Helping Children Achieve: Summary of the Study 2007–2010*, Research Report no. DFE-RR185b, London: Department for Education.

Bedard, K. and E. Dhuey (2006) 'The persistence of early childhood maturity: International evidence of long-run age effects', *The Quarterly Journal of Economics* 121: 1437–1472.

Blatchford, P., Bassett, P., Brown, P., Koutsoubou, M., Martin, C., Russell, A. and Webster, R. with Rubie-Davies, C. (2009) *Deployment and Impact of Support Staff in Schools: The Impact of Support Staff in Schools (Results from Strand 2, Wave 2)*, DCSF Research Report no. DCSF-RR148, London: Department for Children, Schools and Families.

Burgoyne, K., Duff, F.J., Clarke, P.J., Buckley, S., Snowling, M.J. and Hulme, C. (2012) 'Efficacy of a reading and language intervention for children with Down syndrome: A randomised controlled trial', *Journal of Child Psychology and Psychiatry* 53: 1044–1053.

Cassen, R. and Kingdon, G. (2007) *Tackling Low Educational Achievement*, York: Joseph Rowntree Foundation.

Cassen, R., Feinstein, L. and Graham, P. (2008) Educational outcomes: Adversity and resilience, *Social Policy and Society* 8(1): 1–13.

Chitiyo, M., Makweche-Chitiyo, P., Park, M., Ametepee, L.K. and Chitiyo, J. (2011) 'Examining the effect of positive behaviour support on academic achievement of students with disabilities', *Journal of Research in Special Educational Needs* 11(3): 171–177.

Coard, B. (1971) *How the West Indian Child is Made Educationally Subnormal in The British School System: The Scandal of the Black Child in Schools in Britain*, London: New Beacon for the Caribbean Education and Community Workers' Association.

Crawford, C. and Vignoles, A. (2010) *An Analysis of the Educational Progress of Children with Special Educational Needs*, no. 10–19, London: Department of Quantitative Social Science, Institute of Education, University of London.

DfES (Department for Education and Skills) (2001) *Special Educational Needs Code of Practice*, Nottingham: Department for Education and Skills.

DfES (2003) *Every Child Matters*, Nottingham: Department for Education and Skills.

DfES (2011) *Support and Aspiration: A New Approach to Special Educational Needs and Disability – A Consultation*, Green Paper CM 8027, London: Department for Education and Skills.

DfES (2013) *Evaluation of Pupil Premium*, Department for Education Research report, London: Department for Education and Skills.

Donovan, M.S. and Cross, C.T. (eds) (2002) *Minority Students in Special and Gifted Education*, Washington, DC: National Academy Press.

Dunn, L.M. (1968) 'Special education for the mildly retarded: Is much of it justifiable?', *Exceptional Children* 23: 5–21.

Erlbaum, B., Vaughn, S., Hughes, M.T., Moody, S. W. and Schumm, J.S. (2000) 'How reading outcomes of students with disabilities are related to instructional grouping formats: A meta-analytic review'. In R. Gersten, E.P. Schiller and S. Vaughn (eds) *Contemporary Special Education Research: Syntheses of the Knowledge Base on Critical Instructional Issues*, Mahwah, NJ: Lawrence Erlbaum Associates, pp. 105–135.

Evans-Lacko, S., Knapp, M., McCrone, P., Thornicroft, G. and Mojtabai, R. (2013) 'The mental health consequences of the recession: Economic hardship and employment of people with mental health problems in 27 European countries', *PLoS One* 8(10): 13–71.

Farrell, P., Dyson, A., Polat, F., Hutcheson, G. and Gallannaugh, F. (2007) 'The Relationship between inclusion and academic achievement in English mainstream schools', *School Effectiveness and Improvement* 18(3): 1–18.

Hansen, K. and Vignoles, A. (2005) 'The United Kingdom education system in a comparative context'. In S. Machin and A. Vignoles (eds) *What is the Good of Education?*, Princeton, NJ/Woodstock: Princeton University Press, pp. 13–36.

Hanushek, E.A., J.F. Kain and S.G. Rivkin (2002) 'Inferring program effects for special populations: Does special education raise achievement for students with disabilities?', *Review of Economics and Statistics* 84: 584–599.

Heckman, J., Stixrud, J. and Urzua, S. (2006) 'The effects of cognitive and noncognitive abilities on labor market outcomes and social behavior', *Journal of Labor Economics* 24(3): 411–482.

House of Commons Education and Skills Committee (2006) *Special Educational Needs*, Third Report of Session 2005–06, vol. I, HC 478–I. Available at: www.publications.parliament.uk/pa/cm 200506/cmselect/cmeduski/478/478i.pdf (accessed 1 January 2012).

Humphrey, N. and Squires, G. (2011) *Achievement for All National Evaluation*, Department for Education research report DfE RR 123, London: Department for Education and Skills.

Keslair, F. and McNally, S. (2009) *Special Educational Needs in England: Final Report for the National Equality Panel*, London: Centre for Economic Performance, London School of Economics.

Keslair, F., Maurin, E. and McNally, S. (2012) 'Every child matters? An evaluation of "Special Educational Needs" programmes in England', *Economics of Education Review* 31(6): 932–948.

Knapp, M., Perkins, M., Beecham, J., Dhanasiri, S. and Rustin, C. (2008) 'Transition pathways for young people with complex disabilities: Exploring the economic consequences', *Child: Care, Health and Development* 34(4): 512–520.

Lamb (2010) *The Lamb Inquiry: Special Educational Needs and Parental Confidence*, Nottingham: DCSF.

Levy, F., Hay, D.A., McStephen, M., Wood, C. and Waldman, I. (1997) 'Attention-deficit hyperactivity disorder: A category or a continuum? Genetic analysis of a large-scale twin study', *Journal of the American Academy of Child and Adolescent Psychiatry* 36: 737–44.

Lindsay, G. (2007) 'Educational psychology and the effectiveness of inclusive education/main-streaming', *British Journal of Educational Psychology* 77: 1–24.

Meltzer, H., Gatward, R.,Goodman, R. and Ford, T. (2003) *Persistence, Onset, Risk Factors and Outcomes of Childhood Mental Disorders*, London: National Statistics.

OECD (2004) *Equity in Education: Students with Disabilities, Learning Difficulties and Disadvantages*, Paris: OECD.

OECD (2008) *Students with Disabilities, Learning Difficulties and Disadvantages: Policies, Statistics and Indicators*, Paris: OECD.

Ofsted (2006) *Inclusion: Does it Matter Where Pupils are Taught?* London: HMI.

Ofsted (2010) *The Special Educational Needs and Disability Review*, HMI: 090221. Available at: www.ofsted.gov.uk/Ofsted-home/Publications-and-research/Browse-all-by/Documents-by-type/Thematic-reports/The-special-educational-needs-and-disability-review (accessed 1 January 2012).

Olds, D., Sadler, L. and Kitzman, H. (2007) 'Programs for parents of infants and toddlers: Recent evidence from controlled trials', *Journal of Child Psychology and Psychiatry* 48: 355–391.

Peacey, N., Lindsay G., Brown P. and Russell, A. (2009) *Increasing Parents' Confidence in the Special Educational Needs System: Study Commissioned to Inform the Lamb Inquiry*, Warwick, UK: University of Warwick.

Rapport, M.D., Scanlan, S.W. and Denney, C.B. (1999) 'Attention-deficit hyperactivity disorder and scholastic achievement: a model of dual developmental pathways', *Journal of Child Psychology and Psychiatry* 40: 1169–1183.

Rapport, M.D., Denney, C.B., Chung, K.M. and Hustace, K. (2001) 'Internalizing behavior problems and scholastic achievement in children: Cognitive and behavioral pathways as mediators of outcome', *Journal of Clinical Child Psychology* 30: 536–551.

Rivkin, S.G., Hanushek, E.A. and Kain, J.F (2005) 'Teachers, schools, and academic achievement', *Econometrica* 73(2): 417–458.

Rix, J., Hall, K., Nind, M., Sheehy, K. and Wearmouth, J. (2009) 'What pedagogical approaches can effectively include children with special educational needs in mainstream classrooms? A systematic literature review', *Support for Learning* 24: 86–94.

Rutter, M., Tizard, J. and Whitmore, K. (1970) *Education, Health and Behaviour*, London: Longmans.

Rutter, M., Giller, H. and Hagell, A. (1998) *Antisocial Behaviour by Young People*, Cambridge: Cambridge University Press.

Snell, T., Knapp, M., Healey, A. Guglani, S., Evans-Lacko, S., Fernandez, J.L., Meltzer, H. and Ford, T. (2013) 'Economic impact of childhood psychiatric disorder on public sector services in Britain: Estimates from national survey data', *Journal of Child Psychology and Psychiatry* 54(9): 977–985.

Strain, P.S. and Bovey, E.H. (2011) 'Randomised, controlled trial of the LEAP model of early intervention for young children with Autism Spectrum Disorders', *Topics in Early Childhood Special Education* 31(3): 133–154.

Strand, S. and Lindsay, G. (2009) 'Evidence of ethnic disproportionality in special education in an english population', *Journal of Special Education* 43: 174.

10

ICT IN THE CLASSROOM

Robert Cassen

Introduction

This chapter reviews the extent of use of ICT in schools; what the research has to say about its impact, not least on pupil motivation; the teaching of computer science; the use of ICT for school management and improvement; and possible future scenarios. In the course of the discussion a number of specific programmes and technologies are referred to, with relevant research findings where they are available.

State of play

There is a widespread – and justifiable – belief that Information and Communication Technology (ICT) should be playing a big part in the classroom. But we are still well behind the potential. There is much agreement that technology is no substitute for teachers, that pedagogy is important for successful use of ICT, and that the use of ICT has to be student-based as well as teacher-based. There are opportunities to increase school efficiency. There is a lot of discussion of the teaching of computer science as a subject. There is also is a certain amount of visionary literature, saying what the future might be like, with schools employing extended and integrated use of ICT – and a number of schools that are already pursuing the vision.

Here is an example about Simon, a modern language teacher in England:

> The school ICT technician has connected Simon's laptop to the data projector ready for the Year 7 French lesson. Simon's introducing some new vocabulary and uses a slide show of images taken from a pool of ready-made resources. The technician has also placed the images on the network so that pupils can add the new words and images to their electronic vocabulary book

at some point during the lesson. In his non-contact period, Simon updates the school's information management system with the latest marks for his year 10 groups. The system automatically generates profiles of strengths and weaknesses. He uses this information to identify where pupils are having specific difficulties with oral work and builds this into the plans for working with the foreign language assistant. The information will also be useful when he's submitting predicted grades to the head of department.

Simon has booked the computer suite for the Year 9 French lesson on 'at the restaurant'. He uses a short video clip of people at a restaurant taken from the Internet and the pupils watch this as a whole class. Simon demonstrates some of the new language, using the software to pause, listen again to difficult phrases, and remove the sound track so pupils can play the part of one of the customers. The French Club meets at the end of the day. They are preparing a presentation for pupils in a partner school in France, which they intend to deliver during their next video conferencing session. Simon has set up a class email link and the pupils log on to read the responses from the partner school to the pupils' latest version.[1]

This is all very different from the teacher with his back to the class, writing on a blackboard. The interactive whiteboard is in fact widely used and comes off well in research specific to it, though in some studies teachers do not make effective use of it, or do not know how to do so.[2] Unfortunately we don't really know in general how many schools are doing what with computers and other technology, or what the impact is.

In 2003 the DfES said, 'the vast majority of schools are only beginning to tap the potential of ICT to enhance teaching and learning and to modernise the way in which schools are run and organised.'[3] Things have obviously improved since then, and in some respects the pace of improvement has been quite rapid, in others not. But a 2010 report said there had been little improvement in technology access for pupils 'in the last few years', with a pupil-to-computer ratio in UK secondary schools of 3 to 1, 5 to 1 in primary schools (laptops and desktops combined). The figures were unchanged by 2013, but tablet availability had risen considerably, more than trebling between 2012 and 2014, reaching 8–9 per primary school and nearly 60 per secondary school. These figures for tablets are still not huge per pupil, who average over 230 in primary and around 940 in secondary schools.[4] But it is predicted that tablets will rise to over 50 per cent of hardware by 2020.[5]

There is a clear picture of what 'good' schools are doing, if not of the results. They have a 'head of technology' or technology co-ordinator; they have effective leadership and implement a school-wide strategy for using technology, whose primary aim is to improve educational outcomes. They have technical teams to make sure software and hardware perform without glitches. They use learning platforms to engage pupils, parents and teachers, encouraging out-of-school work with a variety of 'learning partners'. A 'learning platform' is a set of interactive online services that can allow content management, curriculum planning and assessment, learner engagement and administration, and communication and collaboration via emails, chat, blogs, notices etc. It includes communication with parents, but is unique and private to each school. Teachers can post lesson plans, homework, coursework tasks and resources on the platform.[6] Clearly it is quite demanding to get it all right, and hardware and software are expensive; perhaps these are the reasons why progress has been slow.

Where have we got to in terms of actual use of ICT in UK schools?

Based on a survey of some 1,240 schools, the British Educational Suppliers Association (BESA) forecast a record level of expenditure on ICT of £14,220 per primary school and £65,570 per secondary school in 2014/2015. But this was only a slight increase over 2008/2009 levels; in between expenditure had fallen significantly till 2012/2013.[7] The proportions in both primary and secondary schools were roughly 12.5 per cent for technical support, 10 per cent for ISP charges, over 14 per cent for system software, 16 per cent for peripherals and networking, and over 46 per cent for laptops and desktops. There were additional expenditures for 'other software and digital content'. A proportion of the expenditure on hardware is of course for replacement; at the same time the productivity of new ICT equipment is constantly rising, and its price often falling.

Nearly half of all schools anticipated more than 50 per cent of pupil-time being exposed to teaching and learning using ICT by 2012/2013. About 10 per cent noted that nearly 100 per cent of all pupil time will involve exposure to ICT. But there are somewhat different estimates of use by different criteria: in a 2010 study, 93 per cent of secondary schools reported use of a learning platform, but only 67 per cent of primary schools and 56 per cent of special schools. (This compares with a government target announced in 2005 of all schools using them by 2010.)[8] In 2009, more than 80 per cent of primary teachers and 70 per cent of secondary and special school teachers used 'display technologies' at least once a day.[9] Nearly 9,000, roughly one half, of primary schools were using Espresso in 2010.[10] Performance is variable.

Impact

Strikingly, there is little robust evidence about how effective ICT in schools has been. There seem to be only a few studies with any kinds of controls or measured outcomes in terms of test or exam scores; many studies just report how ICT has been implemented or teacher and learner reactions to using it. The reactions are broadly positive, often very positive. But we have relatively little firm basis for knowledge of effectiveness, other than for specific technologies.

Part of the problem is the dependence of 'impact' on so many things: teachers' knowledge of the technology and ability to use it, learners' stage of development and prior knowledge of ICT, curriculum issues, etc. When we have large-scale studies of impact, we usually do not know which specific ICT technologies have been used. There are studies just showing that schools with more computers are associated with higher test scores, even after allowing for student intake, social background, etc.; but in these cases we don't know what they are doing with the technology. Nor do we know whether more successful schools use more technology or if greater use of technology causes better school performance. Further, besides test-scores, we rarely have hard-to-measure outcomes such as students' methods of thought and knowledge representation.[11] There is a real problem even with studies using controls: models generally do not allow for differences in teacher quality. If more effective teachers tend to use technology less then this may hide a positive impact from ICT; or better teachers may make more effective use of technology, so we don't know what is due to the technology and what to the teacher.

The literature suggests that it is easier to reach conclusions about impact when looking at specific curriculum subjects; but even here there is little certainty: one older study concluded, 'Our answer to the research question that we set ourselves: "What is the effectiveness of different ICTs in the teaching and learning of English (written composition), 5–16?" has to be – "Not much." '[12] Most of the research reviewed in the study quoted was only looking at word processing and its impact on written composition, and very little of the research was statistically robust. It was also conducted several years ago. But there was some modest evidence of positive effects.

There is evidence of positive effects of ICT more broadly on English learning; but 'the results are very inconsistent and restricted by the rate of ICT use and access in schools'.[13] One American programme for which positive results have been claimed in a controlled study is Time To Know. This is a relatively recent creation; it is an interactive laptop-based programme, designed for English and maths teaching, in the first instance for 9- to 11-year-olds. The teacher monitors her pupils as they go through exercises contained in the programme and it helps the teacher assess pupils' individual needs. The evaluation showed teachers using Time To Know spent more time with individual pupils than in the control group; the programme helped and allowed them to do that.[14]

We are on slightly firmer ground when it comes to maths and science. Studies do show positive correlations – though rarely causal significance – between ICT use and performance in maths.[15] And a number of studies cited show positive effects of specific technologies (the popular Logo, for example),[16] or contributions to the learning of specific mathematical skills, in algebra, graphs, programming and the like. Significantly though, perhaps, the 2008 Williams Review of primary maths teaching had very little to say about the role of ICT and the need for teacher training in it, even if what it did say was supportive.[17]

The reviews referred to do not cover some now common tools, such as the YouTube-based worked examples of the 'Khan Academy', designed to be followed by students on their own and then gone over with teachers. The videos are free and can be followed in groups devoted to a topic; they can be loaded on a touch-screen tablet, linked to interactive whiteboards, and students can test themselves and watch their own progress. The Khan Academy resources are not just for maths and by 2014 over 4 million of its exercises worldwide were being completed each day, according to figures on the Academy's website.[18] Even if such resources are not evaluated in terms of their impact on achievement, there is certainly an appetite for their use.

As a 2011 study said about maths progress over the preceding eight years, 'The world has moved on . . . and there are now far more resources available to mathematics teachers.'[19] One US controlled study shows a positive impact of modest use of maths-based computer games on students' scores in general maths tests.[20] A further controlled study in Texas schools found significant gains from the use of SimCalc for teaching 12- to 13-year-olds fairly complex mathematics. Interestingly there was some control for the quality of teaching and the study also found the programme had positive results for students of all backgrounds and levels of prior attainment, without being very demanding of training time for teachers.[21]

The literature suggests some clear results for science, partly because software has been developed for teaching specific science skills and knowledge, also making it easier to study outcomes. Quite a number of statistically significant findings are shown, for example between the extent of ICT use in schools and results in science tests – though as elsewhere there are less positive results in other studies, even negative ones where mastery of the software takes longer than learning the topic without it.[22]

Home use of ICT has broadly positive effects, especially when integrated with in-school teaching; though there are also reports of negative effects, such as sometimes excessive use of 'leisure' programmes and gaming, or reduction in spelling abilities, uncritical cutting and pasting, etc.[23] Parents can contribute to the effectiveness of students' home use of ICT.[24]

There are also reports, similarly mixed, of results in the teaching of humanities subjects, modern foreign languages, history,[25] geography, art, design and technology[26] and computer science itself (see below).

Some progress has been made with what are known as 'assistive technologies', software designed to help pupils with various kinds of disabilities. One that has been evaluated is My Accessible School, a set of programmes from Dolphin Technologies designed to help pupils with reading or print impairment. The software turns textbooks into screen-readable texts, or on-screen facsimiles of textbooks and pupils' laptops can 'read' selected passages aloud, make spelling corrections based on 'sounds like' rather than 'similarly spelled'; and so forth. Reportedly pupils with quite severe reading disability suddenly find themselves able to access texts and make progress hitherto denied them, though this is based only on a few personal reactions.[27] (For further specific applications used in the teaching of reading, see Chapter 7.)

Another example of assistive technologies is HANDS (Helping Autism Diagnosed [Teenagers] Navigate and Develop Socially), a set of smartphone apps designed to help students with Autism Spectrum Disorder (ASD). It has been studied only in a modest number of individual cases, but appears to be helpful in allowing young people with ASD to cope with a variety of behavioural problems.[28] The authors note, however, that it requires considerable inputs from teachers and cooperation with families.

In summary, ICT for pedagogical use does appear to have the potential to improve students' achievement, and is particularly well supported by research for mathematics and science. However, the impact of such technology on pupil outcomes is specific to the type of ICT being adopted and appears to vary by subject area.

Motivation

Various studies show positive effects of ICT use on motivation and engagement, including with the difficult-to-engage student.[29] Here is an example:

> The teacher displayed a set of plotted co-ordinates on the interactive whiteboard with four statements underneath, only one of which was correct in relation to the example shown. The pupils had to use the buttons on their devices to select the correct answer. A bar chart then appeared on the interactive whiteboard that showed the percentage of the class getting the correct answer.

A considerable amount of 'excitement' was generated as the percentage on the bar chart gradually rose to 100 with successive problems. There is also a virtue for the pupils as they enter their 'votes' anonymously, not risking exposure if they get a wrong answer. As in so many other studies, the example makes clear the relationship between the technology and its effective use by the teacher.[30]

The studies report motivational gains among disaffected pupils, in Pupil Referral Units, even 'indications' of improved behaviour in and outside the classroom, reductions in truancy, offending and so forth – though saying that these need further research. It is also claimed that where investigated, there is little evidence of a 'novelty' effect, that is, the technology's immediate appeal does not seem to wear off, even with the same programmes being successfully used over periods of years. (It is not hard to see why: if you look at the software, it is often appealing and compares very favourably with what the average teacher can produce without it. The mystery once you experience it is why it has been so hard to demonstrate its effectiveness.)

There is anecdotal evidence of motivational effects on reading with tablets and e-readers. A Welsh education Minister spoke of a project between the Swansea council and a local primary in 2013 that had a 'transformational' effect on reading.[31] Similarly the Book Trust reported that of 100,000 students who took part in 'Reading for my School' in 2013, almost half read books online; teachers polled said the results were particularly good for boys and less proficient readers.[32] But only about 2 per cent of schools surveyed in 2012 reported 'extensive' use of e-readers in the classroom: less than 1 per cent in local authority maintained schools, but about 4 per cent in academies.[33]

Broadly the limited evidence available indicates that the impact of ICT on learning is independent of ethnic group or social background, with the obvious problem that disadvantaged individuals and groups and less well-resourced schools may have relatively limited access to ICT.

The teaching of computer science

It is widely accepted that computer science is a proper discipline at university level, and can and should be a school subject in its own right, contributing to learners' autonomy and fulfilment, as well as their learning in schools, their later effectiveness in the workplace, and their contribution to society.[34]

The picture of the teaching of computer science is mixed. It is important not only for giving students the skills needed in an increasingly digital world – the subject has been a statutory requirement in the National Curriculum – but also because it can and should feed into students' use of ICT in the rest of their learning. But criticism of the teaching of ICT in schools has been extensive. An Ofsted study of 177 maintained schools between 2005 and 2008 produced varied findings. In primary schools 'The pupils observed generally used ICT effectively to communicate their ideas and to present their work', but were found to be less skilled in other ways. Pupils' achievement was 'good' in half the schools visited. In secondary schools achievement was 'good' in 45 per cent, 'satisfactory' in the same percentage, and 'inadequate' in the remaining 10 per cent.

In both the primary and the secondary schools, things improved between 2005 and 2008. But for many students – high-flying and otherwise – there was insufficient challenge, especially when the students knew more about the technology than did the teachers.[35] It was a little better two years later: a further Ofsted study of 167 primary, secondary and special schools in 2011 found performance good or outstanding in two-thirds of primary schools, but only a half of secondary schools. But 'In 30 of the 74 secondary schools visited, nearly half the students reached the age of 16 without an adequate foundation for further study or training in ICT and related subjects.'[36] A particular complaint is that teaching is often confined to the familiar rudiments of the subject, with students not frequently enough given a grounding in valuable and demanding skills such as writing code, or programming.

Further, the National Curriculum for primary ICT had not been revised since 1999, though the Rose Report on the primary curriculum made recommendations for it. The computer science exam specifications at GCSE 'seem to offer little by way of challenge to students', and require various forms of enrichment.[37] Different forms of software offer promise and are already being used successfully in many schools: for example, Bee Bots, Roamers, Logo (already mentioned), Game Maker and Lego. But use and teachers' capacity is enormously varied. Relatively few teachers of computer science have degrees in the subject: an NFER survey in 2008 found 59 per cent had no qualification in it beyond A-level;[38] though such a qualification may not necessarily be essential, and many of course do get their teaching skills upgraded in Continuing Professional Development (CPD), including online CPD resources.[39]

The Royal Society report of 2012 is a rich resource for information and advice on teaching Computer Science, too detailed to be rehearsed here. One of their recommendations was for suitable technical resources to be made available in all schools to support this teaching. These could include pupil-friendly programming environments such as Scratch, educational microcontroller kits such as PICAXE and Arduino, and robot kits such as Lego Mindstorms.[40] (Lego and Scratch at least are already fairly widely used.)

In 2011 the *NextGen* report had given a damning assessment of computer science teaching, arguing forcefully that Britain has been a leader in digital media, with considerable employment opportunities – but schools and universities were not turning out qualified people of the right calibre.[41] By 2012 it was openly recognised that teaching of the subject in schools was mostly fairly dismal; the education Minister, Michael Gove, gave a speech in January in which he said, 'Schools, teachers and industry leaders have told us that the current curriculum is too off-putting, too demotivating, too dull.' The relevant Programme of Study was withdrawn as of September 2012, and a new curriculum was published in 2013, to be taught from September 2014.[42] Certainly there was much to be desired: a 2012 survey for the *Guardian* showed only 33 per cent of boys and 17 per cent of girls had learned any computer coding skills at school.[43]

At the same time, there are now numerous resources for teachers and schools to improve the teaching of ICT. For example, various programmes for continuing professional development (CPD) in ICT teaching are offered by universities and other institutions. A number of these are listed in the 'Network of Teaching Excellence in Computer Science' on the website of Computing at School, www.computingatschool.org.uk. The National Association of Advisors for Computers in Education, NAACE, offers a free online CPD course. A NESTA (National Endowment for Science Technology and the Arts) study has suggested further methods and resources, including the use of computer-building kits such as Hummingbird, for students to learn coding.[44]

ICT for school improvement

There is clearly a capacity for ICT to help manage curricula, enhance assessment and feedback with learners, save teachers' time and increase their productivity, etc., but in a small survey (39 schools), Ofsted found, 'In most schools, ICT had not yet become integral to teaching and learning or a driver for school improvement.'[45] Obviously there has been considerable progress since this 2005 survey, but it is not clear how much. In one school where it was used to good effect,

> information such as timetabling, school diary, attendance and behaviour records, academic targets and tracking could be accessed online at any time and from anywhere. Staff, pupils and parents were expected to log on regularly

to access relevant information and to communicate with each other through email and online forums.[46]

The Stephen Perse Foundation School was reported in 2014 to be building a pathway that others could follow. Homework can be downloaded and teachers make their own online library of lessons and course materials for GCSE, A-levels and International Baccalaureates. These are interactive resources, with video links and lesson notes, customised for the specific needs and speeds of their classes. There are extension exercises and links to further reading and ideas. Everything is made to be shared on iTunes U, the academic version of the iTunes download service, so pupils can access them at school or at home or anywhere else.[47]

Touch-screen tablets, as noted, may well be the wave of the future, with many interesting developments. One such is Group Scribbles, which allows users to 'write' on on-screen 'notes' rather like Post-it notes, and share them with each other or post them on a whiteboard, particularly useful for maths where typing is cumbersome. The programme allows easy interaction between teachers and their classes and can also accommodate a variety of on-screen learning games.[48] There are also suggestions that technology can promote school to school collaboration. In the 'Dissolving Boundaries' programme schools use online programmes, wikis[49] and Moodle[50] for between school collaboration. This has led to 'improved literacy, oracy, ICT and communication skills.'[51] But once again, we have little firm knowledge of impact, or the extent to which such technology is used.

Visions of the future

It seems axiomatic that the younger generation are far more involved with ICT and digital media than their elders; they are so-called 'digital natives'.[52] Yet it is evident from the above that education has not at all fully caught up with the fact, or the promise. Perhaps this is not surprising; a large proportion of today's teachers are not digital natives, and the teachers who trained *them* mostly came to the digital revolution late in life. Also much of the subject matter and technique can take long periods for teachers and learners alike to master and internalise. There is a considerable need for investment both in skill and equipment.

Books such as Vander Ark's *Getting Smart* spell out prospects for very different kinds of schools, with 'blended classrooms' where ICT use is substantial, combining at-home and in-school practice with teacher supervision and guidance, different forms of assessment, etc.[53] A few such schools, mainly in the US, already exist. One of the most complete is the Carpe Diem School in Yuma Arizona, offering online and on-campus studying in a wholly new type of environment.[54] The not-for-profit Rocketship Education runs three elementary schools in California, where pupils 'spend a quarter of their day in a computer lab and the rest in a traditional classroom'. Kunskapsskolan in Sweden operates 32 innovative schools based on blended learning and in 2011 opened a Charter School in New York. Its schools are designed for a variety of forms of collaborative work; they have 'a web portal that outlines the steps for each subject and the tasks involved in each step' and students can choose between lectures, workshops and online resources to follow them. These Swedish schools gain above average scores in national tests, but of course that may not be just due to technology.[55]

Learners may get 'badges' (like scout badges) for specific skills mastered rather than being graded by standard forms of assessment. The school may be designed from scratch to be far more inclusive of ICT in the classroom and at home, with school management, assessment, self-assessment, learner feedback, and communication with parents all systematically handled online. Schools not wishing to go so far can adopt more or fewer of such practices. The model is adaptable to the personalised learning ambition of English schools referred to in Chapter 6. Many teachers already manage a Virtual Learning Environment, offering resources and tools for use outside the classroom, and can provide students with a 'Passport to independence (P2i)', a digital booklet that lets them monitor their learning progress and 'take ownership of their own learning'.[56] The UK has in fact a number of schools already noted for well-integrated and fairly comprehensive use of ICT. They include the Bridge Academy in London, Cramlington Learning Village in Northumberland, the ESSA Academy in Bolton, Kemnal College Trust in Bromley, Sandbach School in Cheshire and Wildern School in Southampton.[57]

There are of course commercial interests in ICT in schools – though in the case of the study by Microsoft Partners in Learning just cited, one of the Partners is the London Knowledge Lab, which is associated with the University of London Institute of Education. Computer companies do make free software available, such as Texas Instruments' much used Math Nspired.[58] But there is a variety of free software with no ties to commercial companies – for example, Mangahigh in the UK is a prominent provider in maths.[59] Other well-known maths tools are Cabri 3D for 3-dimensional geometry and Autograph for graphing, not to mention graphic display calculators, Fathom for learning data analysis, and so forth.

Yet moving to a more ICT-intensive world is far from simple; it will require a great deal of learning by teachers, a great deal of organisation by schools and potentially changes in national procedures. For example, there can be conflicts between using ICT innovatively and current forms of assessment: a teacher in England is quoted as saying, 'I can't do something interesting and let results slip. You just do not have that freedom.' (That is much less of a problem in Finland, where there is very limited compulsory testing for students up to age 15.)[60] We are doing it. But we seem to have a long way to go. There is an amazing array of available equipment and software, but not always sufficient evidence about effectiveness to make it easy for schools and teachers to buy and adopt it with confidence.

Key findings

- Information and Communications Technology (ICT) has considerable potential to improve student outcomes. Schools doing well with ICT have a technology coordinator, effective leadership, and implement a school-wide strategy. But use of ICT and the knowledge of how best to use it are enormously varied throughout the school system.

- Research on the impact of ICT with really robust findings is quite limited, but there is some, mainly for specific technologies or in specific subjects. At the same time a range of studies suggest many positive effects, on learning and motivation. Numerous educational ICT programmes are referred to in the chapter, including 'assistive' technologies for working with special needs pupils.

- There is widespread agreement that ICT is not a substitute for good teaching; on the contrary, it is usually reliant on pedagogy to be effective. In particular it helps teachers assess the needs of individual pupils, and allows them more time to attend to those needs.

- The teaching of computer science has, with exceptions, had a poor record, with relatively few students acquiring skills in computer coding. The subject was withdrawn from the Programme of Study in the National Curriculum in 2012, with a new curriculum issued in 2013, to be taught from September 2014.

- Technology is available for school improvement, managing curricula, sharing resources online, enhancing teachers' productivity and the like, but is not yet well deployed in every school.

- A number of schools have been consciously created from the start to maximise use of ICT, or are well advanced in across-the-board integrated use of technology – in the United States and Scandinavian countries, and a few in the UK. They have had interesting results, but it is not clear that such departures are the wave of the future.

Key policies

- Making better use of the potential in ICT is basically a matter of learning from much positive experience. More emphasis is needed in initial teacher training and CPD to spread understanding and mastery of the technology. School leaders who have not already initiated focussed approaches should take steps to do so.

- Budgetary help is needed to provide students with the appropriate hardware and software.

Notes

1 DfES (2003: 23).
2 Moss *et al.* (2007).
3 DfES (2003: 3).
4 BECTA (2010); latest figures from BESA (2013).
5 BESA Press Release 1 July 2014, www.besa.org.uk/news/besa-press-release-tablet-adoption-continues-rise.

6 DfE (2011b): this is a small scale study by the Department's 'Effective Practice Team' of fifteen schools making good use of technology.
7 BESA Press Release 1 September 2013 www.besa.org.uk/news/besa-press-release-besa-releases-ict-uk-state-schools-research.
8 BECTA (2010).
9 BECTA (2009b: 10).
10 Passey (2011a: 5).
11 Passey (2011b) attempts to explore this in maths; more broadly see Cox and Marshall (2007).
12 Andrews et al. (2005: 36).
13 Cox and Marshall (2007: 16); see also Gambrell et al. (2007) on literacy teaching.
14 For the evaluation research, see Rosen and Beck-Hill (2012); Rockman and Scott (2012). The main evaluation was done with matched samples of Texas fourth and fifth graders. (Somewhat confusingly, the programme is described as a digital teaching platform. See further Dede and Richards (2012).)
15 Cox and Marshall (2007). See also Ofsted (2008b); Oldknow and Knights (2011).
16 See also Clements (2000); Kalas and Blaho (2003).
17 Williams (2008: 54–55).
18 www.khanacademy.org.
19 Tetlow (2011: 136). See further Hoyles and Lagrange (2009).
20 Kebritchi et al. (2010).
21 Roschelle et al. (2007b).
22 See BECTA references already cited; Cox and Marshall (2007); DfES (2001 and 2003).
23 Valentine et al. (2005).
24 Day et al. (2009).
25 Ofsted (2008a).
26 Ofsted (2011a).
27 DfE (2011a).
28 Mintz et al. (2012). The book reports on a variety of technologies besides HANDS.
29 Passey and Rogers (2004: 1); DfES (2003); also many of the studies of attainment already cited.
30 Passey and Rogers (2004: 20).
31 www.bbc.co.uk/news/uk-wales-22806246 (accessed 16 June 2013).
32 See www.booktrust.org.uk. One of the present authors was told by the Head of Learning Support in a Hertfordshire school that pupils found reading on tablets was 'cool'.
33 BESA Press Release 23 November 2013, www.besa.org.uk/news/press-release-besa-releases-classroom-learning-resources-english-schools-research.
34 NAACE (2010).
35 Ofsted (2009).
36 Ofsted (2011b: 5).
37 NAACE (2010: 6).
38 NFER (2008).
39 NAACE (2010: 11); see further Chapter 5.
40 Royal Society (2012).
41 Livingstone and Hope (2011).
42 www.gov.uk/government/publications/national-curriculum-in-england-computing-programmes-of-study.
43 Tickle (2012).
44 Luckin et al. (2012). For Hummingbird, see www.hummingbirdkit.com.
45 Ofsted (2005: 3).
46 DfE (2011b: 4).
47 BBC News, 5 March 2014, www.bbc.co.uk/news/business-26249041.
48 Roschelle et al. (2007a). Group Scribbles is a free programme, available from http://group scribbles.sri.com.
49 Wikis are online collaborative areas that allow anyone with access to contribute to and edit the online-workspace.
50 Moodle (abbreviation for Modular Object-Oriented Dynamic Learning Environment) is a free source e-learning software platform, also known as a Course Management System.
51 DfE (2011c: 1).
52 Palfrey and Gasser (2008); Thomas (2011).

53 Vander Ark (2011). On blended learning, see Staker (2011).
54 See www.carpediemschools.com.
55 Vander Ark (2011: Chapter 6).
56 Microsoft Partners in Learning (2011: 16).
57 See www.bridgeacademy.hackney.sch.uk/; www.cramlingtonlv.co.uk/; www.essaacademy. org/; http://sandbachschool.org; www.wildern.hants.sch.uk/. Further detailed suggestions for schools to make better use of ICT can be found in Mäkitalo-Siegl *et al.* (2012).
58 www.ti-mathnspired.com.
59 www.mangahigh.com.
60 Microsoft Partners in Learning (2011: 25).

References

Allen, J. and Potter, J. (2011) *Primary ICT: Knowledge, Understanding and Practice*, Exeter: Learning Matters.

Andrews, R., Dan, H., Freeman, A., McGuinn, N., Robinson, A. and Zhu, D. (2005) *The Effectiveness of Different ICTs in the Teaching and Learning of English (written composition), 5–16*, Research Evidence in Education Library, London: EPPI Centre, Institute of Education.

BECTA (British Educational Communications and Technology Agency) (2008) *Harnessing Technology Review 2008: The Role of Technology and its Impact on Education*, Coventry: British Educational Communications and Technology Agency.

BECTA (2009a) *Harnessing Technology Review 2009: The Role of Technology in Education and Skills*, Coventry: British Educational Communications and Technology Agency.

BECTA (2009b) *Harnessing Technology Schools Survey 2009: Analysis Report*, Coventry: British Educational Communications and Technology Agency.

BECTA (2010) *School Use of Learning Platforms and Associated Technologies*, London: Institute of Education.

BESA (2013) *Information and Communication Technology in UK State Schools: Provision and Spending*, Full Report – vol. 2, London: British Educational Suppliers Association.

Carlacio, J. and Heidig, L. (2009) 'Teaching digital literacy digitally: A collaborative approach', paper presented at Media in Transition Conference, Cambridge, MA: Massachusetts Institute of Technology, April.

Clements, D.H. (2000) 'From exercises and tasks to problems and projects: Unique contributions of computers to innovative mathematics education', *Journal of Mathematical Behaviour* 19(1): 9–47.

Cox, M. and Abbott, C. (eds) (2003a) *ICT and Attainment: A Review of the Research Literature*, DfES/0792/2003, London and Coventry: British Educational Communications and Technology Agency for the Department of Education and Skills.

Cox, M. and Abbott, C. (eds) (2003b) *ICT and Pedagogy: A Review of the Research Literature*, DfES/0793/2003, London and Coventry: British Educational Communications and Technology Agency for the Department of Education and Skills.

Cox, M. and Marshall, G. (2007) 'Effects of ICT: Do we know what we should know?', *Education and Information Technology* 12: 59–70.

Day, L., Williams, J. and Fox, J. (2009) *Supporting Parents with their Children's 'At Home' Learning and Development*, Research Report DCSF-RR138, London: Department of Children, Schools and Families.

Dede, C. and Richards, J. (eds) (2012) *Digital Teaching Platforms: Customizing Classroom Learning for Each Student*, New York: Teachers College Press.

DfE (2011a) *Accessible Resources Pilot Project: Final Report*. Available at: www.altformat.org/mytextbook/ (accessed 2 February 2012).

DfE (2011b) *Using Technology to Improve Teaching and Learning in Secondary Schools: Draft Report*, Effective Practice Team, London: Department for Education.

DfE (2011c) *What is the Evidence on Technology Supported Learning?* London: Department for Education.

DfE (2012) *Michael Gove Speech at the BETT Show*. Available at: www.education.gov.uk/inthe news/speeches/a00201868/michael-gove-speech-at-the-bett-show-2012 (accessed 13 February 2012).

DfES (2001) ImpaCT2: *Emerging Findings from the Evaluation of the Impact of ICT on Pupil Attainment*, London: Department for Education and Skills.

DfES (2003) *Fulfilling the Potential: Transforming Teaching and Learning Through ICT in Schools*, DfES/0265/2003, London: Department for Education and Skills.

Enochsson, A. and Rizza, C. (2009) 'ICT in initial teacher training: research review', *OECD Education Working Papers no. 38*, Paris: OECD.

ETI (Education and Training Inspectorate) (2006) *Information and Communication Technology in Primary Schools*, Bangor: Crown, for Education and Training Inspectorate.

Gambrell, L., Morrow, L., Neuan, S. and Pressley, M. (eds) (2007) *Best Practices in Literacy Instruction*, New York: The Guilford Press.

Harrison, C., Comber, C., Fisher, T., Haw, K., Lewin, C., Linzer, E., McFarlane, A., Mavers, D., Scrimshaw, P., Somekh, B. and Watling, R. (2002) *ImpaCT2: The Impact of Information and Communication Technologies on Pupil Learning and Attainment*, Coventry: British Educational Communications and Technology Agency.

Hattie, J. (2009) *Visible Learning: A Synthesis of Meta-Analyses Relating to Achievement*, London: Routledge.

Hoyles, C. and Lagrange, J.-B. (eds) (2009) *Mathematics Education and Technology: Rethinking the Terrain*, London: Springer.

Ito, M., Horst, H., Bittanti, M., Boyd, D., Herr-Stephenson, B., Lange, P.G., Pascoe, C.J. and Robinson, L. (2009) *Living and Learning with New Media*, Summary of Findings from the Digital Youth Project, Cambridge, MA: MIT Press.

Kalas, I. and Blaho, A. (2003) 'Exploring visible mathematics with IMAGINE'. In G. Marshall and Y. Katz (eds) *Learning in School, Home and Community: ICT for Early and Elementary Education*, Boston, MA: Kluer, pp. 54–64.

Kebritchi, M., Hirumi, A. and Bai, H. (2010) 'The effects of modern mathematics computer games on mathematics achievement and class motivation', *Computers and Education* 55: 427–443.

Leask, M. and Pachler, N. (eds) (1999) *Learning to Teach Using ICT in the Secondary School*, London: Routledge.

Livingstone, I. and Hope, A. (2011) *NextGen*, London: National Endowment for Technology, Science and the Arts. Available at: www.nesta.org.uk/library/documents/NextGenv32.pdf (accessed 22 February 2012).

Luckin, R., Bligh, B., Manches, A., Ainsworth, S., Crook, C. and Noss, R. (2012) *Decoding Learning Report: The Proof, Promise and Potential of Digital Education*. Available at: www.nesta.org.uk/home1/assets/features/decoding_learning_report.

Mäkitalo-Siegl, K., Zottmann, J., Kaplan, F. and Fischer, F. (eds) (2010) *Classroom of the Future*, Rotterdam: Sense.

Microsoft Partners in Learning (2011) *Innovative Teaching and Learning Research: 2011 Findings and Implications*. Available at: www.itlresearch.com (accessed 1 January 2012).

Mintz, J., Gyori, M. and Aagaard, M. (eds) (2012) *Touching the Future: Technology for Autism?* Amsterdam: IOS Press.

Moss, G., Jewitt, C., Levacic, R., Armstrong, V. Cardini, A. and Castle, F. (2007) *The Interactive Whiteboards, Pedagogy and Pupil Performance Evaluation*, Research Report 816, London: Department for Education and Skills.

NAACE (National Association of Advisers for Computers in Education) (2010) *Response to the Royal Society's Call for Evidence on Computing in Schools*, Nottingham: National Association of Advisers for Computers in Education.

NFER (National Foundation for Educational Research) (2008) *2007 Secondary School Curriculum and Staffing Survey*, NFER for the DCSF. Available at: http://publications.education.gov.uk/default.aspx?PageFunction=productdetails&PageMode=publications&ProductId=DCSF-RR026&.

Ofsted (2003) *Boys' Achievement in Secondary Schools*, HMI 1659, London: Office for Standards in Education.

Ofsted (2005) *Embedding ICT in schools: A Dual Evaluation Exercise*, HMI 2391, London: Office for Standards in Education.

Ofsted (2008a) *Education for a Technologically Advanced Nation: Design And Technology In Schools 2004–2007*, Ref. no. 070224, London: Office for Standards in Education.

Ofsted (2008b) *Mathematics: Understanding the Score*, Ref. no, 070063, London: Ofsted Office for Standards in Education.

Ofsted (2009) *The Importance of ICT: Information and Communication Technology in Primary and Secondary Schools, 2005/2008*, Ref. no. 070035, London: Office for Standards in Education.

Ofsted (2011a) *History for All: History in English Schools 2007/2010*, Ref. no. 090223, London: Office for Standards in Education.

Ofsted (2011b) *ICT in Schools 2008–2011*, London: Office for Standards in Education.

Oldknow, A. and Knights, C. (eds) (2011) *Mathematics Education with Digital Technology*, London: Continuum.

Oldknow, A., Taylor, R. and Tetlow, L. (2011) *Teaching Mathematics Using ICT*, London: Continuum Books.

Palfrey, J. and Gasser, U. (2008) *Born Digital: Understanding the First Generation of Digital Natives*, New York: Basic Books.

Passey, D. (2011a) *Independent Evaluation of the Uses of Espresso Online Digital Resources in Primary Schools*, Lancaster University: Department of Educational Research.

Passey, D. (2011b) 'Learning mathematics with digital resources: Impacts on learning and teaching for 11- to 14-year-old pupils'. In A. Oldknow (ed.) (2011) *Mathematics Education with Digital Technology*, London: Continuum, pp. 46–60.

Passey, D. and Rogers, C. with Machell, J. and McHugh, G. (2004) *The Motivational Effect of ICT on Pupils*, Research Report RR523, London: Department for Education and Skills.

Rockman, S. and Scott, B. (2012) 'Evaluating Time to Know: Research concepts and practical decisions'. In C. Dede and J. Richards (eds) (2012) *Digital Teaching Platforms: Customizing Classroom Learning for Each Student*. New York: Teachers College Press, pp. 188–200.

Roschelle, J., Tatar, D., Raj Chaudhury, S., Dimitriadis, Y., Patton, C. and DiGiano, C. (2007a) 'Ink, improvisation and interactive engagement: Learning with tablets', *Computer* 40(9): 42–48.

Roschelle, J., Tatar, D., Shechtman, N., Hegedus, S., Hopkins, B., Knudsen, J. and Stroter, A. (2007b) *Can a Technology Enhanced Curriculum Improve Student Learning of Important Mathematics?* Menlo Park, CA: SRI International.

Rosen, Y. and Beck-Hill, D. (2012) 'Intertwining digital content and a one-to-one laptop environment in teaching and learning: Lessons from the Time To Know program', *Journal of Research on Technology in Education* 44(3): 225–241.

Royal Society (2012) *Shut Down or Restart? The Way Forward for Computing in UK Schools*, London: The Royal Society.

Selwyn, N. (2011a) *Education and Technology*, London: Continuum.

Selywn, N. (2011b) *Schools and Schooling in the Digital Age: A Critical Analysis*, Abingdon: Routledge.

Staker, H. (2011) *The Rise of K-12 Blended Learning*, San Francisco, CA: Innosight Institute.

Thomas, M. (2011) *Deconstructing Digital Natives: Young People, Technology and The New Literacies*, Abingdon: Routledge.

Tickle, L. (2012) 'Upgrade expected . . . in 2014', *The Guardian*, 21 August 2012.

Valentine, G., Marsh, M. and Pattie, C. (2005) *Children and Young People's Home Use of ICT for Educational Purposes: The Impact on Attainment at Key Stages 1–4*, Research Report RR672, London: Department for Education and Skills.

Vander Ark, T. (2011) *Getting Smart: How Digital Learning is Changing the World*, San Francisco, CA: Jossey-Bass.

Wheeler, S. (ed.) (2005) *Transforming Primary ICT*, Exeter: Learning Matters.

Williams, P. (2008) *Independent Review of Mathematics Teaching in Early Years Settings and Primary Schools*, Final Report, London: Department for Education.

11

VOCATIONAL EDUCATION

Anna Vignoles

Introduction

Practical or vocational education is important from an economic perspective, both for the individual and for the economy as a whole. In recent decades the rapid technological advances in the economy, particularly in computing power, have resulted in a substantial increase in the demand for more skilled workers. Firms therefore need individuals who are highly skilled to do the more complex jobs available.[1] If the education system is to meet this demand we need to ensure that a greater proportion of our workforce has higher level skills. Some of this increased demand for skill will clearly come from graduates, a group that has been increasing globally. In England however, only just over a third of the cohort pursue the university route and we therefore need to be equally concerned to increase the skill levels of the half of the population that does not go on to higher education, and particularly the large proportion of the work force that takes practical or vocationally oriented education.

This chapter therefore considers the effectiveness of a vital part of the English education system, namely practical or vocational education. It starts with a brief overview of the current policy context in England, describing some of the concerted recent attempts to improve vocational education and some likely directions for policy over the next few years. However, to understand the impetus behind these policy initiatives we need to first consider why vocational education in England is seen as problematic in the first place. The first part of this chapter therefore examines, from an historical perspective, why the status of the English vocational system remains relatively low compared with the academic route. We then move on to consider effectiveness. Much vocational education takes place in classrooms in the Further Education sector and we start by discussing the effectiveness of the FE sector and in particular the value of the vocational education and qualifications that it produces. Vocational education also takes place in the work place and the final part of the chapter focuses on the effectiveness of work-based provision. We go on to describe the crucially important role of the apprenticeship system in providing the technical skills needed for the UK economy. We end the chapter with a discussion of the effectiveness of training schemes for the low skilled and unemployed.

The current policy context

In England, as in many other countries, there has been long standing concern about the nature and quality of vocational education. In recent decades there have been repeated efforts by governments of all political persuasions to reform the vocational education system, with the unfortunate effect of leading to a huge amount of policy churn and a proliferation of different qualifications, routes and initiatives in this sphere. There have along the way been quite radical suggestions for reform, primarily with the aim of improving the status of vocational education and achieving parity of esteem with academic education. In particular, in the mid-2000s there was a serious attempt to integrate vocational and academic education in secondary schools, originating from a review by Mike Tomlinson,[2] which suggested replacing GCSEs and A levels with an overarching diploma that could incorporate both academic and vocational elements. These suggestions were rejected by the Labour government as being too radical. Though this particular policy proposal was not adopted, it was by no means the end of policy interest in vocational education.

Most recently, the Government asked Professor Alison Wolf to undertake a comprehensive review of the vocational education system and it subsequently committed to implement most of her recommendations: this will lead to further significant changes to the system.[3] The Wolf review (2011) emphasised the need for genuine progression for those who take both academic and vocational options, i.e. there needs to be a measurable increase in their skill level as a result of taking such courses whether in school or beyond. She also argued that progression to a minimum level of numeracy and literacy in particular is essential for all workers, and those pursuing a vocational route must still continue to develop these core skills at least to level 2 (GCSE equivalent). She stressed the need for students to be better informed about the available options (both vocational and academic) and specifically for them to understand the consequences of early choices made at GCSE for their future options. For such choices to be better informed, some simplification of what is a horrendously complex web of vocational qualifications is clearly required. She also noted her desire to encourage 'innovation and efficiency' in vocational education, which included an emphasis on employer involvement in the design of qualifications.

Over and above the impact of the Wolf Review, there are other reasons why practical or vocational education is increasingly important in policy terms. First, the Great Recession has ensured that policy-makers focus more on practical education, because unemployment is higher among unskilled workers and among those who pursue vocational qualifications, as distinct from those on the higher education route. Second, and pre-dating the impact of the Great Recession, there has also been a polarisation of jobs in the labour market, which has led many commentators to wonder whether our vocational education system is fit for purpose. This polarisation has increased the demand for skill and produced a rapid growth of higher-level professional jobs.

One challenge is to supply the graduates and high skilled vocational workers to undertake these roles. At the same time, there appears to have been a decline in the types of jobs that used to be done by technicians and intermediate skilled workers, i.e. those who had vocational education and apprenticeship qualifications. Thus intermediate skilled workers compete for the greater number of jobs that require very little skill at all, in turn displacing unskilled workers. This has been described as a 'hollowing out' of the labour market. It is an issue that causes concern, with fears that we have fewer opportunities at intermediate skill level and hence an even more pressing need for those pursuing a vocational route to achieve very high levels of skill. Whether these problems reflect the inability of the English vocational education system to provide the intermediate and higher level technical skills that firms desire or whether it is driven by insufficient demand from firms for such skills is not entirely clear. Either way, it has increased policy attention on the effectiveness of the vocational route.

Why is the status of the English vocational education system not higher?

Given all this policy concern, one might wonder why the status of vocational education continues to be quite low. The disparity has long been recognised as undesirable but despite more than 30 years of trying, vocational studies post-16 continue to be seen as inferior, at least relative to pursuing the route to a degree. The history of the system gives some insight into this.

Prior to the 1960s in England, we had a highly segregated and tracked education system. At age 11 students took an examination that provided the more academically able with entry into grammar schools and most of these students then proceeded on the 'academic track' either to O levels (examinations taken at age 16), A levels (taken at age 18) or, for a relatively small minority, university. Those who were less academically able attended either secondary modern schools or technical schools, though the latter were few in number. Students on the secondary modern route were in turn more likely to take a vocational education. This system of early tracking was cause for major concern given evidence that education systems with early tracking tend to be more socially segregated, with poorer students more likely to take the vocational route. This system also had the disadvantage that pursuing a vocational education was generally seen in a rather negative way, as an option for less able students, at least in contrast to the high status of vocational education in countries such as Germany.

In the 1960s the tripartite system described above started to be dismantled and most areas of England switched to a comprehensive schooling system, whereby all students attended the same schools. At age 16 students had three options. They could either drop out of school altogether, since that age was the end of compulsory schooling, or they could continue down the academic route and take A levels before going on to university, or they could opt for vocational education. Even with these changes, vocational education was seen as a second best option to the academic route. In 2014 the system changed again, and now all students are required to participate in education and training to the age of 18 (the policy is known as the raising of the participation age or RPA). This policy change does not however, require full-time education until the age of 18 but rather that students undertake a minimum number of hours of part-time or full-time education or training (quite broadly defined). It is likely that despite students remaining in some kind of education or training for far longer now, it will remain the case that the less academically able students are the ones who are more likely to take practical education routes.

Unfortunately, therefore, this stratification of the education system has left the vocational route as the 'poor relation' of the academic route, though an important one in numerical terms. In the late 1980s around half of all students in a given year dropped out of education altogether at age 16. Now, the proportion remaining in full-time education past the age of 16 has grown dramatically to around 85 per cent of the cohort in 2012. Much of this growth has been in vocational education. Going forward we need to know what works for students who follow this path and the effectiveness of the FE sector is crucial in that regard, an issue we now turn to.

What do we know about the effectiveness of the Further Education system?

Most vocational education in England that is classroom based takes place in Further Education (FE) colleges, though schools can also offer vocational options from age 14. Around 600,000 students age 16–18 enrol in colleges each year.[4] Some of these students will be taking A levels and may well continue on to university down the academic route. However, a majority will be pursuing practical education or a combination of academic and vocational education. There have periodically been concerns about the effectiveness of this FE system, particularly since those who teach in it do not have the same terms and conditions as teachers in schools. They are lower paid and on average are less qualified than those who teach in schools. Some studies have found that the FE system is indeed marginally less effective than schools, for students taking A levels at least,[5] but generally the evidence does not suggest that the quality of FE colleges is necessarily the major problem despite the rhetoric.[6]

A more significant problem relates to the disparity of esteem between vocational and academic education discussed above. Generally socio-economically disadvantaged students are, on average, lower achieving at GCSE and hence they are less likely to pursue A levels and more likely to take the vocational route.[7] Thus any problem with our vocational education system disproportionately affects the most socio-economically disadvantaged students and contributes to low social mobility. Put another way, given that poorer students are more likely to take a vocational option it is essential that the vocational offer is of sufficiently high quality that it provides a route to a good job and higher income for these students.

The other problem with this system is that those who take the vocational route through FE appear to face greater difficulties as they attempt to enter the labour market, though actually it is a long-standing problem for young people generally when they try to find work, whatever their qualifications. Around one in five young people age 18–24 years old are NEET (not in employment, education or training). This is a structural problem that preceded the Great Recession, though young people have undoubtedly suffered more during the economic downturn.[8] The Wolf Review highlighted in particular the pressing need for evidence on, and indeed effective policies for, young people's transitions into the world of work. Wolf also questioned the vocational system's effectiveness in helping young people into work. This concern stems from the fact that while the unemployment rate among graduates has risen, it remains low relative to the unemployment rate for those attempting to enter the labour market at an earlier age, largely with qualifications from the vocational system.

There are a number of other potential problems with vocational education in England, over and above the fear that it is not equipping young people with the skills and qualifications they need to make the transition into work. As discussed above, we have ended up with huge numbers of different vocational qualifications. While many of these qualifications are regulated and we do have a framework within which they fit – having hundreds, let alone thousands, of qualifications available, all with different requirements – just confuses students, parents and employers alike. It is hard for students and parents to determine which vocational qualifications are valuable and which are not. Employers, who may not be clear about the value of some vocational qualifications, find it even more confusing if they are changed repeatedly. Further Education colleges in turn find it harder to provide appropriate advice on what qualifications a student should take. So while taking vocational qualifications appeals to some students, and may motivate them to remain in the education system longer, we need to ensure that such qualifications really are valued and help young people into the world of work.

The National Vocational Qualifications (NVQs) illustrate the problem of designing vocational qualifications that are fit for the world of work. NVQs were introduced in the late 1980s and were designed not so much to impart knowledge and skill but to certify the types of occupational knowledge and skill that those in particular jobs have. As a result many have criticised NVQs for not being of a high enough level and for not providing workers with a sufficient level of skill. At the other extreme we had some qualifications, such as the General National Vocational Qualifications (GNVQs), that were primarily classroom based and hence subject to the criticism that they were no longer vocational education in a true sense.

Concerns about the low level of NVQs and the academic nature of GNVQs then led to the introduction of vocational GCSEs, largely offered in schools. The aim was to introduce qualifications that explicitly had the same status as their academic GCSE counterpart and that students taking them could then proceed to FE to take higher level vocational qualifications. Vocational GCSEs, and indeed the thousands of other qualifications deemed equivalent to one or more GCSEs, proved popular with schools in a potentially unfortunate way. In many instances these vocational qualifications were seen as easier to achieve. Since such qualifications could count towards schools' totals in the GCSE league tables, this encouraged schools to enrol pupils on these vocational qualifications to secure GCSE points, even if the qualifications were not necessarily right for and valuable to the student. Wolf highlighted the quite startlingly rapid growth in the numbers taking these vocational qualifications as a major problem. The Government has now removed GCSE equivalence from many thousands of qualifications, leaving around 70 as equivalent to GCSE, though most do not count towards some performance measures such as the 'English Baccalaureate'. (The English Baccalaureate is made up of English, mathematics, history or geography, the sciences and a language, though in 2014 it will include a somewhat wider range of qualifications as long as they are in these subject areas and lead on to A level progression.) Removing GCSE equivalence should cause the expansion in vocational GCSEs to be reversed.

As a corollary to concerns about the achievement level of vocational qualifications offered in schools and in FE, there are worries here in the UK, and indeed in many other countries, about the low economic value of many vocational qualifications. Some vocational qualifications appear not to boost workers' earnings by a significant amount. Since earnings reflect worker productivity, this implies some vocational qualifications may not have positively boosted workers' productivity.

It is perhaps important to put this in context. The evidence on the value of basic skills like literacy and numeracy is compelling. Individuals who achieve higher levels of literacy and numeracy earn more in the UK labour market than those with lower level skills and indeed basic literacy and numeracy is valued more highly in the UK than in many other countries.[9] This clearly indicates that there is an elevated demand for skills and potentially insufficient supply. Given this strong demand for even quite low-level skills, it comes as somewhat of a surprise that the value of vocational qualifications is so variable. Some vocational qualifications, particularly those at higher level (level 3) and those that are quite familiar to employers (e.g. the Higher National Diploma (HND)) are indeed highly valued in the labour market. By contrast, the economic value of some lower level vocational qualifications, such as NVQ2s, is mixed and often estimated to be quite low.[10] This is of concern not just because of the waste of resources implied by this finding but also because poorer students are disproportionately likely to take these lower level qualifications.

Vocational qualifications are also often compared unfavourably to academic qualifications such as GCSEs or degrees, which continue to have a high value in the labour market. It is not always true, however, that vocational qualifications are less valuable than academic ones. For example, some apprenticeships, particularly those at higher level, have a great deal of economic value and indeed some yield a wage return that exceeds that to a degree. Many vocational qualifications also have additional value if they are in a particular subject area, such as mathematics, engineering or technology. Indeed a recent report by the Royal Academy of Engineering showed that these low and intermediate level vocational qualifications in science, technology, engineering and mathematics (STEM) often have additional value if they are then used in a related occupation.[11] Even in the STEM area however, not all qualifications are alike and hence some vocational qualifications in STEM have far more economic value in the labour market than others.

What does this imply? First, that some of our vocational qualifications, particularly at the lower level, are not useful in the labour market. Second, that we need to be far more diligent in informing young people about the value of the different vocational options. This is harder than providing equivalent advice for those trying to navigate the academic system. We cannot simply say that all vocational qualifications are good or bad, nor indeed that all STEM subjects are good or bad. What we can say however, again from the Royal Academy of Engineering report, is that working in science, engineering or technology occupations at intermediate or even lower levels often yields good earnings. Many of these occupations require particular types of vocational education and are higher paying than the equivalent in other subject areas, again endorsing the view that we have a clear need for high quality vocational education to feed the demand for high skilled, practically trained workers in science, technology and related areas.

What is the role of the apprenticeship system?

There are some high quality and persistent features of the vocational education system: overall apprenticeships are one such feature, though they too are not without their problems. The content of an apprenticeship and the way that apprenticeships are delivered and regulated has changed out of all recognition since the 1960s. At that time they were run by various industry groups, considered to be very high quality and consisted of largely training on the job with some 'day release' whereby the trainee got some time out of the work place in the class room. West and Steedman (2003) have noted that following the decline of this apprenticeship system in the 1970s and 1980s, attempts to reinvigorate the apprenticeship scheme resulted in an array of different awarding bodies all certifying different types of vocational qualifications (within the National Qualifications framework), some of which have very little in the way of work-based component. This has, many argue, undermined the value of vocational education generally and apprenticeships specifically. Partly in response to this, there have been ongoing efforts to reinvigorate apprenticeships, and in the mid-1990s a Modern Apprenticeship scheme was introduced, modelled explicitly on the German dual system of apprenticeship and aimed at getting young people to achieve a higher level of skill. Modern apprenticeships have certainly proved successful in attracting students. They have been rather less successful in attracting employers, a point we return to in the next section.

In the UK apprenticeships have been, and continue to be, an important part of the vocational education system, and a way for young people to enter the labour market with the necessary skills to pursue higher-skilled vocational jobs. Apprenticeships are in many respects the success story in the vocational education system, particularly Modern Apprenticeships, which enable the pupil to achieve clear levels of achievement that relate to the National Qualifications framework. Currently apprenticeships can be at intermediate level (level 2 – equivalent to 5 GCSEs), advanced level (equivalent to 2 A level passes) or higher level (leading to NVQ4 or a Foundation Degree). The work of McIntosh (2005; 2007) and others such as Jenkins *et al.* (2007) has confirmed that in the UK such apprenticeships, particularly at higher level, provide a valuable route for young (and not so young) people into well-paid employment. Unfortunately a large proportion of apprenticeships starting in the UK are at a lower level (level 2) (see Figure 11.1) and hence do not necessarily provide access to high quality jobs and good wages for young people. The need to ensure we develop more, higher level apprenticeships is an on-going issue.[12]

On average however, individuals who acquire an apprenticeship qualification go on to have good labour market prospects, earning more than their peers and with better employability. This is a situation found in many other countries too: apprenticeships often provide good economic value in terms of boosting individuals' earnings and employment prospects. In many other countries however, apprenticeships are a more major route into employment than in the UK, particularly in those systems that segregate young people relatively early into vocational or academic tracks, the so-called 'dual systems' (Germany, Austria, Switzerland). In these dual systems, vocational education generally and apprenticeships specifically

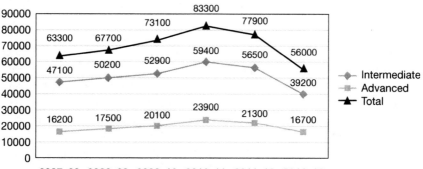

FIGURE 11.1 Apprenticeship achievements for 16- to 18-year olds 2007–2013

Note: Does not show higher-level apprenticeship achievement. In 2012/2013 there were just 500 higher-level apprenticeship starts.

Source: SFR20, October 2013, 2012–2013 data provisional.

have high status and more than half of each cohort proceeds into employment via an apprenticeship. It has long been the aim of policy-makers in this country to emulate such systems though this has clearly not yet been achieved.

Apprenticeships have particular features that make them more valuable in the labour market. First, apprenticeships by their nature impart a broad range of skills, including so called non-cognitive skills, such as work attitudes, which may be less easy to develop in formal education or on short training courses. There is now a body of work that confirms the high value of these non-cognitive skills in the labour market.[13] Second, as already noted, the shortage of apprenticeship places means that firms can be selective about who they recruit. Thus some of the value of apprenticeships may arise because of the selective nature of the people who train as apprentices. This is consistent with the fact that in contrast to apprenticeship programmes, universal state interventions of a practical nature that are designed to boost the skills of less educated/skilled workers have often proved ineffective and in many cases simply replace what firms would have done in the way of training anyway.[14] However, as a consequence of the selective nature of apprenticeships, lower achieving students are less likely to secure an apprenticeship as compared with their higher achieving peers. This may be beneficial for the programme as a whole as it keeps quality high, but poses some problems in terms of using apprenticeships to up-skill the least skilled, who are also often the poorest students.

There are of course potential disadvantages with apprenticeships. There is evidence that systems with early specialisation and tracking into vocational routes tend to produce workers who may be relatively less flexible later on in their careers.[15] In other words, the vocational route may help workers get jobs related to their training in the short run. In the longer run however, with the needs of the labour market changing, those who took apprenticeship training may have fewer generic skills and therefore be less adaptable to change. Certainly the research suggests that in the longer term vocationally trained workers experience more unemployment than others.

Another problem is that in the UK, as in some other European countries, insufficient numbers of firms want to take on apprentices, and large numbers of young people would like an apprenticeship but are unable to secure one.[16] If apprenticeships are valuable for the individual, this implies that individuals who take apprenticeships become more productive and yet firms still seem reluctant to take them on. This is an ongoing problem that vexes policy-makers and was the subject of a recent review of apprenticeships by Richard.[17] The Richard Review, building on the Wolf Review, emphasised the need for employer-led rather than provider-led training for apprenticeships. This means allowing employers more flexibility in how they train apprentices yet also being rigorous in ensuring that apprenticeships really do provide substantial and high-level training rather than a source of cheap labour. The Review also stressed the need for clear industry standards to maintain the high quality of training. Again building on Wolf, the Richard Review reiterated the need for all apprentices to reach a good standard in English and mathematics before completion. Critically, there was also recognition of the cost to firms of training apprentices. The Review stressed that the Government would need to incentivise this kind of training and provide employers with the means to control what kind of training was purchased as part of an apprenticeship.

Hilary Steedman (2005) has investigated this issue in detail in other European countries and focussed in particular on the dual systems that exist in Germany, Austria and Switzerland. These dual systems have apparently achieved parity of esteem between the academic route into Higher Education (HE) and the practical route leading to an apprenticeship or even to a degree via an apprenticeship. Despite this, and contrary to what is often reported, these systems are in fact under pressure too. Just as in the UK, too few employers are willing to offer apprenticeship places. Since offering apprenticeship training is quite costly, particularly if it is of high quality, firms in these countries appear less willing to offer apprenticeships than in the past, perhaps responding to the need to be competitive and keep costs down. Muehlemann et al. (2007) provide some evidence that cost does impact on employers' willingness to take on apprentices. Subsidising firms who do not offer apprenticeships may therefore induce them to do so. Equally subsidies aimed at firms who currently offer apprenticeships may not induce them to take on more and hence could be quite wasteful as a policy. Certainly we need a system that rewards employers for training apprentices, perhaps by providing them with the means to retain apprentices for longer after the end of their training in order to ensure that the firm gets a good return on their investment. Equally we need to protect apprentices from exploitation.

Thus the future for apprenticeships is unclear. On the one hand they are widely seen as effective in terms of providing workers with the skills they need, and certainly they are economically valuable in the labour market for workers. On the other hand, the global economy requires firms to be low cost and to respond quickly to changes in the market. Apprenticeships are costly, may lead to over-specialised workers and certainly are not easy to adapt to short run changes in demand. As such, it is not clear, even in the countries with the best systems in the world, how apprenticeships will evolve. Certainly countries are shying away from compelling firms to train and provide apprenticeships, for fear that this would make them uncompetitive. Rather governments are considering different ways to encourage firms to provide apprenticeships and this will inevitably mean sharing the costs of training between the state and the firm to a greater extent than previously.

In any case, it is a difficult time at the moment with most economies growing only weakly if at all. Firms tend to offer more apprenticeships when the economy is stronger. This is the opposite situation to regular off-the-job training. Generally when there is a recession firms tend to train their workers if they are under-utilised rather than fire them, at least in the short run. By contrast, in a downturn firms are understandably reluctant to take on new apprentices. Hence we may have to wait until the economy is growing again before exploring ways in which we can entice firms to offer more apprenticeship positions. The research evidence on this issue would suggest that countries with strong employers' bodies and fora for social partnership between employers and employees are likely to find this easier.[18] We should also be mindful that apprentices need to develop a sufficient level of general skills to equip them for different jobs in later life and indeed for further training. This means vocational education should not start too early, and partly because of this potential risk, some countries, the US among them, do not offer substantial vocational education in secondary school at all.

How effective are work-based training schemes?

The fact that apprenticeships are potentially so valuable is consistent with other evidence that firm-provided training in general can be highly beneficial to individuals and indeed even more so to firms.[19]

Hence a major source of practical or vocational training is employers themselves. As is the case with apprenticeships however, firms tend to train people who are already quite skilled. Thus you are more likely to receive this kind of training if you have left full-time education with a reasonably high level of general skill. How we tackle low skills among those who leave school without good GCSEs and with low levels of basic skill, is far more challenging.

Over the years, particularly when youth unemployment is very high in the middle of a period of very slow economic growth, governments have tried various schemes designed to up-skill young people and up-skill the unemployed. However, such schemes have a very mixed track record. While some job schemes that help young people get real life and substantial work experience have been successful, many if not most training schemes for unemployed youth have often shown minimal positive effects both in the UK and elsewhere.[20] For example, the Youth Training Scheme that was introduced in the UK in the 1980s in the face of very high youth unemployment was not very successful in enhancing young people's chances of getting work and securing high quality jobs, though there is some evidence it did improve employment for young females.[21] More recently the last Government introduced a programme to encourage firms to provide training to the low skilled, namely Train to Gain. Work by the Institute for Fiscal Studies[22] has shown that this programme did not produce substantial gains in skill for workers and in the end the state was subsidising a lot of training that firms would have done anyway.

This does not of course mean that we are incapable of designing vocational training programmes for very low skilled and unemployed workers, but the evidence base thus far implies that this is a far harder task than designing training for workers who have higher levels of general skill. The evidence therefore supports the general tenor of the Wolf Review, namely that it is crucial that young people acquire a sufficient level of general skills in school, so that they are then able to access higher level training when they leave school and hence make easier transitions into the labour market.

Conclusions

Vocational or practical education can certainly be valuable in the labour market. High quality vocational education delivered by firms, or in partnership with firms, often yields good financial prospects for the individual and benefit to firms. In particular, vocational training for somewhat higher skilled workers appears to be particularly valuable. Apprenticeships, for example, work for many students, particularly when undertaken at a higher level (e.g. level 3) by those who have already got skills (e.g. a set of good GCSEs). They are a proven and successful way to train workers for the labour market. That said, such training is expensive and in order to encourage more firms to provide it, we will need to provide better financial incentives for firms to do so. We also need to be mindful that apprenticeship training is valuable if it is genuinely high level, not least because firms are selective about who receives such training. It is not clear that opening up apprenticeships to workers with much lower levels of initial skill would produce the same result, nor that firms would be willing to take on such workers. There is therefore tension between expanding the apprenticeship scheme to draw in lower skilled school leavers and keeping the rigour and value of apprenticeships.

In general, the evidence suggests that designing vocational or practical education for lower skilled workers is far harder. The minimal labour market value of some lower level vocational qualifications may simply reflect the fact that the demand from firms for such workers is quite limited. However, equally it is also likely that the problem is in the actual content of the programmes aimed at low-skilled workers. Perhaps what also needs to be better recognised is that if individuals spend a great number of years in the school system and yet emerge with very low levels of skill, it will always be more difficult to up-skill them in young adulthood. Often we are expecting short term and relatively cheap training schemes to produce the skills that many years of full-time education failed to do. This will always be difficult. Further work to develop programmes for such low-skilled workers is clearly needed and the emerging evidence would indicate that focusing on developing these young people's non-cognitive skills, such as their attitudes to work and inter-personal skills, may be both feasible and particularly fruitful in terms of enhancing their prospects.

One of the other big decisions that needs to be made for the English system is the age at which vocational specialisation should start. There has recently been an encouragement of relatively early specialisation. Schools have been allowed to offer vocational and practical options from age 14, and it has been argued that this motivates some students better than a purely academic offer. The evidence on this is not compelling however. University Technical Colleges (UTCs) for secondary school pupils wishing to study vocational subjects have also been developed, 17 of them by 2013, again reinforcing the idea that relatively early vocational specialisation can and should happen in the secondary education phase. UTCs are designed for 14- to 18-year-olds, to study vocational and practical subjects side-by-side. They are too new to have been evaluated, but international evidence suggests that there could be a penalty later in life from early specialisation and hence workers who pursue the vocational route very early may end up without the general skills required to adapt to labour market changes later on. At an absolute minimum, we must remember the recommendation of both Wolf and Richard that those pursuing a vocational route need to gain the necessary level of general skill in mathematics and English too.

In conclusion:

- In England, it is generally lower achieving students who pursue the vocational route. This has left the vocational route as a poor relation to the academic route.
- Attempts to bring about parity of esteem between the vocational and academic routes have led to excessive policy change and a proliferation of vocational qualifications, many of which are low level and not recognised nor particularly valued by employers.
- Some vocational education in England is of high quality and does provide skills that are valuable in the labour market. Higher level vocational qualifications are generally valued by firms, reflecting the increasing demand for higher skilled workers.
- Designing lower level vocational education and qualifications that produce genuine gains in skills for very low skilled workers is the major challenge facing the UK vocational education system.
- Apprenticeships, particularly at higher level, are an effective means of training workers. We need to find ways to encourage more firms to offer high quality apprenticeships, potentially by providing them with greater financial incentives.
- There is a need to avoid vocational specialisation too early, and to ensure that individuals achieve a minimum level of general skill in mathematics and English.

Notes

1 Goldin and Katz (2009).
2 http://webarchive.nationalarchives.gov.uk/20050301194752/www.dfes.gov.uk/14–19/documents/Final%20Report.pdf.
3 Wolf (2012).
4 Meschi *et al.* (2014).
5 Meschi *et al.* (2014).
6 Tymms (1992); Belfield and Thomas (2000); Martinez (2002); Morris *et al.* (1999); Owen and Fletcher (2005); Schagen *et al.* (2006); Stanton and Fletcher (2005 and 2006); Meschi *et al.* (2012).
7 Clark *et al.* (2005); Rice (1999); Micklewright (1989); Dickerson and Jones (2004); Andrews and Bradley (1997); Clark (2002 and 2011).
8 OECD (2000).
9 Machin and Vignoles (2005).
10 Dearden *et al.* (2004); Dickerson (2005).
11 www.raeng.org.uk/news/releases/pdf/The_Labour_Market_Value_of_STEM_Qualifications_and_Occupations.pdf.
12 See the Richard Review for a full discussion of this issue, as well as other commentators on social mobility such as The Sutton Trust, for example www.suttontrust.com/our-work/research/item/real-apprenticeships/.

13 Carneiro and Heckman (2003); Cunha and Heckman (2007).
14 Abramovsky *et al.* (2011). Economists refer to the phenomenon of state funding for activities that would have happened anyway as 'dead weight loss'.
15 Hanushek *et al.* (2011).
16 Leitch (2006); Wolf (2011).
17 www.gov.uk/government/news/the-richard-review-of-apprenticeships.
18 Wolter and Ryan (2011).
19 Blundell *et al.* (1999); Goux and Mourin (2000); Feinstein *et al.* (2004).
20 Heckman *et al.* (1999); Dolton *et al.* (1994); Kluve (2010); Sianesi (2008).
21 Dolton *et al.* (1994); Main and Shelley (1990).
22 Abramovsky *et al.* (2011).

References

Abramovsky, L., Battistin, E., Fitzsimons, E., Goodman, A. and Simpson, H. (2011) 'Providing employers with incentives to train low-skilled workers: Evidence from the UK employer training pilots', *Journal of Labor Economics* 29: 153–193.

Adda, J., Dustmann, C., Meghir, C. and Robin, J-M. (2009) 'Career progression and formal versus on-the-job training', *IFS Working Paper* no. W09/06, London: UCL.

Andrews, M. and Bradley, S. (1997) 'Modelling the transition from school and the demand for training in the United Kingdom', *Economica* 64: 387–413.

Belfield, C. and Thomas, H. (2000) 'The relationship between resources and performance in further education colleges' *Oxford Review of Education* 26(2): 239–253.

Blundell, R., Dearden, L. and Sianesi, B. (2005) 'Evaluating the effect of education on earnings: Models, methods and results from the National Child Development Survey', *Journal of the Royal Statistical Society: Series A (Statistics in Society)* 168: 473–512.

Blundell, R., Dearden, L., Meghir, C. and Sianesi, B. (1999) 'Human capital investment: The returns from education and training to the individual, the firm and the economy', *Fiscal Studies* 20(1): 1–3.

Brunello, G. (2009) 'The effect of economic downturns on apprenticeships and initial workplace training: A review of the evidence' *Journal of Empirical Research in Vocational Education and Training* 1(2): 145–171.

Carneiro, P. and Heckman, J. (2003) 'Human capital policy'. In J. Heckman, A. Krueger and B. Friedman (eds) *Inequality in America: What Role for Human Capital Policies?* Cambridge, MA: MIT Press, pp. 77–240.

Cassen, R. and Kingdon, G. (2007) 'Understanding low achievement in English schools', *CASE Papers*/118, London: Centre for Analysis of Social Exclusion, London School of Economics and Political Science.

Clark, D. (2002) 'Participating in post-compulsory education in England: What explains the boom and bust?', CEE *Discussion Paper* no. 24. Available at: http://eprints.lse.ac.uk/19516/1/Participation_in_Post_Compulsory_Education_in_England_What_explains_the_Boom_and_Bust.pdf (accessed 1 January 2014).

Clark, D. (2011) 'Do recessions keep students in school? The impact of youth unemployment on enrolment in post-compulsory education in England', *Economica* 78(311): 523–545.

Clark, D., Conlon, G. and Galindo-Rueda, F. (2005) 'Post-compulsory education and qualification attainment'. In S. Machin and A. Vignoles (eds) *What's the Good of Education? The Economics of Education in the United Kingdom*, Princeton, NJ: Princeton University Press, pp. 71–98.

Cunha, F. and Heckman, J. (2007) 'The technology of skill formation', *American Economic Review* 97(2): 31–47.

Dearden, L. Leslie McGranahan, L. and Sianesi, B. (2004) 'Returns to education for the marginal learner: Evidence from the BCS70', *CEE Discussion Papers* 0045, London: Centre for the Economics of Education, LSE.

Dickerson, A. (2005) *A Study on Rates of Return to Investment in Level 3 and Higher Qualifications*, London: Department for Trade and Industry.

Dickerson, A. and Jones, P. (2004) *Estimating the Impact of a Minimum Wage on the Labour Market Behaviour of 16- and 17-Year-Olds*, London: Office of Manpower Economics.

Dickerson, A. and Vignoles, A. (2007) *The Distribution and Returns to Qualifications in the Sector Skills Councils*, SSDA Research Report no. 21, Wath-upon-Dearne: Sector Skills Development Agency.

Dolton, P., Makepeace, G. and Treble, J. (1994) 'The youth training scheme and the school-to-work transition', *Oxford Economic Papers* 26(4): 629–657.

Dustmann, C. (2004) 'Parental background, secondary school track choice and wages', *Oxford Economic Papers* 56: 209–230.

Feinstein, L., Galindo Rueda, F. and Vignoles, A. (2004) 'The labour market impact of adult education and training', *The Scottish Journal of Political Economy* 51(2): 266–280.

Fersterer, J., Pischke, J-S. and Winter-Ebmer, R. (2008) 'Returns to apprenticeship training in Austria: Evidence from failed firms', *Scandinavian Journal of Economics* 110(4): 733–753.

Goldin, C.D. and Katz, L.F. *The Race between Education and Technology*, Cambridge, MA: Harvard University Press.

Goos, M. and Manning, A. (2007) 'Lousy and lovely jobs: The rising polarization of work in Britain', *Review of Economics and Statistics* 89(1): 118–133.

Goos, M., Manning, A. and Salomons, A. (2009) 'The polarization of the European labor market', *American Economic Review Papers and Proceedings* 99(2): 58–63.

Goux, D. and Maurin E. (2000) 'Returns to firm provided training: evidence from french worker-firm matched data', *Labour Economics* 7: 1–19.

Hanushek, E.A., Woessmann, L. and Zhang, L. (2011) 'General education, vocational education and labor-market outcomes over the life-cycle', NBER *Working Paper* 17504. Available at: www.nber.org/papers/w17504 (accessed 6 January 2014).

Heckman, J., Lalonde, R. and Smith, J. (1999) 'The economics and econometrics of active labor market programs'. In O. Ashenfelter and D. Card (eds) *Handbook of Labor Economics*, first edn, vol. 3, San Diego, CA and Amsterdam: Elsevier, pp. 1865–2097.

Jenkins, A., Greenwood, C. and Vignoles, A. (2007) 'The Returns to qualifications in England: Updating the evidence base on level 2 and level 3 vocational qualifications', *Discussion Paper* CEEDP0089, London: Department for Innovation, Universities and Skills and Centre for the Economics of Education, London School of Economics.

Leitch, S. (2006) *Prosperity for All in the Global Economy: World Class Skills. Final Report*, London: The Stationery Office.

Kluve, J. (2010) 'The effectiveness of European active labor market programs', *Labour Economics* 17(6): 904–918.

Machin, S. and Vignoles, A. (eds) (2005) *What's the Good of Education? The Economics of Education in the UK*, Princeton, NJ: Princeton University Press.

McIntosh, S. (2004) *The Impact of Post-School Vocational Qualifications on the Labour Outcomes of Low-Achieving School Leavers in the UK*, London: Centre for Economic Performance, London School of Economics.

McIntosh, S. (2005) 'The returns to apprenticeship training', *Journal of Education and Work* 18: 251–282.

McIntosh, S. (2006) 'Further analysis of the returns to academic and vocational qualifications', *Oxford Bulletin of Economics and Statistics* 68(2): 225–251.

McIntosh, S. (2007) 'A cost-benefit analysis of apprenticeships and other vocational qualifications', Department for Education and Skills, *Research Report* 834.

Main, B. and Shelly, M. (1990) 'The effectiveness of the youth training scheme as a Manpower Policy', *Economica* 57(228): 495–514.

Marangozov, R., Bates, P., Martin, R., Oakley, J., Sigala, M. and Cox, A. (2009) *Research to Shape Critical Mass Pilots to Address Under-Representation in Apprenticeships*, Institute for Employment Studies. Available at: www.employment-studies.co.uk/pdflibrary/lsc_1109.pdf (accessed 6 January 2014).

Martinez, P. (2002) 'Effectiveness and improvement: School and college research compared', *Research in Post-Compulsory Education*, 7(1): 97–118.

Meschi, E., Vignoles, A. and Cassen, R. (2014) 'Post-secondary school type and academic achievement', *The Manchester School* 82(2): 183–201.

Micklewright, J. (1989) 'Choice at sixteen', *Economica* 56(221): 25–39.

Micklewright, J., Pearson, M. and Smith, S. (1990) 'Unemployment and early school leaving', *Economic Journal* 100(400): 163–169.

Mohrenweiser, J. and Zwick,T. (2009) 'Why do firms train apprentices? The net cost puzzle reconsidered', *Labour Economics* 16(6): 631–637.

Morris, A., Davies, P. and Bromley, R. (1999) *Sixth Form Centres in FE Colleges*, Report for the DfEE, London: FEDA.

Muehlemann, S., Schweri, J., Winkelmann, R. and Wolter, S. (2007) 'An empirical analysis of the decision to train apprentices', *Labour* 21: 419–441.

OECD (2000) *From Initial Education to Working Life: Making Transitions Work*, Paris: OECD.

Owen, G. and Fletcher, M. (2005) '*The Funding Gap: Funding in Schools and Colleges for Full Time Students Aged 16–18*', LSDA *Research Report*, London: LSDA.

Peacock L. (2008) 'Black and minority ethnic apprentice numbers are dramatically low', *Personnel Today* 23 July.

Pischke, J-S. (2001) 'Continuous training in Germany', *Journal of Population Economics* 14(3): 523–548.

Rice, P. (1999) 'The impact of local labour markets on investment in further education: Evidence from the England and Wales youth cohort studies', *Journal of Population Economics* 12(2): 287–312.

Ryan, P. (2001) 'The school-to-work transition: A cross-national perspective', *Journal of Economic Literature* 39(1): 34–92.

Schagen, I., Lopes, J., Rutt, S., Savory, C. and Styles, B. (2006) *Do Post-16 Structures Matter? Evaluating the Impact of Local Patterns of Provision*, London: LSN.

Sianesi, B. (2008) 'Differential effects of active labour market programs for the unemployed', *Labour Economics* 15(3): 370–399.

Stanton, G. (2004) 'The organisation of full-time 14–19 provision in the state sector', Nuffield Review *Working Paper* 13. Available at: www.nuffieldfoundation.org/14-19review (accessed 6 January 2014).

Stanton, G. and Fletcher, M. (2005) 'National institutional patterns and the effects of these on aspects of participation, attainment and progression', Nuffield Review Institutional Dimension series, *Discussion Paper* 2. Available at: www.nuffieldfoundation.org/14-19review (accessed 6 January 2014).

Stanton, G. and Fletcher, M. (2006) '14–19 Institutional arrangements in England: A research perspective on collaboration, competition and patterns of post-16 provision', Nuffield Review of 14–19 Education and Training, *Working Paper* 38, September. Available at: www. nuffieldfoundation.org/14-19review (accessed 6 January 2014).

Steedman, H. (2005) *Apprenticeship in Europe: 'Fading' or Flourishing?* CEPDP, 710, London: Centre for Economic Performance, London School of Economics and Political Science.

Styles, B. and Fletcher, M. (2006) *Provision for Learners Aged 14–16 in the FE Sector – An Initial Analysis*, LSDA Research Report, London: LSDA.

Thelen, K. (2007) 'Contemporary challenges to the German vocational training system', *Regulation and Governance* 1: 247–260.

Tymms, P.B. (1992) 'The relative effectiveness of post-16 institutions in England (including Assisted Places Scheme schools)', British Educational Research Journal 18(2): 175–192.

West, J. and Steedman, H. (2003) *Finding Our Way: Vocational Education in England*. London: Centre for Economic Performance, London School of Economics and Political Science.

Wolf, A. (2011) *Review of Vocational Education: The Wolf Report*, London: Department for Education.

Wolter, S. and Ryan, P. (2011) 'Apprenticeship'. In *Handbook of the Economics of Education*, vol. 3, San Diego, CA and Amsterdam: Elsevier.

Wolter, S., Mühlemann, S. and Schweri, J. (2006) 'Why some firms train apprentices and many others do not', *German Economic Review* 7: 249–264.

INDEX